NEW CURRENTS THROUGH JOHN

Society of Biblical Literature

Resources for Biblical Study

Acquisitions Editor:
Sharon H. Ringe

Series Editor:
J. Ross Wagner

Number 54
NEW CURRENTS THROUGH JOHN
A Global Perspective

NEW CURRENTS THROUGH JOHN
A Global Perspective

Edited by

Francisco Lozada Jr.

and

Tom Thatcher

Society of Biblical Literature
Atlanta

NEW CURRENTS THROUGH JOHN

Copyright © 2006 by the Society of Biblical Literature

All rights reserved. No part of this work may be reproduced or transmitted in any form or by any means, electronic or mechanical, including photocopying and recording, or by means of any information storage or retrieval system, except as may be expressly permitted by the 1976 Copyright Act or in writing from the publisher. Requests for permission should be addressed in writing to the Rights and Permissions Office, Society of Biblical Literature, 825 Houston Mill Road, Atlanta, GA 30329 USA.

Library of Congress Cataloging-in-Publication Data

New currents through John : a global perspective / edited by Francisco Lozada Jr. and Tom Thatcher.
    p. cm. — (Resources for biblical study ; no. 54)
  Includes bibliographical references and indexes.
  ISBN-13: 978-1-58983-201-5 (paper binding : alk. paper)
  ISBN-10: 1-58983-201-9 (paper binding : alk. paper)
  1. Bible. N.T. John—Criticism, interpretation, etc. 2. Bible. N.T. John—Criticism, interpretation, etc.—Methodology. 3. Theology—Methodology. I. Lozada, Francisco, 1965-. II. Thatcher, Tom, 1967-.
  BS2615.52.N48 2006
  226.5'06—dc22   2006025530

14 13 12 11 10 09 08 07 06   5 4 3 2 1
Printed in the United States of America on acid-free, recycled paper conforming to ANSI/NISO Z39.48-1992 (R1997) and ISO 9706:1994 standards for paper permanence.

Contents

Abbreviations vii

The New Current through John: The Old "New Look"
and the New Critical Orthodoxy
Tom Thatcher 1

Part 1. New Currents through History and Theology

"I Will Raise [Whom?] Up on the Last Day": Anthropology
as a Feature of Johannine Eschatology
Jaime Clark-Soles 29

The Role of John 21: Discipleship in Retrospect and Redefinition
Carsten Claussen 55

Sources in the Shadows: John 13 and the Johannine Community
Mary L. Coloe 69

"Salvation Is from the Jews": Judaism in the Gospel of John
Brian D. Johnson 83

Another Look: Johannine "Subordinationist Christology" and
the Roman Family
Beth M. Sheppard 101

Part 2. The New Current of Readers and Readings

John 2:12–25: A Narrative Reading
Armand Barus 123

New Jewish Directions in the Study of the Fourth Gospel
Matthew Kraus 141

The Johannine Community: Caught in "Two Worlds"
    Yak-hwee Tan 167

PART 3. REFLECTION AND FORECAST

Social Location and Johannine Scholarship: Looking Ahead
    Francisco Lozada Jr. 183

Looking Downstream: Where Will the New Currents Take Us?
    R. Alan Culpepper 199

Works Cited 211

Contributors 229

Index of Ancient Sources 231

Index of Authors and Subjects 239

ABBREVIATIONS

1 Apol.	Justin Martyr, *First Apology*
1QH	*Hodayot (Thanksgiving Hymns)*
1QpIsa[a]	*Pesher Isaiah*
AB	Anchor Bible
ABD	*Anchor Bible Dictionary.* Edited by David Noel Freedman. 6 vols. New York: Doubleday, 1992.
AGJU	Arbeiten zur Geschichte des antiken Judentums und des Urchristentums
ATANT	Abhandlungen zur Theologie des Alten und Neuen Testaments
BDAG	Bauer, W., F. W. Danker, W. F. Arndt, and F. W. Gingrich. *Greek-English Lexicon of the New Testament and Other Early Christian Literature.* 3rd ed. Chicago: University of Chicago Press, 1999.
BETL	Bibliotheca ephemeridum theologicarum lovaniensium
BibInt	Biblical Interpretation series
Bib	*Biblica*
BSac	*Bibliotheca sacra*
BZNW	Beihefte zur Zeitschrift für die neutestamentliche Wissenschaft
CBQ	*Catholic Biblical Quarterly*
CQ	*Classical Quarterly*
Comm. Ezech.	Jerome, *Commentariorum in Ezechielem libri XVI*
Conf.	Augustine, *Confessionum libri XIII*
CurBS	*Currents in Research: Biblical Studies*
Dig.	Justinian, *Digestae*
DJG	*Dictionary of Jesus and the Gospels.* Edited by Joel B. Green, Scot McKnight, and I. Howard Marshall. Downers Grove, Ill.: InterVarsity Press, 1992.
DNTB	*Dictionary of New Testament Background.* Edited by Craig Evans and Stanley Porter. Downers Grove, Ill.: InterVarsity Press, 2000.

ExpTim	*Expository Times*
FCNTECW	Feminist Companion to the New Testament and Early Christian Writings
Gen. Rab.	*Genesis Rabbah*
HNT	Handbuch zum Neuen Testament
HTKNT	Herders theologischer Kommentar zum Neuen Testament
HTR	*Harvard Theological Review*
Imm	*Immanuel*
Inst.	Gaius, *Institutiones*
JBL	*Journal of Biblical Literature*
JQR	*Jewish Quarterly Review*
JSNTSup	Journal for the Study of the New Testament Supplement Series
Mek. Exod.	*Mekilta Exodus*
Midr. Qoh.	*Midrash Qohelet*
NovT	*Novum Testamentum*
NovTSup	Supplements to Novum Testamentum
NTL	New Testament Library
NTS	*New Testament Studies*
OECS	Oxford Early Christian Studies
RevExp	*Review and Expositor*
RSR	*Recherches de science religieuse*
Sat.	Horace, *Satirae*
SBLBSNA	Society of Biblical Literature Biblical Scholarship in North America
SBLDS	Society of Biblical Literature Dissertation Series
SBLSCS	Society of Biblical Literature Septuagint and Cognate Studies
SBLSymS	Society of Biblical Literature Symposium Series
SBT	Studies in Biblical Theology
SNTSMS	Society for New Testament Studies Monograph Series
StABH	Studies in American Biblical Hermeneutics
StPB	Studia post-biblica
T. Ab.	*Testament of Abraham*
TBT	*The Bible Today*
TDOT	*Theological Dictionary of the New Testament*. Edited by G. Kittel and G. Friedrich. Translated by G. W. Bromiley. 10 vols. Grand Rapids: Eerdmans, 1964–76.
Tract. Ev. Jo.	Augustine, *In Evangelium Johannis tractatus*
TZ	*Theologische Zeitschrift*
USQR	*Union Seminary Quarterly Review*
WUNT	Wissenschaftliche Untersuchungen zum Neuen Testament

THE NEW CURRENT THROUGH JOHN: THE OLD "NEW LOOK" AND THE NEW CRITICAL ORTHODOXY

Tom Thatcher

At the conference on "The Four Gospels in 1957," John A. T. Robinson delivered a milestone paper entitled "The New Look on the Fourth Gospel." In this essay, an essential component of any survey of the history of recent research, Robinson reviewed five major presuppositions that had functioned as a sort of "critical orthodoxy" in Johannine scholarship since the turn of the twentieth century (Robinson 1962b, 94). Robinson sought to demonstrate that these five pillars of research were crumbling and that the collapse of the edifice was clearing ground for new paths of study. He proceeded to outline this emerging perspective, or "new look," on the Fourth Gospel and to plot anticipated trajectories into the next several decades of research. History has verified several of Robinson's key predictions, and to a large extent the many significant commentaries and monographs produced during the last "golden age" of Johannine scholarship (ca. 1960–90) may be neatly categorized on the rubric of his five trends.

But today, only fifty years later, Robinson's careful and comprehensive outline has become strikingly obsolete. Another "new look" has emerged, one that differs dramatically from anything Robinson could have envisioned. Like Robinson's historic essay, this volume seeks to chart the new currents running through the study of the Johannine literature. The contributors to this book, taken as a group, epitomize the developing "new current through John" in their methods, perspectives, and personal backgrounds. But at the same time, the essays in this volume will also show the ongoing continuity in Johannine scholarship by taking Robinson's "New Look" article as a common point of departure. In this respect, *New Currents through John* will illustrate how the next generation of Johannine scholars will put new wine into old wineskins.

Because each of the essays in this volume will interact with aspects of Robinson's "New Look" essay, the remainder of this introduction will review this historic paper, briefly illustrate the concerns of the generation of scholarship that it described, and underline the most obvious differences between the "new look" perspective and the emerging trends of the future.

The "New Look" 1957

Robinson began his presentation by stressing that the "new look on John" did not represent a radical departure from the past but rather "may best be understood as a questioning of certain presuppositions that have underlain this [traditional] approach [to the Gospel of John] in all its multifarious manifestations." Five such presuppositions, when taken together, formed the "current critical orthodoxy on the fourth Gospel" in the mid-twentieth century (Robinson 1962b, 95). Robinson proceeded to review these five pillars of scholarship and to describe the contrasting "new look" perspective on each issue. Throughout his presentation, Robinson attempted to highlight points of continuity between the New Look and the old critical orthodoxy. Each section of his paper followed a "yes ... but" outline, acknowledging the general validity of a consensus position before questioning its details and/or application. For example, after outlining presupposition two, Robinson noted, "Now the kind of [New Look] reaction that I am describing would not deny that *in a real sense this was true*"; the next paragraph then opens with the phrase, "And *yet, though this may be true* ... that is not to say that...," followed by a discussion of the "new look" perspective on the issue in question (1962b, 98; emphasis added). The "new look," then, represented a gradual yet noticeable shift in the way five key questions about the Johannine literature were being answered.

In the organization of Robinson's paper, the first of the five pillars of the old critical orthodoxy—the assumption that John used the Synoptic Gospels as sources for his own book about Jesus—carried with it the largest number of implications. The remaining four pillars represent a complex of common assumptions about the nature and provenance of the Fourth Gospel's witness to Jesus. Broadly speaking, then, Robinson's first pillar covered all issues pertaining to the composition history of the Fourth Gospel (FG), while the remaining presuppositions addressed John's relationship to the historical Jesus. For sake of convenience, the following review will follow Robinson's topical outline, addressing presupposition one first and then considering presuppositions two, three, four, and five together. It should be stressed at the outset that this review does not represent an exhaustive survey of New Look scholarship, and in many cases other, and perhaps better, illustrations of the trends in question might have been cited. Those included here will, however, serve as adequate examples of the types of issues and concerns that Robinson accurately predicted.

The New Look on Sources

The first key presupposition of the old critical orthodoxy was the assumption "that the fourth Evangelist is dependent on sources, including (normally) one or more of the Synoptic Gospels" (Robinson 1962b, 95). One can scarcely disagree with Robinson's assessment here, the main issue in the early twentieth century being not so much *whether* the Fourth Evangelist used the Synoptics but *the extent to which* Synoptic material was reshaped in the composition of FG. Scholars such as B. W. Bacon had argued that many of FG's stories and discourses can still be directly correlated to the sections of Mark and Luke on which they were based (1910, 365–80). Others, such as B. H. Streeter, contended that John's use of Synoptic material was influenced by extensive meditation and visionary experiences, so that clear links between FG and the Synoptics can no longer be identified (1964, 365–425). But Bacon's book had been published in 1910, Streeter's in 1924; Robinson quickly noted that, of the five pillars, this "is perhaps the presupposition into which the acids of criticism have themselves eaten most deeply" (1962b, 96). In 1957, the theory of Synoptic dependence was already showing the wear of twenty years of erosion by the forces of P. Gardner-Smith's *St. John and the Synoptic Gospels*, a volume that should perhaps win the all-time award for "an academic book whose influence was entirely disproportionate to its length." In less than one-hundred pages, Gardner-Smith dismantled what had been the dominant approach to FG's composition, arguing that the extent and nature of the differences between the Gospel of John and the Synoptics suggest that "all the evangelists drew upon the common store of Christian [oral] tradition." As a result, FG should be viewed as "an independent authority for the life of Jesus," meaning that the Synoptic Gospels were not to be seen as primary sources for its contents (Gardner-Smith 1938, 91, 96).

But while the Synoptics were losing pride of place as presumed sources for FG, the issue remained as to whether John had used other literary sources that are no longer extant. Robinson noted particularly Rudolf Bultmann's source theory, which included a discourse source and a narrative source (Robinson 1962b, 97). Bultmann had argued that FG was produced through a combination of oral tradition (including pieces of the tradition underlying the Synoptics) and extensive citations from, and revisions of, at least three major documents: a passion source (behind the death story), a *sēmeia* source or "signs source" (behind the miracle stories), and the *Offenbarungsreden*, a collection of revelatory sayings of Jesus (Bultmann 1971). Bultmann had not, however, offered a detailed reconstruction of any of these sources and occasionally expressed doubt that it would be possible to do so.[1] Perhaps for this reason, Robinson noted "an increasing reluctance to admit any really objective evidence for such sources" and cited the classic studies of Schweizer, Ruckstuhl, and Noack as evidence for FG's overall "unity of style." "In John," he concluded, "we are dealing with a man who is not piecing together written sources but placing his stamp upon the oral tradition of his community with a sovereign freedom" (Robinson 1962b, 97–98).

The first mark of the New Look, then, was the emergence of a new perspective on the possible sources behind FG. While scholars in the early twentieth century had assumed that the Gospel of John was derivative, drawing much of its material from the Synoptics or unknown documentary sources, the New Look would be skeptical of source-critical approaches, preferring to think of the Johannine tradition as an independent trajectory of Jesus material. Robinson's forecast would prove largely accurate in the decades to follow, but subsequent developments have shown an ongoing diversity of opinion on the two key issues he noted in discussing the problem of FG's sources.

Old Look	New Look
John used the Synoptics as sources	John used independent traditions and sources

First, in the decades since 1957, a true consensus has never been reached on the question of FG's relationship to Matthew, Mark, and Luke. On one hand, an academic hall of fame could be filled from the ranks of scholars who operated under the New Look assumption that John did not use the Synoptics as primary sources. Aside from Robinson himself, the list would include such luminaries as Peder Borgen, Raymond Brown, D. A. Carson, Oscar Cullmann, Alan Culpepper, C. H. Dodd, Robert Fortna, Ernst Käsemann, Robert Kysar, J. Louis Martyn, Francis Moloney, Leon Morris, Rudolf Schnackenburg, D. Moody Smith, and Urban von Wahlde. But even in 1957, Robinson noted that no less an authority than C. K. Barrett had refused to jump ship on the theory of Synoptic dependence (Robinson 1962b, 96). Twenty years into the New Look era, Barrett would continue to stress that "there crops up repeat-

---

1. Note Bultmann's comment, "*It goes without saying that the exegesis must expound the complete text*, and the [source-]critical analysis is the servant of this exposition" (1971, 17; emphasis original). On the possibility of reconstructing sources, Bultmann's remarks on John 15:18–16:11 are typical: "The text of the [discourse] source, which the Evangelist has frequently expanded with his own comments, cannot always be recognized with complete certainty, but is clearly visible in outline" (1971, 548).

edly in John evidence that the evangelist knew a body of traditional material that either was Mark, or was something much like Mark." Since the existence of "something much like Mark" cannot be demonstrated, it is most reasonable to proceed under the assumption that the Fourth Evangelist reworked Mark's material (Barrett 1973–74, 231–32).[2] The theory of Synoptic dependence also enjoyed ongoing support in both Europe and North America through the influence of Werner George Kümmel's popular textbook *Introduction to the New Testament*, which informed its student readers that "obviously the author [of John] knew the Gospels of Mk and Lk from memory and utilized them as seemed to him useful, according to his recollection" (1975, 204). By the mid-1970s, Barrett and Kümmel were joined by Franz Neirynck and the "Leuven school," who operated under the guiding principle that, "in questions of literary [source] criticism, one ought to give priority to the hypothesis explaining the literary data without claiming the existence of unknown sources" (Sabbe 1977, 234). The Leuven school was notable for its application of the results of redaction criticism to the problem of apparent parallels between FG and the Synoptics. In Neirynck's words, if John seems to have incorporated or alluded to Matthew and Luke's peculiar "editorial compositions"—details or themes that originated with Matthew or Luke themselves rather than their common sources—"we should have to conclude to the dependence [of FG] on the Synoptic Gospels" (1977, 73). More recently, Bacon's earlier approach, which viewed portions of FG as mutations of specific passages from the Synoptics, has reemerged in the work of Thomas Brodie, bringing the debate full circle in less than a century (Brodie 1993).

In some cases, the question of FG's relationship to the Synoptic Gospels has been complicated by newer understandings of the notion of "literary dependence" and more complex theories about the interface between written sources and oral traditions. A number of scholars who acknowledge that the Fourth Gospel and the Synoptics are related in some way insist that this relationship cannot be explained simply in terms of one Evangelist copying material from another's book. These scholars have not, however, reached a consensus on how this interaction should be understood. Leon Morris, for example, propounded the theory of "interlocking," arguing that both FG and the Synoptics "needs the other for its complete understanding." Hence, while John did not depend on the Synoptics, "the traditions with which he [John] was familiar and the traditions with which they [the Synoptic Evangelists]

---

2. A more extensive application of Barrett's approach appeared soon afterward in the second edition of his commentary, *The Gospel according to St. John* (Barrett 1978). Robinson later referred to the 1955 first edition of Barrett's commentary as "the last of the 'old look' " (1985, 11).

were familiar at many points supplement each other.... [W]hat he [John] writes in many places serves to fill out and explain what they have written" (Morris 1969, 40–63; quote 62–63). Paul Anderson has argued for a "bi-optic" approach, seeing the Markan and Johannine strains as two distinct yet "interinfluential" traditions. In Anderson's view, the evident similarities and differences between the Gospel of John and the Synoptics imply that "there may *never* have been just one, singular tradition, interpreting Jesus' words and works in a uniform way.... Rather, it is highly likely that from the beginning, Jesus' ministry was interpreted differently, even by some of his followers, and that [the current texts of] Mark and John reflect some of those differences" (1996, 256). Perhaps the most complex theory of the relationship between FG and the Synoptics has been proposed by M. E. Boismard, who argues that all four canonical Gospels underwent several stages of development, with each drawing material from the others at the various stages: intermediate versions of Mark and Luke drawing on an early version of FG, then subsequent revisions of FG in turn borrowing from the intermediate editions of Mark and Luke (1977). More recently, Michael LaBahn has addressed the relationship between John and the Synoptics against the backdrop of first-century media culture. Appealing to the work of Walter Ong, LaBahn suggests that John and the Synoptics may be related through "secondary orality," with material from the written Synoptic Gospels reentering the stream of oral tradition from which the Fourth Evangelist later drew. In LaBahn's model, the Fourth Gospel is independent of the Synoptics but dependent on a tradition that was influenced by those texts (1999). Overall, while these scholars are united in the view that the relationship between the Fourth Gospel and the Synoptics cannot be explained simply in terms of one Evangelist copying material from another, they remain divided in their understandings of the specific lines of influence.

Contrary to Robinson's prediction, the New Look era also saw a marked renewal of interest in the possibility that John used literary sources other than the Synoptics, sources that are no longer extant. Discussion of this issue was revived in 1970 by Robert Fortna's *The Gospel of Signs*, which argued that the narrative portions of FG were derived from a primitive "Signs Gospel." Fortna avoided the criticisms leveled earlier against Bultmann's source theory by utilizing a more detailed source-critical method that depended on "aporias"—narrative, linguistic, and theological inconsistencies—in the text of FG. Fortna extended and applied his arguments in a series of articles and a second monograph that described the final evolution of his model (1988, 1–10), alongside a number of important essays on the Signs Gospel and the history of the Johannine community by D. Moody Smith (Smith 1984). A similar reconstruction, based on a source-critical method that attempted to accommodate FG's discourse material as well as the narratives, was developed by Urban von Wahlde (see esp. 1989). This renewal of interest in Johannine source criticism, especially notable in view of the cold reception Bultmann's proposal had earlier received, was supported by the popularity of J. Louis Martyn's theory that the Johannine community included a number of Jewish Christians who had at one point been excommunicated from the synagogue (1968, 18–22). Martyn's reconstruction provided a reasonable life setting for a possible literary source behind FG's narratives, and Fortna explicitly stated that the Signs Gospel was produced in the context of "an early and pure Christian Judaism" to serve as "a missionary tract with a single end, to show [Jews]… that Jesus is the Messiah" (1988, 214–15; also 1970, 225).

In the last decade, however, Robinson's prediction has been fulfilled in the waning interest in a Signs Gospel or other possible literary sources behind the Gospel of John. The Jesus Seminar includes the Signs Gospel in its reconstruction of the composition history of FG (Funk and Hoover 1993, 17), and Alan Culpepper alludes to the possibility of a signs source in a recent popular textbook on the Johannine literature (1998, 56–58). In general, however, little new research is currently being done into possible independent literary sources, the weight of interest having shifted once more to connections between the Fourth Gospel and the Synoptics.

The New Look on John and Jesus

In Robinson's view, the repercussions of this striking shift on the source-critical question were beginning to ripple into the problem of the Fourth Gospel's historical value. Alongside the conclusion that John did not use the Synoptics as sources, Robinson noted a correlating tendency to "emphasize the independence of the Johannine tradition, which in the nineteenth century was the main count *against* its authenticity" (1962b, 96). In other words, while John's unique vision of Jesus had once been a strike against its historicity, the New Look interpreted "independent tradition" to mean that FG could be treated, like the Synoptics, as a potential primary source of information about Jesus. "[O]ne can [therefore] put the same questions, with the expectation of comparable results, to the Johannine tradition as one can to the Synoptic [tradition] … with an open mind as to which, at any given point, may be the most primitive." Of course, this did not mean that one could naïvely embrace large portions of FG as authentic. Robinson added the caveat, "we shall still give priority to material that is confirmed by two independent traditions" and give "very careful" scrutiny to material attested by only one source, meaning that the vast majority of FG must still remain suspect. But such would be the case with any other ancient witness as well, the primary point being that "we should not adopt different criteria *just because* it [a unit of tradition] is Johannine" (Robinson 1962b, 97; emphasis added).

The second, third, fourth, and fifth pillars of the "new look on John" were all facets of this new perspective on the Johannine tradition. With FG and its underlying sources now seen as independent, it became necessary to develop new understandings of the provenance and value of John's unique presentation of Jesus. If the Gospel of John did not come from the Synoptic Gospels, where did it come from? Because the various issues and perspectives related to this problem are intertwined, for purposes of this review it will be convenient to summarize all four of the presuppositions Robinson addressed before briefly illustrating how the "new look" on these issues impacted subsequent research.

The second pillar of the old critical orthodoxy was the assumption that the Fourth Evangelist's personal "background is other than that of the events and teaching he is purporting to record" (Robinson 1962b, 95). Robinson noted that the previous generation's "legion" of theories about John's biography "all have this in common that they locate him [the Fourth Evangelist], whether in time or place or mental environment, at a distance from the milieu and thought forms of Palestine prior to the Jewish war." Robinson was quick to clarify that the New Look would not argue that FG was written in Palestine or to a Palestinian audience; the issue here is not the provenance of the Gospel of John but rather the provenance of the Fourth Evangelist and/or the Johannine tradition. Robinson detected "a growing readiness to recognize that [the origin of] this [perspective] is not to be sought at the end of the first century ... in Ephesus or Alexandria." Instead, New Look scholars were willing to locate the Johannine tradition, and possibly even John himself, within "a fairly limited area of southern Palestine in the fairly limited interval between the Crucifixion and the fall of Jerusalem" (Robinson 1962b, 98–99). Robinson attributed much of the impetus for this shift to new research on the Dead Sea Scrolls, which had been discovered just a decade before his paper was delivered. The apparent parallels between the scrolls and FG are "decisive" because "*they* [the scrolls] *present us with a body of thought which in date and place ... as well as in fundamental ... theological affinity, may really represent an actual background ... for the distinctive* [theological] *categories of the* [Fourth] *Gospel*" (Robinson 1962b, 99; emphasis original). At the very least, the fact that parallel thought forms could now be documented in pre-70

OLD LOOK	NEW LOOK
John not from pre-70 C.E. Palestine	John and/or his tradition maybe from pre-70 C.E. Palestine

C.E. Palestine silenced the argument that John's theological perspective was incompatible with Judaism in the time and region of Jesus.

The second pillar of the New Look, then, was the emergence of a new perspective on the provenance of the Johannine tradition. Even if FG were written in the late first century in a major Greco-Roman city (such as Ephesus), it might still reflect the outlook of the pre-70 C.E. Palestinian churches. While this perspective impacted New Look scholarship in a number of ways, it should be noted that Robinson's exuberance over the Dead Sea Scrolls now appears dated, despite the ongoing usefulness of volumes such as James Charlesworth's *John and the Dead Sea Scrolls* (1990). Links are, however, still occasionally drawn between ancient heterodox Judaism and FG. For example, in a recent essay on John 1:1–18, Stephen Patterson argues that the prominence of John the Baptist in several strains of heterodox Jewish thought suggests that the Prologue to FG may have been linked at some stage to the Baptist movement in pre-70 C.E. Palestine (2001, 330–32). At present, however, studies of this kind are relatively rare.

The third pillar of the old critical orthodoxy was the assumption that the Fourth Evangelist "is not to be regarded, seriously, as a witness to the Jesus of history, but simply to the Christ of faith" (Robinson 1962b, 95). As Robinson pointed out, this maxim follows logically from the first two presuppositions. The earlier generation's working premise that the Gospel of John was fashioned from the Synoptics by a late first-century Christian automatically implied that FG is primarily a theological treatise rather than a history book.

OLD LOOK	NEW LOOK
John not an associate of Jesus	John maybe an associate of Jesus

But if, as the New Look suggested, FG was not dependent on the Synoptics and shows ideological parallels with pre-70 C.E. Palestinian Judaism, it becomes theoretically possible that John may have been an actual witness to the historical Jesus. The New Look was therefore marked by "an openness to recognize that in the Johannine tradition we may at points be as near to the Jesus of history as in the Synoptic Gospels." Of course, as with the Synoptics, one must unwrap a good bit of theological gauze to get back to this more primitive witness, but the results of these efforts "are often such as to uncover tradition [that is] at least as primitive as in comparable Synoptic material, and sometimes more so" (Robinson 1962b, 100).

In Robinson's view, the possibility that the Johannine tradition might be based on a primitive witness is supported by at least two features of FG. First, Robinson felt that theological parallels between FG and the Dead Sea Scrolls indicate that the source person for the Johannine tradition may have been involved in John the Baptist's movement, as John 1:35–42 can be taken to suggest. Obviously, if the Fourth Evangelist were an associate of John the Baptist, one could scarcely doubt that he might also have witnessed some of Jesus' deeds and teachings. Second, Robinson was struck by John's "knowledge of the topography and institutions of Palestine prior to the Jewish war" (1962b, 101). In general, John provides considerable detail about names and places in Palestine, and archaeological evidence often seems to confirm these references. These apparently accurate reminiscences, alongside John's theological interest in historicity, suggested to Robinson that FG should be taken seriously as a possible witness to the historical Jesus (1962b, 101–2).

The fourth pillar of the old critical orthodoxy was the assumption that the Gospel of John "represents the end-term of theological development in first-century Christianity" (Robinson 1962b, 95). This hypothesis is a natural corollary to the third presupposition: if John had no real connection to pre-70 C.E. Palestine and subscribed to the theological perspective of the late first-century church, then one may assume that "even as regards the Christ of faith he [the Fourth Evangelist] stands at the furthest remove from the primitive witness." In other words, in the view of the old critical orthodoxy, not only was John historically and geographically distant from Jesus, but his theological views were also more distant from the views of Jesus than were those of the other New Testament authors. But the New Look would see in FG's theological tensions both the beginning and the end of New Testament thinking, treating the Fourth Evangelist's perspective as both primitive and developed *at the same time*. New Look scholars could therefore operate under the assumption that John's theology is "extraordinarily mature" but also "stands very near to the primitive apostolic witness" (Robinson 1962b, 102). In conjunction with the other pillars of the New Look, this meant that an admission that aspects of John's theology are highly developed would not require one to conclude that all of John's theology was necessarily very different from that of Jesus.

Old Look	New Look
John's theology reflects late first-century beliefs	John's theology is both primitive and developed

Finally, the fifth pillar of the old critical orthodoxy was the assumption that the Fourth Evangelist "is not himself the Apostle John nor a direct eyewitness" to Jesus (Robinson 1962b, 95). As Robinson noted, this premise must follow from the first four conclusions. The Old Look had set John at such a distance from Jesus in time, space, and thought that it was impossible to imagine that the author of the Fourth Gospel might be the apostle

John who is mentioned in the Synoptics. Robinson did not foresee a rush to argue in favor of apostolic authorship, but he did anticipate "a shift in the questions asked." Specifically, whereas earlier discussions of FG's authorship had focused on the identity of the author—John the apostle or not John the apostle—the New Look would focus more on "the Johannine *tradition* as such and … the community behind it" (Robinson 1962b, 104–5). "The decisive question," Robinson argued, is not the specific identity of the Fourth Evangelist but rather "the status and origin of the Johannine tradition. Did this [perspective on Jesus] come out of the blue around the year AD 100? Or is there a real continuity, not merely in the memory of one old man, but in the life of an on-going community, with the earliest days of Christianity? What, I think, fundamentally distinguishes the 'new look' on the fourth Gospel is that it answers that question in the affirmative" (Robinson 1962b, 106).

Old Look	New Look
The Fourth Evangelist was not the apostle John	The Fourth Evangelist's specific identify is not an issue; maybe more than one person

Overall, then, alongside the view that the Gospel of John was not dependent on the Synoptics, the "new look" approach reflected a willingness to move John closer to Jesus in time, space, and theological outlook than the previous generation had allowed. But this move would not depend on the traditional view that the Fourth Evangelist must have been the apostle John. Instead, by shifting the authorship question to the broader issue of the provenance of the Johannine tradition, it would be possible to connect FG to Jesus on the grounds that the text at times reflects a pre-70 C.E. Palestinian perspective. This approach, as Robinson predicted, impacted New Look scholarship in a wide variety of ways. For sake of illustration, several scholars whose work reflects Robinson's proposed paradigm shift will be surveyed here.

The New Look in Action

Many New Look scholars, assuming that the Gospel of John was based on an independent tradition, attempted to identify early, and possibly authentic, pieces of Jesus material in the current text of FG. Premiere among these studies is C. H. Dodd's milestone monograph *Historical Tradition in the Fourth Gospel*, a book that represents, in many respects, the epitome of New Look thinking. Dodd did not believe that FG was based on the Synoptics and expressed little interest in source-critical theories. In fact, whether or not such sources ever

Old Look	New Look
John used the Synoptics as sources	John used independent traditions and sources
John not from pre-70 C.E. Palestine	John and/or his tradition maybe from pre-70 C.E. Palestine
John not an associate of Jesus	John maybe an associate of Jesus
John's theology reflects late first-century beliefs	John's theology is both primitive and developed
The Fourth Evangelist was not the apostle John	The Fourth Evangelist's specific identify is not an issue; maybe more than one person

existed, "I am not concerned with them; I am trying to discover where, if at all, the finished work [FG] still betrays the existence and character of the oral tradition upon which ... it depends" (Dodd 1963, 8–9, 423–24; quote 424). Dodd found evidence of such an oral tradition through extensive analysis of individual episodes and sayings in FG and concluded that this traditional material "was shaped (it appears) in a Jewish-Christian environment still in touch with the synagogue, in Palestine, at a relatively early date, at any rate before the rebellion of A.D. 66" (1963, 426). Many of these bits of primitive tradition are so "deeply embedded" in passages which explicitly articulate John's theology that they can no longer be distinguished. But in other instances, passages which obviously reflect John's personal perspective include material "framed in purely traditional forms," suggesting that "John did find in [primitive] tradition a direct starting point for the development of his distinctive theology" (Dodd 1963, 431). Do these findings shed any light on authorship? After surveying evidence for the traditional view that the Fourth Gospel was written by the apostle John, Dodd concluded that "the question of authorship is, on the basis of data at present available, incapable of decision" (1963, 10–16; quote 16). This is not, however, an obstacle to historical inquiry, because the Fourth Evangelist's identity "is not as important for the problem of historicity as has been supposed," the more significant issue being whether the traditions underlying FG can be traced back to Jesus (Dodd 1963, 17). In view of these conclusions, it comes as little surprise that Robinson's "New Look" essay refers to Dodd's work with approval several times (see Robinson 1962b, 96 n.7, 98 n. 16, 100 n. 21, 103).

As Robinson noted, the Gospel of John is notorious for apparent theological contradictions. Some passages seem to promote a primitive theological outlook, while others apparently reflect the mindset of the late first century.

New Look reactions to this problem varied widely, and two approaches of note will be reviewed here. First, some New Look scholars located these tensions within John's own theological perspective, or within the perspective of the Johannine tradition. From this approach, FG's theological contradictions were seen as evidence of the complexity of the Fourth Evangelist's personal convictions. A second approach saw in these theological tensions evidence of a series of attempts to adapt the Johannine tradition to contemporary problems in John's community. From this perspective, FG's theological contradictions were seen as evidence of layers of composition and revision, a theory now known as "the developmental approach."

The theory that FG's theological tensions reflect the complexity of John's thought is illustrated by the work of Oscar Cullmann. Cullmann typifies the New Look's ability to place John both close to and far from Jesus at once. Rejecting the theory of Synoptic dependence, Cullmann proposed that John had access to three major sources of Jesus material: "a tradition *common* to *all* branches of early Christianity and made familiar to us through the synoptic gospels," meaning that FG and the Synoptics shared some traditions without directly borrowing from one another; "a *separate tradition* ... which came down to him [the Fourth Evangelist] in the *particular circle* to which he belonged," meaning that John also had access to independent traditions; and, finally, the Fourth Evangelist's own personal reminiscences, for in Cullmann's view "the author [of FG] is identical with the beloved disciple and is therefore a disciple of Jesus" (1975, 7, 84). But if John was in fact an eyewitness to Jesus, should not FG reflect a uniformly primitive theology? Cullmann explains that John believed himself to be inspired by the Paraclete "to reveal the deeper meaning and significance of these facts." Hence, while the Fourth Evangelist offers a primitive witness to Jesus, he can also "develop the discourses beyond what the incarnate Jesus said," placing words in Jesus' mouth to promote his own theological motifs and interests (Cullmann 1975, 8, 18; quote 18). As a result, the text of FG sometimes reflects a very primitive theological perspective but at other times reflects the position of the later Johannine churches. Also typical of New Look scholarship, Cullmann showed little concern for the Fourth Evangelist's specific identity, save to insist that the author "was not the son of Zebedee and was not one of the Twelve" (1975, 78–79; quote 84). Cullmann could thus argue that FG should be treated as a serious witness to the historical Jesus even though the text sometimes promotes a late first-century theological outlook.[3]

---

3. In Cullmann's view, some of the apparent tensions in John's thought are actually reflections of tensions in Jesus' thought and presentation. At several points, Cullmann suggests that FG and the Synoptics sometimes differ because John has preserved "a more intimate teaching

A second group of New Look scholars, focusing on the evolving Johannine tradition rather than an individual author, explained the theological tensions in FG in terms of the ongoing revision and expansion of the text to address new problems in the life of the Johannine churches. This model is called the "developmental approach" because it argues that the Gospel of John was developed over time in response to a series of new and difficult situations. Raymond Brown, one of the most notable proponents of this model, traced the history of the Johannine community and its Jesus tradition from pre-70 C.E. Palestine to the "great church" of the second century. In Brown's view, the Gospel of John began as a body of "traditional [oral] material pertaining to the words and works of Jesus," similar to the Synoptic tradition but independent of it and, at times, more primitive (1966–70, 1:xxxiv, xlviii). This oral material gradually developed distinct patterns and themes that reflected the theological perspective of the Jewish Christians who made up the early Johannine community. But an influx of Samaritans, "Jews of peculiar anti-Temple views" (Brown 1979, 38), and later Gentiles, along with the Johannine community's conflict with the Jewish authorities and expulsion from the synagogue, led to a shift in the community's theological perspective, with subsequent reshaping of the tradition. In Brown's model, this reshaping was not limited to the oral stage of the Johannine tradition: the Fourth Gospel itself underwent at least three revisions under the hand of two different editors (1966–70, 1:xxxiv–xxxvii; 1979, 25–47). In this reshaping process, older theological perspectives were not systematically eliminated or integrated into the newer position, producing, for example, the striking juxtaposition of low Christology and high Christology in the current text of FG (see Brown 1979, 25). On the authorship question, while Brown insisted that the Beloved Disciple was the source of the Johannine tradition and a real associate of both John the Baptist and Jesus, he ultimately concluded that the Fourth Evangelist was neither the Beloved Disciple nor the apostle John (1979, 31–34, 177–78). In Brown's New Look perspective, FG's unique composition history has left the text both primitive and developed, early and late, all at once.

As Robinson predicted, some New Look scholars took the notion of primitive tradition a step further to reconsider the possible historical value of John's witness to Jesus. D. Moody Smith, for example, has recently suggested that "there are a number of points at which it may be argued that John represents, or reflects more accurately [than the Synoptics], the historical situation or events of Jesus' ministry." These historical tidbits may be

---

given by Jesus to the Twelve" or because Jesus used a different style when addressing disciples (such as the Beloved Disciple) from heterodox branches of Judaism (1975, 24, 92–94).

identified at points where (1) FG agrees with the Synoptic portrait of Jesus without directly reproducing it, suggesting independent testimony to the same information; or, (2) FG includes unique narrative details that do not seem calculated to advance John's Christology; or, (3) FG includes details that are "historically plausible in the time, place, and setting of Jesus' ministry" (Smith 2001, 203). These three criteria reveal that "there are a number of instances in which John differs from Mark, and usually also from the Synoptics generally, but is arguably more accurate historically" (Smith 2001, 234). Paula Fredriksen's *Jesus of Nazareth, King of the Jews* also illustrates the impact of New Look thinking on studies of the historical Jesus. Fredriksen notes that "neither the [Fourth] evangelist's narrative nor his speeches [of Jesus] inspire confidence as history" (2000, 220). At the same time, however, the Synoptics should not be seen as three voices against John's single vote in points of apparent discrepancy. Instead, each point of disagreement must be resolved by weighing FG and Mark against one another, with the understanding that both John and Mark developed their respective Gospels in service of theological interests (Fredriksen 2000, 28–34, 237–38). Viewed from this neutral perspective, it appears that John's presentation of Jesus may be more reliable than Mark's at several points. For example, John's claim that Jesus' ministry encompassed both Galilee and Judea, with movement back and forth between the two regions on multiple occasions, is consistent with the pre-70 C.E. Palestinian context and is likely to be accurate (Fredriksen 2000, 238–40). Similarly, John's account of Jesus' Jewish trial is "much more credible" because it lacks Mark's dramatic elements and explicit christological confession (Mark 14:62). Of course, both John and Mark could be wrong about the trial, but "if only one [account] is true, the more likely candidate is John's" (Fredriksen 2000, 223–24).

John A. T. Robinson's own subsequent work represents, in many respects, the pinnacle of New Look principles. His magnum opus *The Priority of John* was driven by a belief that the Fourth Gospel's witness "to the history and the [development of early Christian] theology, is … to be accorded a status of *primus inter pares*" among the Gospels (Robinson 1985, 36–37). After assessing John's ideological orientation and the incidental topographical and historical details in the text of FG, Robinson concluded that "the Fourth Gospel could take us as far back to source [Jesus] as any other" and found no reason to doubt that the Johannine tradition originated with a disciple of Jesus, perhaps even John the apostle. As a result, the Fourth Evangelist should be seen as "internal to his tradition" (Robinson 1985, 36–122; first quote 122, second quote 96). But notably, this does not mean that FG's witness is always the most primitive. For example, typical of the New Look perspective, Robinson defended the historical verisimilitude of a number of FG's discourse units by arguing that "there is no necessary absurdity or contradiction in asserting that the Johannine presentation [of Jesus' words] could be *both* the most mature *and* the most faithful to the original [historical] truth" at the same time (1985, 342). This strange combination of historicity and maturity is the result of John's free merger of Jesus' words with his own theological reflections, so that "the interpretation is thoroughly assimilated and integrated" into the sayings tradition (Robinson 1985, 298). Like Cullmann, Robinson attributed this compositional technique to the Fourth Evangelist's Paraclete doctrine, which "affects what we might call the 'laws of transformation' which determine his [the Fourth Evangelist's] presentation of Jesus in comparison with that of the Synoptists," who in fact generally come closer to transmitting Jesus' actual *ipsissima verba* (1985, 324). Hence, while Robinson placed the Johannine tradition closest to Jesus, he ultimately left aspects of the Fourth Gospel's presentation at the furthest remove from Jesus.

The New "Old Look"

In many respects, the changing tides Robinson forecast in his "New Look" paper marked a major shift in perspective that would clearly distinguish the Johannine scholarship of the second half of the twentieth century from the preceding generation. Certainly, it must have felt like a major shift in 1957, with so many working presuppositions under review. But from the hindsight of today's reader, Robinson's "new look" in many ways appears to be new icing on a stale cake—a different set of conclusions (or preclusions) built up from the same methods that had animated earlier scholarship. The old critical orthodoxy whose death Robinson eulogized and the New Look whose bright future he heralded were driven by the same underlying concerns. These concerns are reflected in two dominant images in the substructure of Robinson's essay: the "line" and the "author." "The line" here refers to the foundational role of chronological timelines as tools for analysis and interpretation, while the "author" refers to the notion that the producer of a text or tradition is its primary locus of meaning. Both of these guiding images reflect a desire to objectify interpretation by measuring a text against something outside itself—history in the former case, an author's intentions in the latter—and this desire was clearly the driving force in both the Old and New Looks on the Gospel of John.

The significance of this observation requires clarification, for much—indeed, most—biblical scholarship today is still driven by these same two concerns, focusing on the biblical text's relationship to history and using the author as an anchor in the historical ocean. As will be seen, many of the essays included in the present volume continue to reflect this perspective in varying degrees, a fact that highlights the overall continuity between contemporary Johannine scholarship and Robinson's generation. But the centrality of the line and the author in both the old critical orthodoxy and the New Look is notable today simply because so many scholars now reject both as canons of interpretation. For those "who are suspicious of the ideology or rhetoric of historiography, it is not necessary to employ historical investigation as the final arbiter of interpretation," because the locus of meaning has shifted from history and author to text and reader (Adam 1995, 164). And today, even scholars who utilize historical methods must, unlike Robinson, do their work in dialogue with others who reject the philosophical underpinnings of their approach. The historical critic of today is, for example, aware of feminist and postcolonial readings and may even absorb techniques from these readings from time to time in service of the historical enterprise. It will therefore be helpful, in contextualizing the chapters to follow, to highlight the role that the line and the author played in the old critical orthodoxy and the extent to which the New Look absorbed and preserved these images and their related methodological concerns.

The Line Game

Robinson's survey of the pre-1957 critical orthodoxy reveals the presence of a line—in this case a timeline—at the core of Johannine studies. This timeline begins on the left with a cross-shaped mark labeled "the historical Jesus" and ends on the right with an arrow labeled "A.D. 100." Each notch between these two endpoints represents a level of development in the early church's theology. Correlated to this temporal arrangement there is a geographical one, with the spaces closest to Jesus labeled "Palestine" and those further to the right designated "the ends of the earth." Things from Palestine, then, may be assumed to be closer to Jesus, while things farther off—in Asia Minor, for example—are more distant from Jesus. Similarly, the older things on the left of the timeline must be closer to Jesus than the newer things that appear on the right. For this reason, the placement of any particular object on this timeline (a written Gospel, for example) immediately carries a number of assumptions about the relative value of that thing in understanding Jesus: texts that are closer to Jesus in time and space must be of greater historical value. This is a matter of no small import, because "historical value" and "value in general" were closely correlated under the old critical orthodoxy—all five pillars of the Old Look relate directly to questions of historicity. In the lexicon of Robinson's "New Look" article, the terms "primitive" (referring to the left end of the timeline) and "mature" (referring to the right) function as a shorthand for this larger set of interpretive values and assumptions.

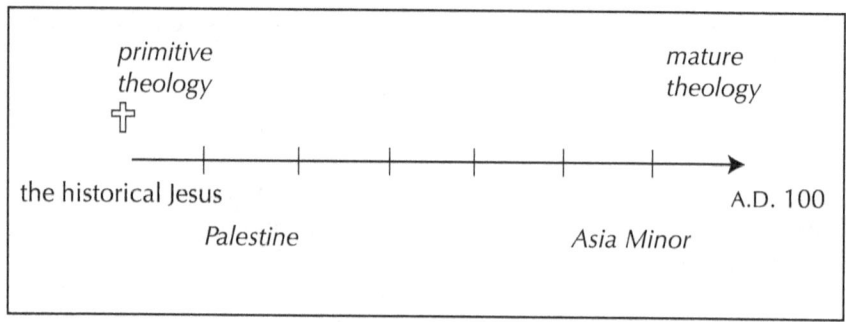

The Old Look Timeline

Such, then, was the infrastructure of the old critical orthodoxy: a line with Jesus at one end, Ignatius at the other, and the books of the New Testament somewhere in between. It was an apparently innocent heuristic tool, this timeline, but one that was wielded with a certain inevitable effect, for it becomes immediately apparent that the old critical orthodoxy was a sort of board game, with this timeline as its playing field. Notably, the board was not laid across the table but was, rather, placed upright against the wall before the contest began. Play proceeded by standing biblical texts on top of one another like so many blocks, and through a peculiar stipulation in the rulebook it was essential that each block be stacked neatly on the one below, there being no room for several texts to stand together side by side. In this respect, the Old Look's game board functioned as a sort of reverse thermometer, by which Gospels may be judged "hot" or "cold." Like a diagram of gnostic cosmology, the texts at the base of the stack were presumed to be closer to the life and teachings of the historical Jesus ("more primitive"), while those at the top were considered "more developed," meaning that they represent primarily the later theological views of the Gentile church. The object of the game was to situate the Gospel of John and its traditions/sources somewhere on this timeline/grid, to locate the Synoptics and other New Testament documents on the same grid, and then to tally the score by comparing the relative distances of all these texts to one another and to Jesus.

Viewed from this perspective, Robinson's outline of the old critical orthodoxy immediately reveals that the Gospel of John had lost the game. All five of the consensus assumptions that Robinson noted placed both John and his Gospel toward the top of the thermometer, well into the cold zone. The Fourth Gospel was found to be: (1) likely dependent on the Synoptics or, even worse, on other texts that history has not seen fit to preserve; (2) geographically and chronologically distant from Jesus and therefore not any kind of real witness to his ministry (much less an "apostolic" witness); and, as a result of numbers 1 and 2, (3) "the end-term of theological development in first-century Christianity" (Robinson 1962b, 95). Such was the unhappy denouement of the thermometer game for the Gospel of John in the era of the old critical orthodoxy.

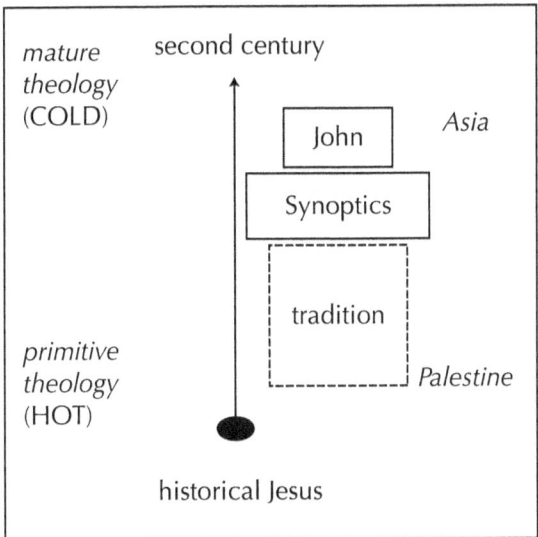

The Old Look Thermometer

Reflecting on this scenario, it seems clear that the Old Look drank deeply of what A. K. M. Adam has called "chronological determination," "a modern fascination with chronology" that is "dominated by the ideal of progress" and a tendency to value things on the basis of their place on an evolutionary spectrum (1995, 24–25). Adam traces the popularization of this model in biblical studies to Wilhelm Wrede, certainly a gatekeeper of the old critical orthodoxy that the New Look sought to displace. Wrede had argued that

> the only appropriate arrangement for a New Testament theology is a developmental scheme. Why? Because the true character of the writings is revealed only by such an arrangement. The various differing testimonies [in the New Testament canon] are only understood correctly when they are set in a developmental order that clarifies the relations of one [theological] position to the others. (Adam 1995, 73–74)

Reflecting this perspective, the Old Look was concerned with John's appropriation of Synoptic material and the theological interests that guided that appropriation. The Fourth Gospel was valued, or devalued, on the basis of this presumed evolutionary relationship and corollary assumptions about the text's historicity.

The reader of today who picks up "The New Look on the Fourth Gospel" for the first time, roughly fifty years after it was written, would perhaps expect Robinson to challenge this linear model and its underlying assumptions, to break the Old Look thermometer. But it quickly becomes clear that he has no such intention. The "new look" Robinson proposes does not seek to displace any of the five presuppositions of the previous generation, nor to rewrite the terms of the discussion, nor to mark out a new set of objectives that might call for new methods of inquiry. Instead, Robinson simply attempts to move the Gospel of John to a lower point on the scale, to make FG appear "more primitive" than was previously supposed. As a result, Robinson's "new look" is primarily a reshuffling of the cards, an act of moving the pieces to a different place on the game board and creating a new stack of texts with the Fourth Gospel closer to the bottom.

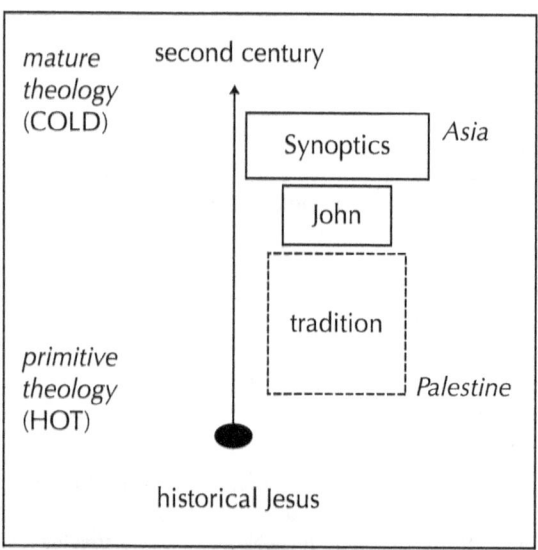

Robinson's New Look Thermometer

This phenomenon is most obvious, and most striking, at the moments when Robinson realizes that the Old Look's linear approach fails to adequately comprehend data from the biblical text. From time to time, today's reader of Robinson's essay may suspect that certain aspects of the Gospel of John defy the interpretive presuppositions of the old critical orthodoxy. These suspicions are sometimes directly confirmed by Robinson's observations. But remarkably, Robinson does not use these observations to question the underlying presuppositions of the Old Look. Instead, he simply reinterprets the conflicting data from FG to fit a slightly reworked version of the timeline. A notable example of this approach appears in Robinson's discussion of presupposition four, where the underlying image of the line actually irrupts into the surface text of his argument. While the old critical orthodoxy had concluded "that the fourth Evangelist represents the end-term of theological development in first-century Christianity," the New Look would argue that, "while it [the Fourth Evangelist's theology] is mature, it also stands very near to the primitive apostolic witness" (Robinson 1962b, 102). One wonders at this paradox: How could John be at the top of the thermometer and the bottom, developed and primitive, close to Jesus and far from Jesus, in Palestine and in Asia, all at the same time? Perhaps John's theology, as deducible from the Johannine literature, is simply too complex and paradoxical to be reduced to a linear model of this kind? Or perhaps John had no particular interest in those modern questions and categories that would tend to bifurcate his beliefs and set them neatly against those of other early Christians, or even against himself, in an evolutionary model? And if we conclude that this is indeed the case, have we threatened to render the entire Old Look project anachronistic? But just when Robinson might have dealt the death blow to the old orthodoxy's linear paradigm, he redeems it by reshaping the line in the form of an alphabet: the Fourth Evangelist "bestrides the whole development of New Testament thinking like a colossus" and "will be seen, I [Robinson] believe, to represent its *Alpha* as much as its *Omega*"—an obvious inconvenience should one need to look John up in the phone book (1962b, 102).

As if to illustrate the virtue of building the New Look on the ruins of the Old, Robinson proceeds to remodel discussion of "the [theological] point above all at which the fourth Evangelist is normally regarded as standing at the end of a line of doctrinal development ... namely, in his [the Fourth Evangelist's] eschatology" (1962b, 102–3). Once again, today's reader might suggest that the shortest route through this problem would be to question the validity of the notion of a monolithic "line of doctrinal development" in the early church's thought, especially one that terminated at a single distinct endpoint. Those who are familiar with the moves typical of today's postmodern readings might observe here that the Old Look reflected a "canonized orientation toward an absolute history," where "history" is understood as a sort of transcendental touchstone against which to evaluate literary texts. But this same postmodern person might further observe that "the discourse of modern historiography is no better equipped to avoid ideological overdetermination than is ... the New Testament's [own] discourse of historiography" (Adam 1995, 153–54), an observation that would place John on a level playing field not only with Mark and Luke but also with modern critics. "On what basis can it be claimed that a twentieth-century historian's version of the events in the first-century Mediterranean basin is truer than Luke's version (or Augustine's)? [Or, for the purposes of this essay, John's?] Only on a basis laid by the twentieth-century discipline of historical inquiry whose [very] authority is [today] in question" (Adam 1995, 156).

Such might be musings of the reader of today. Robinson, however, was content to play the Old Look's game, simply restacking the blocks rather than revising the rulebook. He begins at the bottom of the pile by arguing that "the original eschatology of Jesus ... was much more in the line of the prophets than of the apocalyptists." The question then becomes whether FG or the Synoptics should be placed next on the timeline: Which of the two appears to be more primitive, more directly derivative from Jesus' view? Most Old Look scholars had concluded that the Synoptics should come first, with FG advocating a more mystical or realized view of the kingdom as a sort of corrective to this earlier position—a conclusion entirely consistent with the Old Look premise that John knew and borrowed from the Synoptics. In other words, the Synoptics were written at a point on the timeline when apocalyptic elements were being gradually added to the Jesus tradition, whereas FG was written at a later point when these elements were being phased out. Robinson, however, argues that FG in fact "represents a [primitive] form of the tradition that has never seriously undergone this process [of adding apocalyptic elements] at all." As a result, FG's "picture of the vindication and visitation of the Son of man is still essentially that, I believe, of Jesus himself and of the most primitive tradition." How, then, does one explain the occasional apocalyptic statements in the Fourth Gospel? Robinson resolves this problem entirely in terms of the timeline as well, arguing that these apocalyptic elements point to "the contact of the Johannine tradition with this [apocalyptic] stream of thought after it had been thrown ... into the more cosmopolitan world of Asia Minor" (1962b, 102–3). Whether or not this conclusion is valid, Robinson's mode of argument demonstrates the New Look's resolve to beat the old critical orthodoxy at its own game. While the well-known aporiae in Johannine eschatology could be cited as proof that the notion of an evolving, monolithic early Christian theology is inadequate, Robinson is content simply to relabel portions of the Old Look's timeline and then situate FG at a more favorable position.

From the perspective of today's interpreter, then, both the pre-1957 critical orthodoxy and Robinson's "new look" were characterized by an extreme confidence in the historical-critical enterprise. The postmodernist would challenge this confidence on the grounds that all reconstructions of early Christian history and theology must be viewed with suspicion, especially when these reconstructions are utilized as authoritative interpretive keys. But today, even some scholars who are deeply committed to historical criticism might feel compelled to disagree with Robinson's understanding of the first-century context. This is the case because current scholarship is informed by a more extensive database in reconstructions of Christian origins than Robinson could have utilized in 1957, one that includes newly available materials from outside the canon. Further, today's scholarship generally does not sharply distinguish between the types of materials in this database, explicitly rejecting labels such as "orthodox" and "heretical." By refusing to privilege the canonical texts as historical witnesses, these scholars have, like their postmodern counterparts, challenged the notion of a single, evolving early Christian history and theology, even though they may affirm the basic orientation of Robinson's interpretive method.

The Author Quest

Along with the limitations of the chronological approach, the New Look absorbed a second and related guiding image from the old critical orthodoxy: the image of the author as the locus of a text's meaning. This emphasis on authorial authority is particularly striking because, as noted above, New Look scholars were generally content to think of "the Fourth Evangelist" in vague terms: a nameless disciple, an unknown redactor of lost sources, an entire community with an uncertain history, or a faceless Johannine tradition. Despite this fact, the relationship between the mysterious Fourth Evangelist and his subject, Jesus, was the New Look's central interpretive problem, and each of the five New Look presuppositions touched on some facet of this one larger issue. Taken together, these presuppositions reveal the extent to which both Old and New Look scholarship were obsessed with the pursuit of one set of historical questions—Who is John? Where did he live? What books did he read?—as keys to the ultimate historical question: What does the Gospel of John have to do with Jesus?

Here again, today's reader notes that Robinson did not foresee the emergence of an entirely new critical mindset, one that would locate textual meaning in the reader rather than the author and thus treat the Gospel of John, in the words of Roland Barthes, as a "text" rather than a "work." The concept of a specific "author" allows the interpreter to think of the Gospel of John as a "work," a closed system whose meaning originated in the mind of the person(s) who produced it, a doctrine that drove both the old critical orthodoxy and the New Look (Barthes 1977, 143, 147). But one might instead choose to view FG as a "text," an independent and freestanding "tissue of quotations drawn from the innumerable centres of culture" that does not represent any specific author's intentions. The "text" model would lead the interpreter to approach the Gospel of John as "plural," not in the sense that it has several latent meanings at once, but in the sense that it need not refer to any specific objective reality outside itself. Since the "text" is not viewed as carrying a specific, singular meaning reflecting an author's intention, it is inappropriate to use terms such as "the true, the probable, or even the possible" in evaluating varying readings (Barthes 1974, 6). Judgments of this sort are relevant only to "works," because the determination that an interpretation is "true" or "false" requires the notion of an objective standard that transcends the artistic product, an objective standard that appears in Robinson's essay under the guise of the author of FG, the mysterious Fourth Evangelist. By contrast, the "text," liberated from the constraints of its author's beliefs and intentions, "achieves a state which is possible only in the dictionary or poetry—places where the noun can live without its article—and is reduced to a sort of zero degree, pregnant with all past and future specifications" (Barthes 1967, 54). These "specifications" are generated by the reader of FG rather than the author, moving the locus of meaning and authority away from the Fourth Evangelist and toward the contemporary interpreter.

Of course, one can scarcely fault Robinson for failing to foresee the rise of interpretive moves of this kind (although Barthes's first major book had been released in 1953, and theorists such as I. A. Richards had been moving toward similar models of language and rhetoric since the 1920s). Once again, Robinson's assumptions are notable today only because so many scholars have since rejected the notion that the author may serve as an objective reference point for the "meaning" of the Gospel of John. As early as 1983, well within the *terminus ad quem* of the New Look era, Alan Culpepper observed that "in the majority of [New Look] studies the gospel [of John] has been used as a source for evidence of the process by which it was composed, the theology of the evangelist, or the character and circumstances of the Johannine community." But the emerging influx of interdisciplinary literary models would generate readings of FG that proceed under the assumption that meaning "lies on this side of the text, between the reader and the text," so that "the experience of reading the text is more important than understanding the process of its composition" (Culpepper 1983, 3, 5). Viewed from this perspective, the Gospel of John is less the work of a specific author from the ancient past than a text that provokes meanings in the minds of modern readers.

The New Current through John

As the preceding review has shown, Robinson's "New Look on the Fourth Gospel" was ultimately only that: a new look at questions already established by previous generations, through lenses ground on well-worn methods of criticism, not a remodeling or restructuring of the Johannine puzzle but a rearrangement of familiar pieces. Fifty years later, perhaps the most notable feature of Robinson's "New Look" essay is the absence of a criticism of criticism: no sense of reconfiguring the terms of the debate; no sense of offering not only new answers but also categorically new questions; no sense of appropriating new models, interdisciplinary models, to address these new issues; no sense of asking whether history, authorship, and literary dependence should continue to dominate the discussion; no sense that early Christian theology might be a complex animal that must be viewed in terms of parallel trajectories rather than stages of evolution; no sense that the Gospel of John might echo with voices outside the canon; no sense that methodological heterodoxy might become the next critical orthodoxy.

Of course, today's "new current through John," for want of a better label, maintains sufficient continuity with Robinson's generation to speak of an ongoing tradition of "Johannine scholarship." Several of the trends Robinson identified continue to shape the contours of current discussion, and none of the issues he mentioned have been entirely removed from the table. But alongside these threads, spun on the looms of centuries past, bold new lines have been woven into the fabric by other hands, currents from streams that Robinson and his contemporaries did not foresee. Recent Johannine scholarship has not simply built on its past but has rebuilt its past, recasting old questions and answers in the forge of new approaches. Of course, the history of every academic discipline is marked by change and growth, with new developments often rising in specific opposition to established orthodoxy. Following this rule, the New Look of Robinson's day represented, in many respects, a radical departure from the past. But the striking differences Robinson noted between his generation and the previous generation, significant as they were at the time, pale against the differences one notes in even a cursory comparison of Robinson's era with current scholarship. When comparing the Johannine scholarship of 1957 to that of 2007, one is faced not so much with a "new look" as a polar shift.

Specifically, the emerging "new current" through John, as represented by the essays in this volume, differs notably from the New Look era in at least two key respects. First, the current wave of research is characterized by *methodological diversity*, resulting from the influx of interdisciplinary approaches into biblical scholarship. As a result, whereas Robinson could catalogue Johannine scholarship in terms of major conclusions, any contemporary attempt to catalogue scholarship must also take account of interpretive methods. For example, in 1957 Robinson could conveniently distinguish scholars who believed that FG reflects primitive theology from those who saw FG as the endpoint of early Christian theological development. But one could scarcely use a model of this kind to characterize the differences between a postcolonial reading of John 4, a folkloristic treatise on the Johannine sayings tradition, and an inquiry into the social memory and identity of the Johannine community, even if these three studies somehow arrived at similar exegetical conclusions. Indeed, in the current academic context, the term "exegesis" must be used selectively when describing specific studies, a nuance Robinson could not have foreseen. This diversification of method in Johannine studies has been accompanied by a thorough criticism of criticism, a sustained conscious reflection on the presuppositions and limitations of previous approaches to the text. In general, the New Look was not informed by a true criticism of criticism and therefore did not advocate the kind of realignment of the terms of debate that characterizes contemporary Johannine scholarship.

Second, the "new current" through John is characterized by a *diversity of global perspectives*. A cursory review of recent publications, or of the program book for the Society of Biblical Literature's Annual Meeting, will immediately reveal that the Johannine literature is no longer in the safekeeping of Caucasian males. For a variety of reasons, the ranks of Johannine scholars now include men and women, Catholics, mainline Protestants, evangelicals, Jews, atheists, agnostics, and persons from a wide variety of nationalities: North Americans, Europeans, South and Central Americans, Africans, Asians, Australasians. In summary, whereas Robinson's era was characterized by a diversity of opinions on certain fixed issues, the "new current" through John is characterized by a diversity of methods of research and by the diversity of global voices engaged in dialogue on the key issues. For this reason, when comparing the rising generation of scholars to those from Robinson's era, one must speak not of a "generation gap" but rather of a chasm in consciousness, a complete paradigm shift in theoretical orientations and in the roster of participants in the academic arena.

Despite these significant differences, one key aspect of the New Look's spirit continues to drive the "new current" in Johannine studies. In Robinson's words, "The 'new look', if I may use the term, is characterized by a certain impertinence, which insists that it may be worth asking other, often apparently naïve, questions, which these [older] presuppositions would rule out as ones that the [Fourth] Gospel was never meant to answer. This is partly because if one does ask them one frequently seems to get what look like astonishingly sensible answers, and partly because the foundations of these presuppositions themselves are beginning to appear a great deal less certain than they [once] did" (Robinson 1962b, 95–96). The essays that follow will illustrate the ongoing relevance of this assessment.

Part 1
New Currents through History and Theology

"I WILL RAISE [WHOM?] UP ON THE LAST DAY": ANTHROPOLOGY AS A FEATURE OF JOHANNINE ESCHATOLOGY*

Jaime Clark-Soles

Robinson's paper "The New Look on the Fourth Gospel" enumerates five presuppositions of the (then) "current critical orthodoxy on the fourth Gospel" (1962b, 94–96). Under presupposition number four—that the Fourth Gospel (FG) represents only the latest stage of theological development in first-century Christianity—Robinson addresses eschatology. In his estimation, "critical orthodoxy" assumes that John has finally achieved a realized eschatology; "critical orthodoxy" further asserts that the final form of FG sloughs off the "crude adventism" of an earlier apocalyptic eschatology. In contrast, Robinson argues that neither Jesus nor the primitive church held an apocalyptic eschatology; rather, apocalyptic eschatology, which distinctly emphasizes a future, second advent of Christ, developed only gradually: "The Synoptists witness to a progressive apocalypticization of the message of Jesus" (1962b, 103). Robinson argues against "critical orthodoxy" when he claims that FG actually reflects an earlier, nonapocalyptic phase quite in line with Jesus himself. This would mean, then, that the reference to Christ's return found in John 21 is *not* the remains of an early, first-stratum apocalyptic eschatology that the author has failed to bury entirely; rather, according to Robinson, FG has no future, apocalyptic eschatology in its first stratum of theological thinking (a layer already fully formed but not committed to writing by Paul's time). Instead, Robinson argues, the strains of apocalyptic found in FG crept in only after "the Johannine tradition" (which lies behind and is quite distinct from the text known as FG) originally located in "the relative isolation of its Palestinian milieu" came into contact with "the more cosmopolitan world of Asia Minor" (1962b, 103). That contact, he argues, resulted in the accretion of apocalyptic

---

* I would like to thank Ila Kraft and the Graduate Bible Colloquium of Perkins School of Theology for their contributions to this essay.

elements that were not originally present, thus causing the Johannine tradition finally to participate in the growing trend toward the "apocalyptic *faux pas*" (1962b, 103). The final stage of the Johannine literature, Robinson contends, is represented by the thoroughgoing apocalypticism of Revelation. In this essay, I will argue for "a still more excellent way" to approach the subject of Johannine eschatology.

Robinson's discussion of Johannine eschatology centers exclusively on a diachronic methodology, trying to understand John's eschatology by positing very early layers of theological rumination, followed by the bulk of the written Gospel, followed by an "epilogue" (John 21). To compel, Robinson's idea that the Fourth Evangelist is in conversation with a growing tendency toward a doctrine of the *parousia* (Christ's second coming) would need to be argued in much finer detail: In conversation with whom, specifically? Where? At one level, Robinson answers the question when he refers to "the more cosmopolitan world of Asia Minor," but this answer is too vague to be meaningful. Why would Robinson imagine apocalyptic thought as more prominent in Asia Minor than in Palestine, especially given his heavy reliance on the Dead Sea Scrolls? Robinson would further need to reflect upon whose best interest is served by a doctrine of the *parousia*.

Writing in the 50s, Paul already had a notion of the *parousia* (cf. 1 Cor 15; 1 Thess 4). If FG's initial theology was already developed by the time of Paul, as Robinson maintains, then why should one *not* assume that John also had a doctrine of the *parousia* at the earliest stage? Robinson argues that "the Johannine tradition" followed a wholly independent trajectory ("Indeed, he *is* his own tradition" [1962b, 98]) that bypassed Paul and leads directly back to Jesus. But the presence of apocalyptic elements in FG could just as easily support the conclusion that John and Paul come from a similar trajectory, namely, one that was apocalyptic at an early stage. If Robinson adjudicates the matter by assuming that the southern Palestinian trajectory must be different from the Pauline trajectory, this would be problematic on at least two very different counts. First, as indicated above, the Dead Sea Scrolls community in southern Palestine is extremely apocalyptic, so the notion of southern Palestine as isolated from apocalyptic thought does not stand. Second, the notion of southern Palestine as "isolated" is easily contested by reference to the works of Josephus, if not by Paul's own letters, which attest to social exchange between the Palestinian churches and those outside of Palestine.

Finally, that Robinson looks to Revelation as part of his diachronic picture of the development of Johannine thought is now peculiar, for what has Revelation to do with FG? Though his article is certainly helpful, insightful, and multifariously informative, much of Robinson's eschatological argument is too hypothetical.

In what follows I will avoid the language so prominent in Robinson's article and common to many diachronic analyses, such as "remarkably primitive" versus "extraordinarily mature" or "essential maturity" versus "formal maturity." Furthermore, rather than continue endless debate about source-critical issues or which eschatology the historical Jesus likely held, I will explore the ways in which understanding FG's *anthropology* might illuminate the study of its eschatology. By "anthropology," I refer to a question that occupied the minds of philosophers and theologians alike in antiquity just as it does today: What is a human being? As feminist, gender, and postcolonial studies have taught us, not everyone signifies the same thing when using the language of personhood. In what follows I will provide some preliminary soundings regarding the composition of human beings according to FG, but only with a view to informing the discussion of their fate. The thesis of this disquisition is this: the Fourth Gospel maintains a *bestowed, realized immortality* for believers rather than a doctrine of future resurrection. I will return to this claim at the conclusion of the paper.

The Composition of Human Beings

The Fourth Evangelist does not present her or his anthropology under the categories of logic, ethics, and physics, the traditional triumvirate among Hellenistic philosophers. Rather, one must piece together the Fourth Evangelist's view of the person by attending to the language present in, and perhaps even the language absent from, the text of FG. A large section of Robert Jewett's *Paul's Anthropological Terms* is devoted to an analysis of individual anthropological terms, specifically *sarx* ("flesh"), *pneuma tou anthrōpou* ("human spirit"), *sōma* ("body"), *kardia* ("heart"), *psychē* ("soul"), *nous* ("mind"), *exo/ezo anthrōpos* ("outer/inner person"), and *syneidēsis* ("conscience, consciousness"). I will take a similar approach here, guided by several precautions in my analysis of the relevant Johannine anthropological terms. First, I warn against what Jewett calls "the lexical method," which abstracts words from their literary and historical contexts (1971, 6–8). Instead, one must take into account the literary context of the sentence, the paragraph, and the document as a whole; relate the terms to the historical situation (including the author's battle against opponents, which may dictate some of the terms chosen); and relate the terms to the linguistic horizon of the first century. Second, one must engage in the comparative task. What might be learned from the Hebrew Bible, consolation literature, medical texts, Hellenistic religion and philosophy? Third, one must account not simply for the strict meaning of a term but also for any discernible fluctuation in meaning (Jewett 1971, 6–7). Following these guidelines, I will proceed to analyze FG's anthropological vocabulary, looking particularly for clues to the Fourth Evangelist's eschatological outlook.

The Johannine Terms

Four times the Johannine Jesus repeats his promise to raise up the believer "on the last day" (*en tē eschatē hēmera*), all in chapter 6 (6:39, 40, 44, 54). Jesus refers again to this "last day" at 12:48, where he indicates that his word will *judge* (*krinei*) the nonbeliever. What is the nature of the believer, such that on this "last day" he or she will be raised? When does the author envision the occurrence of this "last day"? Is the believer to continue some sort of existence after he or she has died? In order to answer such questions, one must understand what the author means by such terms as *sarx* ("flesh"; and, closely related, *haima*, "blood"), *pneuma* ("spirit"), *anthrōpos* ("person, human being"), *sōma* ("body"), *psychē* ("soul"), *kardia* ("heart"), *noeō* ("perceive, comprehend"), and *koilia* ("belly, womb").[1]

Due to space restrictions, let me state directly a number of conclusions, moving quickly over the least important to more significant features. (1) The terms *gynē* ("woman, female") and *anēr* ("man, male") do not factor into a discussion of anthropology in a way that affects the Fourth Evangelist's eschatology. (2) *Koilia* and *noeō* occur only infrequently in FG. (3) *Nous* ("mind") does not appear at all in FG, which is surprising given its customary role in anthropological discussions by other biblical authors and also Hellenistic philosophers and the Fourth Evangelist's general interest in knowledge (*ginōskō*; *gnōsis*). (4) The Fourth Evangelist never applies *kardia* to Jesus, only to his disciples, and the term always maintains the Old Testament range of meaning for "heart" (*lēb*), the seat of emotions, understanding, and volition (Wolff 1974, 40–58). (5) *Psychē*, *sarx* (to which *haima* relates closely), *sōma*, *pneuma*, and *anthrōpos* are key features of the Fourth Evangelist's anthropology. (6) Four of the Fourth Evangelist's key anthropological terms—*psychē*, *sarx*, *haima*, and *anthrōpos*—are used of both Jesus and others, whereas *pneuma* and *sōma* are used *only* in reference to Jesus. Thus, the Fourth Evangelist's anthropology categorizes Jesus as both similar to and different from human beings; he is both divine and human, God enfleshed. (7) Aspects of these terms/categories overlap with one another.

While one can imagine various fruitful ways to present the discussion—for example, by discussing the terms in the order of their appearance in the

---

1. "Flesh, in John's anthropology, is not a part of the human but the human being as natural and mortal" (Schneiders 2005, 171).

text—I will analyze FG's anthropological terms in descending order of usage frequency.

The Fourth Evangelist uses *anthrōpos* in six ways.

(1) The Fourth Evangelist sometimes uses *anthrōpos* as the generic word for an individual person or for humanity in general, before value judgments are attached and categories of believers and unbelievers obtain. In John 16:21, the Fourth Evangelist speaks of a woman giving birth to an *anthrōpos*, not to a soul, mind, or spirit. The Samaritan woman testifies about Jesus to *anthrōpoi* (4:28), and Nicodemus wants to know how an *anthrōpos* can reenter the womb (3:27). I initially assumed that passages such as 2:10 and 5:7 fall under this category as well, but now I am not so sure. In 2:10 the steward observes that an *anthrōpos* serves the good wine first. True enough, but, as the reader comes to learn in the unfolding narrative, Jesus, who provides abundant wine for the wedding feast, is much more than *anthrōpos*. This may be an example of Johannine irony. If the steward had known who Jesus was, he might have asked Jesus for living wine, or wine that does not perish. At 5:7 the lame man at Bethesda has no *anthrōpos* to help him attain healing. True enough, but Jesus, who is much more than an *anthrōpos*, is available to heal him. Again, I think this is an example of double entendre.

(2) The Fourth Evangelist sometimes uses *anthrōpos* negatively of human beings. For instance, its usage overlaps that of *sarx* (treated below) in a sinister sense when we learn at John 2:25 that Jesus did not need anyone to testify concerning human beings because he knew what was in the human being, presumably *qua* human being. The author may have Gen 6:5–6 and 8:21 in mind. At John 17:6 *anthrōpos* approximates the more neutral meaning of *sarx* when Jesus designates his followers as the "*anthrōpoi* whom you [the Father] gave to me out of the world."

(3) The Fourth Evangelist sometimes uses *anthrōpos* to refer to a specific individual: "There was a *person* whose name was John" (1:6); Jesus met "a *person* blind from birth" (9:1). The term *anēr* is never used to refer to a specific male individual; only *anthrōpos* is used in such contexts. By contrast, the word *anthrōpos* is never used of a specific female individual. When women are referred to at all, as in chapter 4, the person is referred to by gender, *gynē* ("woman"). Presumably this bespeaks the common cultural assumption that male is the default of "person," while female, as the "other" or unusual part of the equation, requires some secondary or specific identification. Thus in chapter 4 the storyteller displays some discomfort with, or flags some sense of, the Samaritan woman's otherness. Why tell us she is a woman of Samaria rather than an *anthrōpos* of Samaria? If the author had used *anthrōpos* of this character, first-century readers would probably have pictured a male. While I do think the author maintains patriarchal assump-

tions (cf. 6:10), I do not think that these assumptions factor into the Fourth Evangelist's eschatology. Neither the Samaritan woman nor Mary Magdalene (ch. 20) must "become male" (cf. *Gos. Thom.* 114) to receive the rewards the Fourth Evangelist's Jesus has to offer. In other words, although the terms *gynē* and *anēr* do reveal important anthropological assumptions on the part of the author, they do not significantly affect the *eschatological* picture. FG is not the *Gospel of Thomas*.

(4) The Fourth Evangelist sometimes uses *anthrōpos* to refer to Jesus in his role as "Son of Man" (*huios tou anthrōpou*). In John 3:13 Jesus refers to the Son of Man simultaneously as the one who will be lifted up and the one who has already (perfect tense) ascended, thereby collapsing present and future in a way that reflects the author's postnarrative perspective. In addition to collapsing time, the Fourth Evangelist artfully uses titles to collapse the role and reward of Jesus into the role and reward of those who believe in him. Jesus repeatedly calls himself "Son of Man" (1:51; 3:13, 14; 5:27; 6:27, 53, 62; 8:28; 9:35; 12:23, 34; 13:31), the last occurrence of the phrase coming just as he enters his passion. Because Jesus, who is equal to God and *is* God, is also the Son of Man, believers become children, not of flesh and blood, but of God (1:13). Jesus is brought down, but on his way back up believers latch on and become elevated as well.

(5) On several occasions in FG *anthrōpos* is used incorrectly by opponents to label Jesus. There is a vast difference between *huios tou anthrōpou* and *anthrōpos*, a point the author makes through the use of irony. Jesus' incorrigible opponents designate him as *anthrōpos*, but when they do, the Fourth Evangelist indicates that the characters lack understanding of Jesus' true identity. This is true of Caiaphas (11:50), those who question the blind man (9:16, 24), the woman who questions Peter by the gate (18:17), and, famously, Pilate (19:5). This lack of understanding is writ especially large in chapter 5 and at 10:33, where Jesus' opponents accuse him of making himself God when he is only an *anthrōpos*. At 8:40 Jesus calls himself an *anthrōpos*, but only because he is taking up his opponents' line of argument. Surely they should agree that there have been *anthrōpoi* sent by God, but Jesus is not even treated as well as one of those, let alone as one who is united with God (10:33–36).

(6) On several occasions in FG *anthrōpos* is used by potential followers who have not yet arrived at a revelation of Jesus' full identity. When these characters apply the word to Jesus, the Fourth Evangelist always makes it clear, through irony, that such a designation implies, "not enough." Thus, the Samaritan woman mistakes Jesus for an *anthrōpos* in 4:29, as does the man born blind in chapter 9. Although both begin in ignorance, each eventually calls Jesus by more appropriate titles ("prophet" and "Christ," 4:19, 29; "prophet" and "Lord," 9:17, 38).

Pneuma ("spirit") occurs twenty-four times in FG. It can refer to: (1) the Holy Spirit; (2) the category that is the opposite of "flesh," as in the Nicodemus story (John 3) and the bread of life discourse, where the spirit makes alive but the flesh is useless (6:63); (3) the *nature* and *identity* of God ("God is spirit," 4:24); and (4) the *manner* in which God is to be worshiped ("in spirit and in truth," 4:23; dative of manner).

The distinctiveness of the Holy Spirit is addressed in John 7:39: "Now he [Jesus] said this about the Spirit, which believers in him were to receive; for as yet there was no Spirit, because Jesus was not yet glorified." Here we learn that, while Jesus is conducting his earthly ministry, no one except Jesus enjoys the gift of the Spirit. This is quite unlike the Gospel of Luke, then, where little of import occurs without the aid of the Spirit, who has been active in the lives of the characters even before Jesus arrives. In John, the inspiriting of the believers takes place only after Jesus has died and risen, when Jesus bestows the spirit from the cross (19:30) and when he breathes on his disciples and says, "Receive the Holy Spirit" (20:22). The Holy Spirit is available, therefore, only to believers. Jesus calls the Spirit "another Advocate," implying that Jesus is the first Advocate (14:16); in many ways the Spirit serves the same role as Jesus and is intimately related to both God and Jesus.

The word *pneuma* is not used in reference to a part of human composition until John 11:33, where we learn that Jesus is disturbed in spirit and troubled (*tarassō;* cf. 13:21). Here, *pneuma* appears to approximate *kardia*, though the Fourth Evangelist refuses to use *kardia* when speaking of Jesus' agitation, preferring *pneuma* and *psychē* instead. The Fourth Evangelist describes Jesus' death by saying that Jesus "handed over his spirit" (19:30), presumably to the God who inspired Jesus at his baptism. It remains an oddity, however, that Jesus finally gives up his *pneuma* when earlier he has said that he will lay down his *psychē* for his "sheep" (10:17–18). Mary Coloe provides a partial solution to this problem when she insists that Jesus does not "give up" his spirit but rather "bestows" the Spirit from the cross:

> After Jesus' word of completion *tetelestai* ["It is finished"; 19:30], he performs his final sovereign act as he bows his head and hands down (*paredōken*) upon the nascent Christian community the promised gift of the Spirit (v. 30). The phrase *paredōken to pneuma* is frequently seen through a Synoptic interpretative model—Jesus gives up his spirit (i.e., his life). This is not what the Johannine texts says. The term *paradidōmi* is not a euphemism for death; it refers to the handing on or bequest of something to a successor.... At this moment Jesus' words to Nicodemus are realized as a disciple experiences being "born from above" (3:3, 5). (Coloe 2001, 189)

What makes *pneuma* such an interesting category for an anthropological discussion is the way that the Fourth Evangelist has taken one of the most common features of ancient anthropology and made it a specifically Christian category. Hellenistic philosophers, particularly Stoics, hold forth at length about *pneuma* as a feature of a person. For Zeno, fire and breath ("hot breath") are part of soul. Medical writers conceived of *pneuma* as the "vital" spirit transmitted via the arteries. For Chrysippus, *pneuma* is the vehicle of the logos. "Intelligent pneuma" is "something which is both a physical component of the world and an agent capable of rational action" (Long 1986, 155). This approximates FG's usage, where *pneuma* is physical, the disciples can feel it, it blows where it wills (3:8), and it is also responsible for guiding the disciples in all truth (16:13), among other things. For the Stoics, *pneuma* serves a connective function: it "holds together" earth and water. "The universe itself is a sphere, and all its constituents tend to move towards the center; but only earth and water actually possess weight.... The *pneuma*, unlike the passive elements, pervades the whole cosmic sphere and unites the center with the circumference.... This function of *pneuma* in the macrocosm is equally at work in every individual body. Organic and inorganic things alike owe their identity and their properties to the *pneuma*" (Long 1986, 156). The Fourth Evangelist follows suit by arguing that *pneuma* is a connective entity. In FG, however, *pneuma* does not connect the human being with the cosmos; rather, it connects certain human beings (believers) with the *creator* of the cosmos. *Pneuma* is now defined as the Holy *pneuma* whose role is definable (it teaches truth, guides, reminds, and so forth).

For the authors of the Hebrew Bible, spirit (*rûaḥ*) is used in reference to God and human beings (Wolff 1974, 32–39). With respect to God, it signifies God's vital power; with respect to humanity, it signifies breath, feelings, and will. In his *Anthropology of the Old Testament*, Wolff entitles the chapter on spirit "*Rûaḥ*—Man as He Is Empowered" and notes in the very first paragraph, "*Rûaḥ* must from the very beginning properly be called a theo-anthropological term" (Wolff 1974, 32). He concludes the chapter by claiming, "Most of the texts that deal with the r[*ûaḥ*] of God or man show God and man in a dynamic relationship" (1974, 39). While the latter statement, *mutatis mutandi*, could be made of FG insofar as *pneuma* serves as a critical link between God and humanity, there is a crucial difference: Old Testament anthropology, like that of the Stoics, imagines *pneuma* as constitutive of all persons, whereas FG takes great pains to argue otherwise.

To summarize, Jesus is the only character in the narrative of FG who is said to have *pneuma* before the resurrection appearances. *Pneuma* descends on him early in the narrative, and he hands over *pneuma* at the very end. Clearly, *pneuma* is not a natural, normal part of a person's constitution. It is a gift bestowed by God and available only to those who believe in Jesus. The bestowal of the gift on believers takes place by the end of the narrative (John 20:22), so *pneuma* is yet another gift promised to the believing reader and realized in the reader's present. There is no indication that any fullness is lacking here and now for the believing reader, a feature in harmony with the Fourth Evangelist's realized eschatology. Because believers have received the spirit who is connected with truth, they can worship God appropriately in spirit and in truth. There is no hint of an enigmatic Pauline "mirror" (1 Cor 13:12). Light, truth, and clear vision have been granted in fullness with the bestowal of *pneuma* effected by Jesus' death and resurrection.

The Fourth Evangelist uses the word *sarx*, often translated "flesh," thirteen times. On first glance, one might assume that *sarx* is a highly esteemed thing, since Jesus, the "Word," has become *sarx* (John 1:14). More than half of the occurrences of this term appear in chapter 6, the bread discourse, where for the most part it is Jesus' *sarx* that is addressed. By eating Jesus' *sarx* one receives life (6:33). He gives his *sarx* as bread for the sake of the life of the world, the world for whom God sent his Son. In fact, anyone who does *not* eat his flesh (*sarx*) and drink his blood (*haima*) has no life (*zōē*). In this discourse, a comparison of *sarx* with the quail provided by God in the wilderness is probably implied (Exod 16:13; Num 11:31–32). This is especially indicated by the otherwise inexplicable use of *trōgō* for "eat" (6:54, 56, 57, 58; 13:18), instead of *esthiō*, the usual word. *Trōgō* implies chomping, crunching, or gnawing, as the Israelites gnawed the flesh of the quail off of the bone. Just as Jesus, the "bread of life," is superior to the manna given in the wilderness, so Jesus' *sarx* is superior to the *sarx* of the quail.

Negatively, at John 1.13 the Fourth Evangelist links *sarx* with "blood" and "the will of man" in specific contrast to God. One who is "born of flesh" is different from one who is "born of spirit" (3:6). Jesus' opponents "judge according to the flesh," which obviously casts *sarx* in a negative light (8:15; my translation). In 6:63 *sarx* is useless, while *pneuma* gives life, an exception to the discussion of *sarx* in the bread discourse. It is important to note that the category *sarx* need not be negative in and of itself; it is negative only when compared with Jesus. Before Jesus, bread was bread, water was water, and flesh was flesh—certainly nothing to testify about. After Jesus, all of these categories become options for human beings: if one chooses plain bread, water, and flesh over Jesus as bread, water, and flesh, one will miss out on life. This reminds us of Jewett's notion of "fluctuation in meaning" (1971, 6–7). Jesus transforms *sarx*, a negative phenomenon apart from participation in him, into something good and life-giving. *Sarx* alone ends in death, just as bread alone, the kind that Moses gives (6:49), ends in death, and water alone, the kind that Jacob's well gives (4:13), ends in death. Jesus transforms the mundane into the spiritual by his participation in the mundane. Just as the water from Jacob's well is not necessarily negative in and of itself, the *sarx* just *is*, before Jesus transforms it by participating in it. This is the force of 17:2, where Jesus, the Word made flesh, announces that he has authority over *all* flesh. Because of Jesus' participation in *sarx*, those who believe in Jesus no longer live according to *sarx* alone. They align their *sarx* with *pneuma* so that spirit, God, and life are associated with the believer.

All human beings, including Jesus, have *sarx* and *haima* ("blood"). When referring to Jesus, these words have a positive connotation; when referring to other human beings, they represent the human being apart from Jesus. Because of and through Jesus, *sarx* and *haima* can become *redeemed* categories if one chooses to abide in Jesus. The Fourth Evangelist seeks to pull the reader out of the mundane into the sublime. The possibility of the sublime is fully present by the end of the narrative, when Jesus returns.

Psychē ("soul, life") appears ten times in FG. Four of these occurrences refer directly to Jesus' *psychē*. Jesus lays down his *psychē* for the sheep (John 10:11, 15, 17), and Jesus' *psychē* is troubled (12:27). Twice *psychē* refers to what Peter wants to lay down for Jesus (13:37, 38). Three times this term occurs in general statements about would-be disciples: Jesus says that those who love their *psychē* will lose it; those who hate it in this world will guard it for eternal life (12:25). Finally, *psychē* is what one lays down for one's friends (15:13). Jesus, of course, models each of these elements. In every instance save one (12:25), *psychē* can be taken to refer to something like the post-Homeric expanded *psychē* that combines aspects of the free-soul and body-soul (see Bremmer 2002, 1–10). It represents the individual personality (Jesus and Peter declare it to be their own), the seat of emotions (Jesus' soul is troubled), and that which "endows the body with life and consciousness, but does not stand for the part of the person that survives after death" (Bremmer 2002, 2). One could argue, however, that the Fourth Evangelist has been influenced primarily by the LXX, which renders the Hebrew *nepeš* as *psychē*, thus making any discussion of the pagan literature superfluous at this point. For purposes of the present study, two important features of the Fourth Evangelist's use of *psychē* should be noted. First, the Fourth Evangelist imbues the term with a new meaning unparalleled in either the Hebrew Bible or pagan literature. The Fourth Evangelist's *psychē* is far more robust than the Hebrew Bible's *nepeš*, which does not endure for eternity; it is also unitary, unlike the meaning of the term in Platonic-based philosophies. Second, in FG *psychē* has no meaning of its own; it draws meaning from its relationship to *other* Johannine anthropological terms. To those terms we now turn.

The word *kardia* ("heart") appears only seven times in FG, most often in the Farewell Discourse (John 14–17). Before that, it occurs only in the quotation from Isaiah at John 12:40, which, following customary Old Testament anthropology, indicates that the heart is the seat of understanding. The *kardia* is also susceptible to the wiles of the devil (13:2). Chapter 14 opens and closes with virtually identical language in which Jesus exhorts his disciples to let their hearts be untroubled (*tarassō*; 14:1 and 27). The heart is a seat of the emotions. Both the disciples' grief over losing Jesus and their subsequent joy when they see him again will be located in the heart. Interestingly, it is Jesus' *psychē*, not his *kardia*, that is troubled (*tarassō*) in 12:27. Never do we hear a word about Jesus' own heart, and the Fourth Evangelist uses the word less than any other Gospel writer.

The Fourth Evangelist uses *sōma* ("body") only six times, four of which appear in John 19:31–40, the deposition of Jesus' body. *Sōma* first appears in 2:21, where the narrator explains that Jesus had alluded to his resurrection using the phrase "temple of his body." The last occurrence finds Mary Magdalene asking the angels where they have laid Jesus' body (20:12). So, in FG the word *sōma* relates *only* to the body of Jesus, particularly with regard to his death. We hear nothing about anyone else's body—not Lazarus's, not the centurion's slave's, not Peter's, not the Beloved Disciple's. *Sōma* occurs near the beginning of the Gospel and near the end, but not in between. I find highly debatable, then, Sandra Schneider's contention that "bodiliness is the linchpin of resurrection faith" (Schneiders 2005, 168).

Twice the Fourth Evangelist uses the word *koilia* ("belly, womb"), a term also employed by Matthew, Mark, Luke, Paul, and the author of Revelation. In Matthew, Mark, and Revelation, *koilia* refers only to the stomach; in Luke it always refers to a woman's womb; in Paul it can refer to stomach or womb. Consistent with these usages, John 3:4 finds Nicodemus wondering how to reenter his mother's womb. The use of the word in 7:38, however, is quite enigmatic, and much attention has been devoted to deciphering its meaning. The NRSV translation—"Out of the believer's *heart* shall flow rivers of living water"—implies that the word *koilia*, which actually appears in the text here, is synonymous with *kardia*, which cannot be accurate, given the fact that the Fourth Evangelist uses the word *kardia* elsewhere in a more distinctive fashion. It is not even clear whether the rivers of living water are to come out of the believer's heart (most likely) or Jesus' heart. The experienced reader of the Fourth Gospel will immediately think of the water that flowed from Jesus' side on the cross; viewed against this backdrop, 7:38 seems to suggest that those who believe in Jesus will have the same experience, as is often the case in the FG (14:12). Clearly, the language is metaphorical and is tied to other "abundant water" themes in FG. At most, it is an anthropological category relevant only to believers, not human beings in general.

For a text so concerned with knowledge, the lack of noetic (*noeō*) language in FG is striking. Notably, the Fourth Gospel does not include the famous dictum found in the Synoptics, "You shall love the Lord your God with all your heart, and with all your soul, and with all your strength, and with all your mind; and your neighbor as yourself" (see Mark 12:33 and parallels). *Noeō* language appears only once in FG, in the Isaiah quote at 12:40. Noetic language is inconsequential for Johannine anthropology.

SUMMARY

What key ideas should be gleaned from the foregoing discussion of Johannine anthropological terms? First, an *anthrōpos*, or human being, consists of *flesh and blood*, a *psychē*, and a *heart*. It is the *psychē* that bears the primary anthropological weight, since this is the feature of a person that is capable of eternal life, the primary eschatological reward in FG. The Fourth Evangelist connects the *psychē* with *zōē* (12:25), thus avoiding any strict dichotomies between earthly/heavenly, this life/next life. This connection supports the Fourth Evangelist's eschatological project, which seeks to blur, if not entirely erase, the distinction between the present and the future, both for the believer and the unbeliever. *Psychē* and *zōē* each belong to what a Pauline scholar might call *both* realms, the present and the future, the earthly and the heavenly; for the Fourth Evangelist, it is all *one* realm, available in fullness already for the believer and fully unavailable already for the unbeliever. Second, FG uses anthropological language both to unite Jesus with other human beings and to distinguish him from them. Like other human beings, Jesus has flesh, blood, and a *psychē*. But a distinction is created when the author avoids using heart language for Jesus. Thus, the disciples' hearts are the seat of their trouble (*tarassō*), but Jesus experiences trouble in his *psychē*. Third, *pneuma* is a rich feature of Johannine anthropology. Given Jesus' privileged access to spirit throughout the narrative, *pneuma* serves both to distinguish Jesus from other humans and to finally unite Jesus with believers by his inspiriting them at his death and resurrection, which are presented as a single, unified moment in FG.[2] Fourth, Johannine anthropology is distinctive: while points of contact with the Hebrew Bible, Hellenistic philosophy, other New Testament concepts, and even emergent gnostic ideas can be cited, FG coincides exactly

---

2. As Mary Coloe states, "There are not two bestowals of the Spirit [in FG]. I would rather speak of two moments within the one Hour, one moment where the focus is on the believer's relationship to Jesus, and a second moment where the focus is on the believer's relationship to the world, as the agent of Jesus in the world" (2001, 97).

with none of them.³ Perhaps we will not be surprised, then, to learn that this distinctive anthropology contributes to a distinctive eschatology, particularly with respect to the ultimate fate of human beings. The Fourth Evangelist is neither Paul nor Plato.

The Fate of Human Beings

Now that we have some idea concerning what the Fourth Evangelist does and does not think about the *nature* of human beings, we are prepared to ask about the *fate* that this author envisions for human beings. We have already seen that, unlike some Hellenistic philosophers, the Fourth Evangelist does not present any part of a person as inherently immortal. What can the Fourth Evangelist mean, then, when he states that believers will never die, since such a statement seems to imply immortality? To answer this question, we will explore the author's comments relating to life and death; this inquiry will, in turn, help us answer the question of how a human being can *become* immortal (by being inspired). In the process, we will need to discern *which* human beings become immortal. Further, for those who participate in immortality, when does this quality of life begin? Is it available in the present (i.e., realized eschatology) or only in some near or distant future (e.g., at one's own death; at the *parousia*)? If not all human beings become immortal, what happens to those who do not? In this section, I will marshal the evidence necessary to hypothesize soundly that, although all human beings experience physical death, beyond that one's fate depends upon whether or not one believes in Jesus. The author of FG claims a bestowed, realized immortality for believers, an eternal life that begins now. Unbelievers can expect eternal death, which also begins now.

Death and Life Language

The Fourth Evangelist uses a number of terms in reference to death: *thanatos* ("death"), *apollymi* ("to destroy"), *apōleia* ("destruction"), *nekros* ("dead"), *apokteinō* ("to kill"), *koimaomai* ("to sleep"), *koimēsis* ("sleeping"), and *thuō* ("to slaughter in sacrifice"). The last three terms—*koimaomai, koimēsis,* and *thuō*—each occur only once in FG. By far, *apothnēskō* is the term used most often in reference to death in FG: twenty-eight of the 111 total occurrences of *apothnēskō* in the New Testament appear in the Fourth Gospel. This word

---

3. For a full and interesting argument about the relationship between Johannine and gnostic anthropology, see Trumbower 1992.

appears in eight of John's twenty-one chapters, with the majority of occurrences in chapters 8 (six times) and 11 (nine times).

In the Johannine view, all human beings start in death and are given the opportunity to transfer to life. This would be similar to a student starting with a zero and working to earn an A over the course of the semester, rather than starting with an A and trying not to lose it. Thus, the Johannine Jesus says, "Very truly, I tell you, anyone who hears my word and believes him who sent me has eternal life, and does not come into judgment, but has transferred from death to life" (5:24). The perfect tense of the verb "has transferred" (*metabebēken*) indicates that the action has been fully completed with continuing effects in the present.

Death appears to have a double meaning in FG, signifying both physical death, which no one escapes, and Holy-Spiritual death, which only believers escape. By "Holy-Spiritual death" I mean life without receipt of the Holy Spirit, a death that the author describes in 8:24 as death-in-sin. I avoid saying "spiritual death" so as to prevent the reader from thinking of a physical/spiritual dichotomy. As noted above, *pneuma* is not naturally part of any human being; it is bestowed by Jesus on the basis of belief. This differs vastly from Platonic, Stoic, or gnostic ideas, all of which contend that *pneuma* is constitutive of all human beings.

There is no Greek word that directly renders the English word "afterlife," and even if there were, the Fourth Evangelist would never use it. He takes great pains to show no discontinuity between present life and future life. Life before death and life after death are all simply the same life. In FG, such ideas are expressed through the language of "birth" (*gennaō*), "life" (*psychē, zōē, zōopoieō, zaō*), and "resurrection" (*egeirō, anistēmi, anastasis*). Like death, life also has a dual meaning in FG: everyone has physical life (*psychē*), but not everyone has Holy-Spiritual life (*zōē*)—that is, the kind of life that is characterized by receipt of the Holy Spirit. While FG occasionally mentions the former, its emphasis is on the latter. Any person who believes in Jesus will not experience Holy-Spiritual death, and this is the only death that matters. At John 6:50, Jesus says, "This is the bread that comes down from heaven, so that one may eat of it and not die." On the other hand, those who do not believe that Jesus is who he says he is *will* experience Holy-Spiritual death: "I told you that you would die in your sins, for you will die in your sins unless you believe that I am" (8:24). That there are two layers of meaning is evidenced by the ironic exchange at John 8:51–52, where it is clear that Jesus is speaking "from above," with an eye to the present revelation embodied in himself, while his opponents are speaking "from below," with their eyes set on the past. Jesus says, "Very truly, I tell you, whoever keeps my word will *never see death*" (8:51; emphasis added). They answer, "Now we know that you have a demon. Abraham died (*apethanen*), and so did the prophets; yet you say, 'Whoever keeps my word will *never taste death*.' Are you greater than our father Abraham, who died? The prophets also died. Who do you claim to be?" (8:52–53; emphasis added). Clearly, Jesus' opponents have no understanding of Holy-Spiritual death or life.

Jesus' enemies are not the only ones who do not understand the double meanings of "life" and "death"; neither do his disciples. When Lazarus dies, Jesus says, "This illness does not lead to death" (*ouk estin pros thanaton*; 11:4), despite the fact that Lazarus is literally rotting away (11:39). Jesus is speaking a higher truth, a heavenly concept beyond their comprehension. When Jesus says, "Our friend Lazarus has fallen asleep, but I am going there to awaken him" (11:11), the disciples take Jesus' *koimaomai* ("sleep") language literally. Jesus uses "sleep" language to indicate that death is not ultimate. For the duller reader, the narrator explicitly says, "Jesus, however, had been speaking about his death, but they thought that he was referring to dreaming sleep. Then Jesus told them plainly, 'Lazarus is dead'" (11:11–14). Martha appears to be ahead of the disciples in her understanding of life and death when at 11:24 she quotes Jesus' own words on the subject from 6:40: "I know that he [Lazarus] will rise again in the resurrection on the last day." But rather than affirming Martha's regurgitation of his own words, which sound very traditional by Pauline or Synoptic standards, Jesus *corrects* her understanding: "I am the resurrection and the life. Those who believe in me, even though they die, will live, and everyone who lives and believes in me will never die" (11:25–26). It is not that believers do not die, as the opponents in 8:52 had assumed; it is that physical death has been made inconsequential by Jesus' self-revelation. The concessive, "even though," shows that he is coming down to her level, acknowledging rather than denying actual death, but trying to move her toward the only real point: eternal life is found in the person of Jesus.

Jesus' Paradigmatic Death

FG indicates that some of Jesus' experiences will be mirrored by the experiences of the disciples. The world hates him; the world will hate them. The world does not keep Jesus' word; it will not keep theirs. Physical death should be no big deal for Jesus' disciples because, for FG's Jesus, physical death is not a crisis: "For this reason the Father loves me, because I lay down my life (*psychē*) in order to take it up again. No one takes it from me, but I lay it down of my own accord. I have power to lay it down, and I have power to take it up again. I have received this command from my Father" (John 10:17–18). Jesus' death is a sacrifice that glorifies God (11:50; 21:19); that sacrifice is thrown into ironic relief by the comment that the thief seeks to steal and sacrifice (*thuō*) and destroy (10:10). Death holds no surprise for Jesus; the narrator often reminds us that Jesus knows what kind of death he is to die (12:33; 18:32; 21:19). His death is, in fact, an exaltation: no suffering servant of Mark's Gospel here; no *kenosis* hymn (Phil 2:6–11); no "cursed is everyone who hangs on a tree" (Gal 3:13).[4] Instead, Jesus says, "Very truly, I tell you, unless a grain of wheat falls into the earth and dies, it remains just a single grain; but if it dies, it bears much fruit. Those who love their life (*psychē*) lose it, and those who hate their *life in this world* (*psychē*) will keep it for *eternal life* (*zōē*). Whoever serves me must follow me, and where I am, there will my servant be also" (John 12:24–26; emphasis added).

Clearly the author is trying to reeducate believers who might consider death to be a terrifying prospect by having Jesus use consolatory rhetoric: "I have said these things to you to keep you from stumbling. They will put you out of the synagogues. Indeed, an hour is coming when those who kill you will think that by doing so they are offering worship to God" (16:1-2). "But because I have said these things to you, sorrow has filled your hearts" (16:6). "I have said this to you, so that in me you may have peace" (16:33). Why do they need consolation? Jesus' death, their struggle with his absence, and their own persecution have left them fearful. This fear manifests itself in the language of being "alone." Jesus says, "You are going to leave me *alone*" (*kame monon aphēte*; 16:32), but "I will not leave you *orphaned*" (*ouk aphēsō humas orphanous*; 14:18, emphasis added). For the believer, death does not involve being orphaned or forsaken; it has no power to sting, and it need not be considered an "enemy," as Paul puts it in 1 Cor 15:26.

The Distinctiveness of Jesus' Death

While the author provides Jesus as a model of encouragement, it is important to realize that the Fourth Evangelist distinguishes Jesus' death from that of the disciples. Only Jesus' death is presented in sacrificial cult language, and only the resurrected *sōma* of Jesus is addressed. The Fourth Evangelist insists that Jesus' death is a sacrifice that glorifies God (11:50; 21:19). It is widely recognized that FG's passion chronology differs from that of the Synoptics in its emphasis on Jesus as the paschal lamb. There is an ironic comment at John 10:10 that is missed by every English translation. In the statement, *ho kleptēs ouk erchetai ei mē hina klepsē kai thysē kai apolesē* ("the thief comes only that

---

4. John uses *hypsoō* and *doxa* language to make this point; for the former, see John 3:14; 8:28; 12:32, 34; for the latter, see 7:39; 12:23; 13:31.

he might thieve and sacrifice and destroy"), translators typically render *thyē* as "kill." Surely "sacrifice" is closer to the author's meaning, by comparison with Jesus' comment in 16:2, "They will put you out of the synagogues. Indeed, an hour is coming when those who kill (*apokteinō*) you will think that by doing so they are offering worship to God." If at 10:10 the author had simply meant "kill" instead of "sacrifice" in some cultic sense, he would not have added *thyē* to *apollymi*.[5]

Chapter 21, which I take to be an appendix to FG, brings Jesus back to deal with the physical deaths of Peter and the Beloved Disciple. As is widely argued, John 21 serves, in part, to rehabilitate Peter. I am among those who think that this chapter reflects some level of conflict between the Johannine community, whose hero is Beloved Disciple, and the "Petrine church down the street," whose hero is Peter. So elevated does the heretofore invisible Beloved Disciple become that his death is described as glorifying God (21:19), language elsewhere reserved for Jesus' death. The fact that the appendix must deal with the rumor that the Beloved Disciple would not die (21:23) indicates that some in the Johannine community misunderstood Jesus' realized eschatology and expected no physical death. This appendix, then, was a necessary corrective.

FATE OF NONBELIEVERS

Given the fact that the Fourth Evangelist is generally thought to represent a persecuted group of Jews who have been excised from their parent tradition, one might expect the sort of vehement and vindictive invective against nonbelievers that one finds in Matthew, where "hell"—in the form of Gehenna, Hades, outer darkness, and unquenchable fire—abounds. The terms "Gehenna" (*geenna*), "Hades" (*hadēs*), "the outer darkness" (*to skotos to exōteron*), "consign to Tartarus" (*tartaroō*), "Abaddon" (*Abaddōn*), "abyss" (*abyssos*), and "Apollyon" (*Apollyōn*), all perfectly good words used elsewhere in the New Testament, never appear in FG. All the Synoptics use Gehenna; Matthew and Luke also have Hades. The Synoptics all refer to "the unquenchable fire," which Mark pairs with hell (*hē geenna to pyr to asbeston*; 9:43). In FG, fire (*pyr*) appears only once, without the word "unquenchable," and then in the context of a parable (15:6). FG has no Son of Man coming on the

---

5. It is important to note here that an argument could be made against the Jesus-as-paschal-lamb proposition on the basis of the details of the Old Testament texts. Nevertheless, the Fourth Evangelist takes Jesus' death to be sacrificial, and that is what is important here. Note that the author of 1 John 2:2 understands FG to mean that Christ served as an atoning sacrifice.

clouds, no wars and rumors of war, no trumpets sounding where believers are changed in the twinkling of an eye, and no rider on a white horse.

But while there is no hell in FG, there is judgment. Let me highlight two verses in FG that specifically contrast the fates of believers and nonbelievers. John 3:36 contrasts "seeing eternal life" with "having the wrath of God remain upon him," and 5:29 contrasts doing good, which leads to resurrection of life, with doing bad, which leads to resurrection of judgment. The believer sees eternal life; the nonbeliever has the wrath of God remaining (*menō*) upon him. This *menō* language is, of course, not accidental; it is special Johannine vocabulary, and the Fourth Evangelist plays on the word here. In FG, the ultimate reward granted to the believer is to have the Father and Jesus abide, remain, dwell (*menō*) with that believer (see 14:23, *eleusometha kai monēn par' autō poiēsometha*). This is nothing less than eternal life. The nonbeliever, by contrast, has only the *wrath* of God; God's self does not abide (*menō*) with him or her.

What about Satan? Does Satan still hold sway in this world? In John's view, no. "*Now* is the judgment of this world; *now* the ruler of this world will be driven out" (John 12:31; emphasis added). "The ruler of this world has been judged" (*ho archōn tou kosmou toutou kekritai*; 16:11). There is no indication that Satan is a cosmic force opposing God. He is not the strong man whose house Jesus has begun to plunder (cf. Mark 3:27); he is a puny character. Satan does not rule over hell or anything else, although believers do need protection from him (John 17:15).

There is no sense in FG that the judgment is ongoing. Matthew can speak of eternal fire (*to pyr to aiōnion*) and eternal punishment (*kolasin aiōnion*). In FG, however, the phrase "eternal" is never paired with judgment or death but is quite often paired with "life."[6]

The Fate of Believers

Believers inherit eternal life, which starts now. The Fourth Evangelist uses *zōē* (often in conjunction with "eternal," *aiōnios* or *eis ton aiōna*), as well as *zōopoieō* and *zōē* to indicate eternal life. Sandra Schneiders astutely observes that "eternal life" in FG signifies not "indefinite temporal extension of natural life but … a qualitatively different kind of life" (2005, 5). God, Jesus, and the Spirit all enliven (*zōopoieō*) the believer (5:21; 6:63). That Jesus makes alive, with an emphasis on the present, is evidenced by the use of "living" (*zaō*).

---

6. One could also treat the Fourth Evangelist's attitude toward "the world" (*kosmos*) under the heading of "unbelievers." For discussion and bibliography, see Cassem 1972–73, 81–91. Likewise, one might also include the Fourth Gospel's "Judeans" (*hoi Ioudaioi*) in this category.

Jesus' conversation with the Samaritan woman about living water pits past against present (Jacob versus Jesus; John 4). *Zaō* also appears in the living bread discourse, where past is again pitted against present (Moses versus Jesus; John 6), as well as in the story of the revitalizing of the official's son (4:46–54). In FG there is no judgment day for believers in the traditional sense of the Synoptics, Paul, and Revelation. Judgment has already happened, one's fate has been decided, and there is no second chance. In typical Johannine fashion, John uses traditional language but strips it of its traditional significance and infuses it with new meaning.

The word *anistēmi* is used in three contexts in reference to resurrection, always in the future tense. The term appears in the bread discourse (John 6:39, 40, 44, 54), the Lazarus discourse (11:23, 24), and in reference to Jesus' own resurrection (20:9). As noted above, Martha assumes that Jesus' declaration, "I will raise him up on *the last day*" (6:40), refers to a notion of future resurrection, but Jesus corrects her (11:25–26). The "last day" has already come in the package of Jesus' incarnation, death, and resurrection. Thus, Jesus says, "Very truly, I tell you, the hour is coming, *and is now here (kai nyn estin)*, when the dead will hear the voice of the Son of God, and those who hear will live" (5:25; emphasis added). At 5:28, Jesus declares that "the hour is coming when all who are in the tombs (*mnēmeion*) will hear his voice"; the next time the word *mnēmeion* appears, it is in the story of Lazarus, who hears Jesus' voice and comes out of his tomb into the resurrection of life. He has been raised from the dead. In narrative time, of course, this resurrection is incomplete because Lazarus, unlike the postresurrection reader, does not yet have access to the Holy Spirit, since Jesus has not yet been glorified.

Unlike Paul (see 1 Cor 15), the Fourth Evangelist contends that one can have everything that matters here and now. As it is now, so it will be then; as it will be then, so it can be now. After all, what more can be given than Jesus and God making their dwelling place with one? To say that there is some reward to which one does not presently have access is to say that the revelation of Jesus is somehow lacking. There is no language in FG about the Holy Spirit as a down payment for future glory (2 Cor 1:22), or about Jesus as the firstfruits (1 Cor 15:23). Jesus defines eternal life: "And this is eternal life, that they may know you, the only true God, and Jesus Christ whom you have sent" (John 17:3). With Jesus one has all that one needs; without him, one has nothing.

We have already seen that the Lazarus story takes the meaning of "resurrection" out of the future and puts it more firmly into the present. The final uses of tomb language in FG refer to Jesus' burial and resurrection. Clearly, Jesus' resurrection is accomplished in the present as well. All that matters is finished by the end of the story. Keck understands FG's notion of "resurrection on the last day" in the Pauline sense, a reading that leaves him perplexed:

"It is not explained [by John] why resurrection is necessary, but we may assume that the same consideration is at work here as in Paul: 'What God created, the body, God will redeem'" (1992, 93). Keck fails to recognize that FG has taken the tradition's language of future resurrection and corrected it so that the future is completed not at a second coming but rather at Jesus' resurrection. Put differently, for the Fourth Evangelist Jesus' appearance after the resurrection and his bestowal of the Holy Spirit constitute the second coming (John 20:19–22). The Coptic Nag Hammadi Codices remind one that an author can use traditional language but infuse it with untraditional meanings. Even a cursory scan of these texts reveals that they use *very* traditional language for death and the afterlife: "underworld" (*amnte* or *emnte*); "pit" (*hieit*); "day of judgment" (*-mphoou ntkrisis*); and, particularly interesting for our present purposes, "house" (*aei*). The latter term appears, for example, at *Trimorphic Protennoia* 40:19–32, in which we find a wisdom character, First Thought, dwelling with the believer. The Fourth Evangelist is neither the first nor the last theologian to breathe new life into old terms.

Heaven

To denote "heaven," the Fourth Evangelist uses the words *ouranos*, *epouranios*, *anōthen*, and *anō*. Three points deserve mention. First, "heaven" language in FG designates the realm of God the Father; that is, it serves as a metonym for God. Such language is used to emphasize source and agency. Heaven is God's command center. Second, most modern understandings of the Fourth Evangelist's view of heaven seem to rely on the opening verses of John 14: "In my Father's house there are many dwelling places [*monai*, from *menē*]. If it were not so, would I have told you that I go to prepare a place for you? And if I go and prepare a place for you, I will come again and will take you to myself, so that where I am, there you may be also" (14:2–3). People often interpret this to mean one of two things: (1) at the general resurrection, believers will go to heaven, and nonbelievers will not; or (2) at the time of an individual's death, Jesus will take the individual up to a heavenly mansion in the sky.[7] I contend that the Fourth Evangelist has neither in mind. While John uses *ouranos* eighteen times, the term never appears in chapter 14. The Fourth Evangelist's failure to use *ouranos* in chapter 14 is a clue that suggests that the "many dwelling places" do not have anything to do with heaven. Mary Coloe analyzes John 14 in detail and argues quite compellingly that the image (*paroimia*) about the

---

7. See Keck 1992, 93: "In other words, Jesus promises to come to the believers in the hour of death and to take them to where he is—with God in heaven."

father's house (*oikia*) that has many dwelling places (*monai*) "introduces the theme of the abiding of the *divine presence*" and "draws upon and transforms Israel's Temple traditions" (2001, 159). After careful exegesis, with particular attention to the language of John 14 as it relates to the rest of the book as well as to the Hebrew Scriptures, Coloe concludes that "the action therefore is not the *believers* coming to dwell in God's heavenly abode, but the *Father, the Paraclete* and *Jesus* coming to dwell with the believers. It is a 'descending' movement from the divine realm to the human, not an 'ascending' movement from the human to the divine" (2001, 163). In short, John 14 is about a familial relationship, not a castle in the sky (cf. 8:35, "The slave does not have a permanent place in the household; the son has a place there forever").

Third, I want to draw attention to what John does *not* say about "heaven." He indicates no belief in layered heavens, as one finds in Stoic philosophy, the apostle Paul, and Gnosticism. He never uses the language of paradise (*paradeisos*) as do Paul, Luke, and Revelation. He certainly never uses language such as "believers go to heaven when they die."

Summary

It may be useful here to review the most salient points in our discussion about the fate of human beings. FG has a rich vocabulary for death, but its primary concern rests with Holy-Spiritual death. Everyone experiences physical death, including Jesus and the Beloved Disciple, but believers do not experience Holy-Spiritual death. Correlatively, believers gain Holy-Spiritual life (also called "eternal" life), the highest reward possible. Unbelievers do not. For believers, *pneuma* is added to *psychē*. Believers can face death with the same confidence that Jesus exhibits, for death has no power to interrupt Jesus' and God's dwelling with the believer (John 14:23)—the qualitatively abundant life that is available now extends forever. Heaven is not envisioned as a place where believers go posthumously; rather, it serves metonymically to signify God's agency. Likewise, the Fourth Evangelist never imagines an afterlife in which Satan, a fallen angel, rules over a hellish territory to which unbelievers are carried by angels (cf. Matt 13:41–42). With the revelation of Jesus Christ, Satan becomes ultimately impotent. All people receive judgment with its concomitant fate in this life, a fate that continues into the future.

Conclusion

I began this essay by looking at Robinson's approach to eschatology in FG, a heavily diachronic approach. I then decided to take up the issue of eschatology differently, using a more synchronic approach. In Robinson's discussion, to "solve" the puzzle of Johannine eschatology means to determine whether or not there was ever a pure (or at least purer) form of Christianity (which he finds hints of in the earliest layers of FG and refers to as "the Johannine tradition"), located in a particular geographical spot (an isolated Palestine), that was later adulterated by the apocalyptic *faux pas* (due to contact with Asia Minor). Without wholly eschewing the benefits of diachronic investigation (indeed, I have used some diachronic tools in this investigation), I treat the topic more synchronically and assume that one has not "solved" Johannine eschatology until one has presented a hypothesis about the possible *significance* of FG's eschatology rather than its *derivation*. The primary question becomes, What does the author *mean* when he or she makes particular statements throughout the text? rather than, How did the author end up with such ideas? Because my goals are different from those of Robinson, one should expect what we consider important conclusions to be different as well.

To offer a hypothesis regarding the Fourth Evangelist's eschatology, I inquired after FG's view of "the ultimate fate of human beings," a point of interest for Old Testament writers, New Testament writers, and Hellenistic philosophers alike. I noted that such a question cannot be responsibly pursued until one has discerned the author's view of what actually constitutes a human being. Is it a bipartite model? tripartite? monistic? And which "parts," if any, are assumed to perdure beyond the grave? If they do perdure, is that because they are inherently invincible or immortal (Plato), or is such a characteristic bestowed upon a person (FG)? If bestowed, when? Is that which perdures enervated (Old Testament *nepeš*) or robust (Plato's "immortal soul"; FG's pneumatic *psychē*)? Do people or parts of people "go" somewhere in the future (e.g., heaven or hell) after death (as in Paul), or do rewards and punishments accrue and occur in life before death (FG)? Having explored these questions, I now state the most important conclusions regarding FG's anthropological eschatology and their implications with respect to Robinson's essay.

Earlier I claimed that FG evinces a notion of *bestowed realized immortality* for the believer. I am now in the position to elaborate. In the Fourth Evangelist's view, immortality is bestowed, not innate. It is realized, not future. Functionally, death has been rendered inconsequential for the believer—and only for the believer. Death is not the last great enemy. But this notion of immortality must be distinguished both from Platonism and Paulinism. On the one hand, unlike Platonism or Gnosticism, no person or part of a person is inherently immortal in FG; rather, immortality characterizes only the *psychē* of the believer whom God gifts with Holy-Spiritual (i.e., pneumatic) *zōē*, a "life" that starts now and continues uninterrupted forever. On the other hand, unlike Paul's bestowed futuristic immortality, which *follows* resurrection, the Fourth Evangelist claims that the believer never dies and has *already* passed from death to life. Where Paul is insistent that the quality of future life is far different from the present (cf. Rom 8), for the Fourth Evangelist the future is simply more of the same (abundant life). There is no interest in the *parousia* (the term never occurs in FG), no blowing of the shofar, no new heaven and new earth, no spiritual body.[8] Speaking of FG, Robert Kysar has claimed that "in few other pieces of Christian literature is the tension between the present and future dimensions of salvation more evident" (1993, 99). I disagree. John is one of the few New Testament documents to exclude the language of "hope" (*elpis*; *elpizō*). Paul says, "Now hope that is seen is not hope. For who hopes for what is seen? But if we hope for what we do not see, we wait for it with patience" (Rom 8:24). None of this would make sense to a Johannine Christian, who has *seen* Jesus and, therefore, has seen the Father and, in fact, has no need for hope because she has the ultimate *now*. Strange, then, that Robinson would nominate FG as "essentially the Gospel for those who have not seen, because they were not there to see" (1962b, 98). Robinson himself misses the Fourth Evangelist's meaning because, much like Jesus' opponents, he is preoccupied by earthly things, such as the "perfectly clear" notion that the Fourth Gospel is written "for a non-Palestinian situation."

In FG resurrection adds nothing to the believer that she does not already enjoy. FG is not Paul, nor is it the Synoptics. For Robinson, such a statement would require a diachronic explanation with an aim to placing proximate value judgments on the various texts. We would have to decide whether John's distinctiveness lies in his correcting the tradition as represented by Paul or in his ignorance of such a tradition. Robinson is hoping for the latter, so that John's trajectory might be both "mature" and "remarkably primitive" at the same time (1962b, 102). The drive to prove that John is primitive coheres with Robinson's conviction that "primitive" means "closer to the historical Jesus" and, therefore, better. Robinson's enthusiasm for the promises of diachronic

---

8. Contra Mary Coloe, who appears to see John as a hesitant maverick: "Just as the Spirit is a proleptic gift of the eschaton, so also the worshiping, remembering community is a proleptic experience of the eschatological House of God. Stibbe's conclusion is along similar lines: 'The realized eschatology in the rest of John 14 suggests that this house is not so much an eternal home in heaven as a post-resurrection, empirical reality for the true disciples.' I add a qualifying note to Stibbe in presenting the role of the Paraclete as mediating this 'empirical reality' and also in claiming that it is not so fully realized that there is no sense of a further Parousia" (2001, 177). The only textual evidence that Coloe cites for a future eschatology are those passages in John 5 and 6 discussed above that I have already argued do not, in fact, point to a future eschatology. The only truly difficult piece of evidence is John 21:22, but Coloe's monograph does not address this verse because she, like me, considers 21 to be an appendix with certain tendencies that move against the rest of the Gospel.

approaches appears also in his attitude toward the Dead Sea Scrolls: "[F]or *the first time they present us with a body of thought which in date and place (southern Palestine in the first century* BC—AD), *as well as in fundamental, and not merely verbal, theological affinity, may really represent an actual background, and not merely a possible environment, for the distinctive categories of the Gospel*" (1962b, 99; emphasis original). In fact, however, with respect to anthropological and eschatological categories, the Dead Sea Scrolls indicate as much dissimilarity as affinity with FG. The Dead Sea Scrolls community evinces a thoroughly apocalyptic eschatology and certainly does not grant women the place of witness and value that FG does.

Post-Robinson synchronic approaches have reminded us that meaning is not determined by diachrony; diachrony may or may not contribute to meaning, but meaning certainly does not depend on a diachronic approach. Today it seems odd to operate with models of trajectories and growth, primitive and mature—heavily judgmental language that forces biblical texts to compete with one another on the basis of age and development. Robinson's goal is to find his favorite theology at the earliest possible stage of Christianity so that he can validate it as the best theology. Consider this comment, which he makes when critiquing an opposing reconstruction:

> This reconstruction I believe to be correct at one point, namely, that the path into apocalyptic was a *faux pas*. It was not, I am persuaded, the original eschatology of Jesus, which was much more in the line of the prophets than of the apocalyptists, nor was it that of the most primitive Church. The Synoptists witness to a progressive apocalypticization of the message of Jesus ... as the Gospel of Matthew most forcibly illustrates. (Robinson 1962b, 103)

Let me draw attention to a few of the striking elements in this statement. First, notice the force with which Robinson expresses his own theological convictions. It is not enough for him to notice that John does one thing and Matthew another; what Matthew does is unequivocally wrong. Second, his ideal goal is to get back to the original eschatology of Jesus, to get back behind the text. It is not enough to discern the Fourth Evangelist's eschatology; rather, one must dig through the sediment that is FG to get to the real treasure. Third, who are these mutually exclusive "prophets" and "apocalyptists," and where do Daniel and the intertestamental literature fit into such categories? Fourth, scholars no longer axiomatically assume that there was such a thing as "the" (rather than "a") "*most* primitive," capital-C "Church."

Perhaps, contra Robinson, we might opt for a more synchronic approach, informed rather than dominated by concerns external to the text itself. Perhaps we could treat the text as a moment in time and space, a snapshot of one author or community as distinct from, but not better or worse than, another

New Testament author or community. If we did this, we could spend our time uncovering, experiencing, and perhaps even creating meaning from the text, rather than performing an autopsy. Having done so, one just might find that these words were written not that one might understand the original eschatology of Jesus and/or the primitive church, and not that one might see that FG was correct and Matthew a failure, but "that you might come to believe that Jesus is the Christ, the Son of God, and that by believing you might have life in his name" (John 20:31).

The Role of John 21:
Discipleship in Retrospect and Redefinition

Carsten Claussen

In his article "The Destination and Purpose of the Johannine Epistles," John A. T. Robinson argues that "the last chapter of the [Fourth] Gospel bears all the marks of having been added at about the stage when the Epistles were written" (1965, 129). This judgment is based on a reconstruction of the historical milieu that the Johannine Epistles presuppose. Thus, Robinson believes that the Epistles can "be understood if they are seen as necessary correctives to deductions drawn from the teaching of the fourth Gospel by a gnosticizing movement within Greek-speaking Diaspora Judaism" (1965, 138). This statement is typical of Robinson's focus on the community behind the Johannine tradition. As the fifth trend of "the new look on the Fourth Gospel," in 1957 Robinson predicted a shift from the question of authorship toward looking for "a real continuity, not merely in the memory of one old man, but in the life of an on-going community, with the earliest days of Christianity" (1962b, 106). Robinson thus foresaw a shift toward the notion of the continuity of the Fourth Gospel (FG) with Jesus and, at the same time, a change of focus away from the question of apostolic authorship toward an appreciation of the history of the Johannine community.

Both of the above trends became very important just a few years later in studies that remain influential. Reaching back from the Gospel of John to Jesus, C. H. Dodd's *Historical Tradition in the Fourth Gospel* (1963) tried to trace the Johannine tradition to its historical roots. In line with Robinson's prediction, Dodd's case does not rest on apostolic authorship but still argues in favor of a positive and significant relationship between the text of FG and Jesus himself.

I am grateful to Prof. Dr. A. J. M. Wedderburn and Prof. Dr. Jorg Frey for their helpful comments and corrections.

Also in line with Robinson's prediction, J. Louis Martyn's *History and Theology in the Fourth Gospel* (1968) reconstructed a three-stage development of the Johannine community. While the early period was marked by the "the conception of a messianic group within the community of the synagogue" (Martyn 2003, 147–54), Martyn's main contribution is a reconstruction of the crucial middle period, which saw the separation of the Johannine community from the synagogue through the traumas of excommunication and martyrdom (2003, 154–57). For an undoubtedly late text such as John 21, however, Martyn's third stage of community history may be most important. This period "finds the Johannine community forming its own theology and its own identity not only vis-à-vis the parent synagogue, but also in relation to other Christian groups in its setting" (2003, 157; cf. Brown 1978).

While the above authors represent fine examples of the conviction that "the Gospel of John bears clear marks *both* of the historical setting in which it was written *and* of the theological issues that were matters of life and death in the author's community" (Martyn 2003, xiii), the methodological focus of Johannine scholarship has meanwhile shifted quite considerably. In a way that representatives of the "new look" probably could not have envisaged, the emergence of literary approaches has enriched our interpretation of FG tremendously through a greater appreciation of the narrative design that marks the final form of the text. When R. Alan Culpepper published his landmark study *Anatomy of the Fourth Gospel* in 1983, he confronted "Johannine scholars [who] have generally approached the text looking for tensions, inconsistencies, or 'aporias' which suggest that separate strains or layers of material are present in the text." Culpepper conceded that, "on the basis of this stratification, the history of the material, the process by which the gospel was composed, and developments within the Johannine community can all be studied." But he criticized the fact that "little attention has been given to the integrity of the whole [text], the way its component parts interrelate, its effects upon the reader, or the way it achieves its effects" (1983, 3). Against this trend, Culpepper introduced a literary reading of FG that set the agenda for a whole new period of Johannine exegesis.

Now, more than twenty years after Culpepper's milestone study, the interpretation of FG may be characterized by a multiplicity of approaches representing a broad range of historical, theological, and literary questions. One may reasonably view the Gospel of John as literature, history, and theology (see Culpepper 1998, 14–18). Nevertheless, it has proven useful and often necessary not to burden one's interpretation with reconstructions of the history behind the text or with theological judgments or prejudices. Accordingly, the present inquiry into John 21 will start by looking at the interaction of this chapter with other texts in FG. If we refer to these passages as "earlier" than chapter 21, this is simply to acknowledge that the reader has already read through chapters 1–20 before encountering this material. Through this analysis, I hope to demonstrate that a synchronic reading of John 21 reveals many close connections between this chapter and the remainder of the narrative and may also shed light on the historical circumstances in which this chapter was composed.

John 21 and the Literary Unity of the Fourth Gospel

Both the beginning and the end of a text are highly significant for its comprehension and, consequently, to its interpretation. According to what the theory of literary dynamics calls the "primacy effect" and the "recency effect," both the beginning and the end of a text provide a hermeneutical framework that guides or even controls one's understanding (Perry 1979, 53–58). While this point has been established beyond doubt regarding the Prologue (John 1:1–18), for a number of reasons it is more challenging to analyze the significance of FG's ending. Indeed, there is not even a consensus on which verses represent the actual ending of the text. While the vast majority of Johannine scholars still seem to agree with Robinson that John 21 is a secondary addition to the Fourth Gospel, a growing number of interpreters argue that John 21 forms a literary unity with the remainder of the narrative (Thyen 2005, 772).

The majority view is prominently expressed in Rudolf Bultmann's influential commentary on John (1971). Following the path of Julius Wellhausen's *Literarkritik*, Bultmann argues that the original text of FG was expanded by a later redactor who added, among other verses, the eucharistic (John 6:51b–58) or sacramental allusions (19:34b–35) and who also made "corrections" to the text's eschatology (5:28–29; 6:39, 40, 44, 54; 12:48). Bultmann also holds this redactor responsible for the addition of John 21, making the chapter secondary material. A number of features of the text itself may be cited in support of this position.

(1) Those who stress the secondary character of John 21 find it obvious that John 20:30–31 functions as a conclusion to the story. At first sight, then, there is really no need to add another chapter, and it would not have been necessary to end this now final chapter of FG with another literary conclusion (21:25), which is similar to the formulas used in other ancient literature (Brown 1966–70, 2:1130).

(2) The secondary character of John 21 is also underlined by the observation that a number of words and expressions appear here for the first time; the vocabulary of this passage, in other words, seems inconsistent with that of the

earlier chapters (Brown 1966–70, 2:1079–80). These considerations would suggest that some unknown person added another chapter after John 20:30–31.

(3) It seems clear that John 21 does not simply follow up what the readers of FG know from the previous text, and especially from John 20. There the disciples are informed about Jesus' resurrection (20:18) and finally meet the risen Lord himself (20:19); they receive the Holy Spirit (20:22) and are commissioned to forgive or to retain sins (20:23). Even Thomas, who was not present at this meeting, receives a special revelation (or, rather, a visitation) and is reunited with his fellow disciples (20:24–29). All this happens while the disciples are still in Jerusalem, and there is no reason why they should suddenly have returned to their home area by the Sea of Tiberias, as we are informed at John 21:1.

(4) While one has the impression that Jesus' mission statement to his disciples should have left them with a sense of joy and power to start their ministry (20:21), at first sight their spirits seem to have fallen, and the mission seems to be stuck (21:1–3).

(5) Although most of the disciples have already seen the risen Lord twice in the upper room (20:19–23, 26–29), their eyes now seem to be blind. They fail to recognize Jesus on the shore of the lake (21:4), despite the fact that the text specifies that this is the third time he has appeared to them (21:14). Further, in referring to three resurrection appearances, did the author of John 21 forget about the earlier appearance of Jesus to Mary Magdalene (20:11–18), or does this not count as an appearance to the disciples?

(6) Along with the reference to the third resurrection appearance at John 21:14, the phrase "after these things" at 21:1 links this chapter with the similar introductions at 19:28, 38. One may argue that John 21 follows the end of chapter 19 closely, and thus that chapters 20 and 21 "in at least a very general sense … stand in parallel with one another" (Gaventa 1996, 246).

In sharp opposition to such traditional *Literarkritik*, Hartwig Thyen argues in favor of reading the Gospel of John as a coherent text in its present canonical form (2005, 1). Especially in his earlier work Thyen did not deny that an original draft of FG (= *Vorlage*) was altered to produce the current text. But in contrast to Bultmann, Thyen referred to the individual responsible for these alterations as "the Fourth Evangelist" (1977, 267–68). In his recent commentary, however, Thyen moves away from the idea of such a redaction and opts in favor of a purely synchronic reading of the narrative in its canonical form. Consequently, he treats John 21 not as a mere addition but rather as the hermeneutical key for the whole narrative (2005, 772). He confesses "daß ich Joh 21 gegen einen breiten Konsensus … für einen ursprünglichen und unverzichtbaren Teil unseres Evangeliums halte" ("that against a broad consensus … I regard John 21 as an original and indispensable part of our

[Fourth] Gospel"; Thyen 2005, 4). Thyen's position resonates with the earlier judgment of Culpepper that "John 21 is an epilogue, apparently added shortly after the gospel was completed" and as such "the necessary ending of the gospel" (Culpepper 1983, 96–97).

There are, then, essentially two major perspectives on John 21. From a diachronic perspective, it seems very likely that either the Fourth Evangelist himself or a secondary redactor added chapter 21 to a narrative that originally ended at John 20:30–31. This person may or may not also be responsible for a number of other additions throughout FG (e.g., 5:28–29; 6:51b–58). From a synchronic perspective, it cannot be overemphasized that we do not have any extant evidence that FG ever circulated without its twenty-first chapter. Authors such as Culpepper and Thyen even argue that a "correct" understanding of the Gospel of John may be impossible without chapter 21. Nevertheless, they have to concede that even such a synchronic reading assumes that John 21 (re-)interprets earlier portions of the narrative.

Both positions outlined above rest on historic and literary arguments at the same time. On the one hand, any traditional *literarkritische* method draws conclusions by working backwards from literary observations to the historical genesis of the text. On the other hand, even a synchronic reading from the perspective of the reader cannot overlook the fact that John 21 stands in a dialectical relationship with the earlier portions of the narrative. As a consequence, any interpretation of John 21 needs to take into account not only the integrity of the whole Gospel but also this chapter's process of interpreting what has already been said (cf. Zumstein 2004, 297).

In common with Culpepper, Thyen, and a growing number of Johannine scholars (Thyen 2005, 772), we shall temporarily leave aside questions of the source and authorship of John 21 and its possible connection with the historical situation that 1 John presupposes. The main purpose of the present essay is to address the literary role of the final chapter of FG: How does John 21 reinterpret earlier portions of the Johannine narrative? In order to sharpen our focus, we shall have to limit the scope of our investigation. Raymond Brown emphasizes that "discipleship is the primary category in John" (1979, 84). The topic of discipleship is also of primary importance in John 21. We shall therefore concentrate on the way the disciples are introduced to the reader, and particularly on the question of how John 21 influences the reader's understanding of discipleship. In a synchronic manner, our interpretation of FG will look back at relevant passages, particularly the calling of the first disciples (1:35–51), the wedding at Cana (2:1–11), and the feeding of the five thousand (6:1–15), including the subsequent schism among the disciples and the confession of Peter (6:60–71). Such analysis will reveal a strong dialectical relationship between John 21 and the earlier chapters of the text.

John 21:1–14: A New Revelation to the Disciples

The final chapter of FG divides naturally into two sections: 21:1–14 and 21:15–23. While both parts are unified in their overall treatment of the topic of discipleship, they involve different groups of people: the former a group of seven disciples and the risen Lord; the latter only Peter, the Beloved Disciple, and Jesus, followed by a conclusion to the chapter (21:24–25).

John 21:1 opens with the announcement of a theme for the first pericope (cf. v. 14): "Jesus revealed himself." The verb *phaneroō* ("reveal") appears nine times in FG, and from the beginning of the narrative the reader has been informed that it refers to the revelation that happens through Jesus. John the Baptist presents as the aim of his ministry "that he [Jesus] might be revealed to Israel" (1:31); Jesus then "revealed his glory" at the wedding at Cana (2:11). Although his brothers prompt Jesus "to reveal himself to the world" (7:4), this does not happen until John 21:1, and even here the revelation is not to "the world" but only to a small group of disciples. As *phaneroō* is *not* used of the resurrection appearances in John 20, it becomes clear that what follows in chapter 21 is not simply an appendix, an epilogue, or a conclusion to what has been told so far but rather what Beverly Roberts Gaventa has called an "excess ending" (Gaventa 1996, 240). There is something more in the final chapter, something that does not simply summarize what has happened or what has been said so far. It is only here that God's revelation in Jesus comes to its post-Easter fulfillment through Jesus' self-revelation to the disciples.

The Disciples' Return to Galilee

Many interpreters have passed a remarkably severe judgment on the actions of the disciples in this pericope. Why did they return to Galilee and to their old professions after the Lord sent them out and gave them the Holy Spirit (John 20:21–23)? Commentators have called this return to fishing an "aimless activity undertaken in desperation" or even "apostasy" (Brown 1966–70, 2:1096; Hoskyns 1947, 552). But there could be other reasons for the return of the disciples to Galilee. From a diachronic point of view, it seems very likely that the author of FG knew the tradition that the disciples should meet the risen Lord in Galilee. This would certainly be the case if, as I believe, the Fourth Evangelist knew the Gospel of Mark. In Mark 14:28 and 16:7 the disciples are told that Jesus will go ahead of them into Galilee. The secondary ending of Mark's Gospel tries to report the fulfillment of this announcement (16:14–18). Even if one should cast doubt on John's knowledge of Mark and Luke, it is still very likely that the author of FG would have known about a Galilean, post-Easter tradition. But while we might reasonably explain the disciples' return to Galilee in terms of the relationship between FG and the Synoptics, from a synchronic point of view the reader of John 1–20 is surprised to find the disciples in Galilee in John 21. Further consideration reveals, however, a number of themes that link the presentation of the disciples' return to Galilee to earlier portions of the narrative.

At the beginning of the Gospel of John, the reader has been informed about the calling of the first disciples: Andrew and another unnamed character (1:35, 37, 40), Simon Peter (1:40–42), Philip (1:43), and Nathanael (1:44–49). Later on in the narrative other disciples are mentioned, including Judas (6:71; 12:4; 13:2, 26–31; 18:2–5), Thomas (11:16; 14:5; 20:26–29), and the Beloved Disciple (13:23; 20:2), who may be identical with the unnamed character in 1:35–37. The Fourth Evangelist seems to think that there are a total of twelve such disciples (see 6:67–71). But in John 21:2 only seven disciples are mentioned: Simon Peter, Thomas, Nathanael, the sons of Zebedee, and two other unnamed disciples. It has been frequently suggested that the number seven may represent the whole group of disciples and, furthermore, the whole church. There is, however, no direct evidence from the text that would justify such an interpretation. How, then, might a synchronic reading reveal an interaction between the mention of seven disciples at John 21:2 and earlier portions of the narrative?

If we look at John 21:2 a bit more closely, the number seven is not mentioned specifically but is rather deducible only by adding the five specific names with the two unnamed individuals. Such a combination of five plus two may remind the reader of the "five barley loaves and two fish" in the story of the feeding miracle (John 6:9). Further, although there is no hint that the number seven should be compared with twelve in terms of showing a decimation of the number of disciples after Easter, there is nevertheless the possibility that these few disciples may have viewed themselves as far too powerless to obey Jesus' commission at John 20:21. Such an acknowledgment of shortcoming is very much in line with Johannine anthropology (see Böttrich 2001, 379–96, esp. 395), and it is especially instructive to compare this story with the other two miracles of provision: the wine miracle at the wedding at Cana (2:1–11) and the feeding of the multitude (6:1–15). All three stories start with some kind of stocktaking that reveals a shortage. There is no wine left at the wedding at Cana, only six stone vessels filled with water (2:3, 6). In John 6, there is not enough food to feed the masses, only five barley loaves and two fish (6:9). The same situation prevails in John 21: only seven disciples, who are in principle capable of going fishing, but that alone will not do. For all three of these miracle stories, then, the experience of an obvious shortcoming seems to be representative of the human condition before God.

Throughout FG, the theme of "searching" or "seeking" is prominent. Not only the disciples (John 1:38; 13:33) but also a number of other characters are portrayed as people who "search": the crowds (6:24), the "Jews" (7:11, 34–36), the Pharisees (8:21), Judas and the detachment of soldiers and police (18:7–8; cf. 18:3), and, finally, Mary Magdalene (20:15) all "search" (*zēteō*) for Jesus. Although *zēteō* does not appear in John 21, one gets the impression that the disciples first "look for" a job and then for fish (21:2–3), when in fact Jesus has already found them without being searched for (21:4). John the Baptist's early statement, "among you stands one whom you do not know" (1:26), establishes, through the primacy effect, the theme that all sorts of people simply do not recognize Jesus' true identity. However, "searching" is not the final target. The Fourth Gospel also presents people as finding (1:41, 45) and, in the case of the disciples, as believing (1:49–50; 2:11) and thus receiving eternal life (6:35, 54; 10:28; 11:26). But one question remains open regarding this search for Jesus and its ultimate goal: the question of the relationship between "seeing" and faith. The reader of FG could easily get the impression that seeing some kind of miracle (as in the case of Nathanael; 1:48) or touching the wounds of the risen Lord (as in the case of Thomas; 20:25–27) may be essential to belief (1:49; 20:28). For the reader of John 20:29, this view is clearly marked as a misunderstanding: "Blessed are those who have not seen and yet have come to believe." The overall structure of John 21 confirms this statement. As in several of the episodes from chapters 1–20, the confession of faith only follows a miracle (John 21:7). However—and this is significant also for the resurrection experience—it is Jesus who reveals himself (John 21:1). Here as earlier, the risen one decides to whom he grants his self-revelation. There is nothing that even his closest disciples could have done to bring about Jesus' revelation by their own means. The flow of the story is entirely dependent on Jesus' intervention. The persistence of this theme explains why the disciples were simply not able to do anything but return to their day-to-day routine and go fishing: this kind of activity is to be expected of those who are no longer waiting for a special revelation to send them on their way. But this is precisely what John 21 wants to underline: apart from the risen Lord, they can do nothing (cf. John 15:5). Without this final chapter, then, one could easily get the impression that the disciples' return to their former profession is really the fulfillment of John 16:32: "The hour is coming, indeed it has come, when you will be scattered, each one to his home, and you will leave me alone." John 21:1–14 clearly corrects this misinterpretation. The risen Lord reveals himself in the midst of the disciples' day-to-day life, and they are able to recognize him only when he decides to reveal himself (1:26).

The 153 Fish

As we have already seen, FG's three miracles of multiplication (wine, bread, and fish) all begin with an assessment of a shortage that reveals, in turn, the limited capabilities of human beings. The servants at Cana can only provide water (John 2:7), not wine. The disciples are able to get five barley loaves and two fish from a boy, but they simply do not have the money needed to buy enough food for the crowd (more than six months' wages; 6:7). Similarly, in chapter 21 the disciples (who are now for the first time in FG presented as fishermen) cannot find a single fish in their net after a whole night's work (21:3), although one should probably expect more success from such experienced people. In each of these three cases, Jesus addresses the shortage by providing much more than one could have hoped for. Six stone water jars full of the best wine are certainly much more than one may deem necessary, and the fact that the disciples collected twelve baskets of leftover pieces from the five barley loaves suggests that this multiplication surely went over the top as well. Similarly, the 153 large fish of John 21:11 was certainly more than the seven disciples and Jesus needed as their "daily bread." Clearly, in FG there is not only one "miracle in the service of luxury"—as David Friedrich Strauss once commented on the wine miracle at Cana (1860, 2:585)—but at least three of them.

No single detail of these three miracles of provision has puzzled commentators more than the specific mention of "153" fish at John 21:11 (see Beasley-Murray 1999, 401–4). In general, interpretations fall into two categories. A rather large number of interpreters attempt to resolve the problem by referring to information from outside the text of FG, while a smaller group appeals to information provided earlier in the narrative of FG itself. Among the former group, the attempt to read the number of 153 in light of various gematric speculations has not found much overall support. Very different from such guessing, a most remarkable explanation was offered by Jerome in his commentary on Ezek 47. There he refers to ancient writers who say that there are 153 species of fish (*Comm. Ezech.*, PL 25:474C). Although we cannot verify that the author of John 21 knew this tradition, it would nevertheless help to establish the interpretation of this story as a parable for the mission of the apostles to all nations. Here, however, we will seek to establish an interpretation of the 153 fish that is based on a synchronic perspective that highlights details inside the narrative of FG itself.

As Augustine observed (*Tract. Ev. Jo.* 122.8), 153 is the triangular number of seventeen: the sum of the numbers from one to seventeen (1 + 2 + 3 + 4 ... 15 + 16 + 17). Many scholars today therefore suggest that the number seventeen is important for interpreting John's 153 fish. But does the narrative of FG provide evidence in support of such an approach? Matthias Rissi has offered an explanation based on John 6, which mentions that five barley loaves were used for the feeding of the multitude and that twelve baskets of leftover pieces were gathered afterward. The figure 153 thus establishes a link between the feeding miracle and the resurrection. Rissi is certainly correct in seeing a connection between John 6 and 21 (see esp. John 6:11 and 21:13). But while a close connection between these two miracles is also noticeable in the eucharistic overtones of both stories, Rissi's argument leaves certain details unconsidered. Especially, one may wonder why John 21 overlooks the two fish mentioned at John 6:9. Rissi's fascination with a eucharistic interpretation even drives him to regard John 21:13 as "der älteste Beleg für ein eucharistisches Mahl mit Brot und Fisch" ("the earliest evidence for a eucharistic meal of bread and fish"; 1979, 82). Even though the Gospel of John (together with the *Didache*) sheds some light on different kinds of early eucharistic practice (see Claussen 2005, 135–63, esp. 158–62), there is simply no convincing evidence for a fish Eucharist in early Christianity (McGowan 1999, 127–40). Thus, the eucharistic overtones between the two stories cannot support a link between the numbers in John 6 and John 21.

A more convincing interpretation of the number seventeen may be established, however, if we remind ourselves that *discipleship* is really the topic that binds John 21 not only to John 6 (esp. vv. 66–71) but also to the call of the first disciples (1:35–51), an episode that is, in turn, structurally linked to the wine miracle at Cana by the dating formula "on the third day" (2:1). The whole sequence of the call and Cana stories really only ends at John 2:11, when "his disciples believed in him." In John 21:2 the reader is reminded of this earlier scene by the reference to Nathanael, one of the first disciples to be called (see 1:45–51), who is now for the first time said to come from Cana. Does the topic of discipleship in these three contexts (1:35–2:12; 6:1–15, 66–71; 21:1–14) help us to interpret the significance of the numbers seventeen and 153? I suggest that it does, for the following reasons.

In the context of John 1:35–51, only five disciples are mentioned, but in John 6:66–71, after many disciples had "turned back and no longer went about with him," Jesus asks, "Did I not choose you, the *twelve*?" The reader of FG is reminded again at 20:24 that there were twelve disciples. However, as we have already pointed out, their number seems to be reduced to merely seven after the crucifixion (21:2). In this context, the number seventeen reminds the reader of John 21 that Jesus called at first five, then altogether twelve, disciples. Their number was reduced first by Judas's betrayal (John 6:71), and in John 21:2 the group seems to be even smaller. In this situation, where there may also be an emphasis on the shortcoming of the disciples, the number seventeen may be interpreted as a reminder to the reader that there were originally five or, respectively, twelve disciples, but through Jesus' promise there will finally be many more, symbolized by the figure 153 as the triangular number of seventeen (five plus twelve). Further, if anyone fears that such a large number of disciples will bring about friction and disunity, the reader should note that "though there were so many, the net was not torn" (21:11). Such an enormous success of their mission should not, however, lead the disciples to the conviction that it is they who provide what is most important: Jesus already had fish and bread on the charcoal fire before the disciples were able to haul the net ashore (21:9). Such an understanding of Jesus' calling activity is also supported by the use of the verb *elkyō* ("draw") in John 21:6 and 11, which is also used in John 6:44 for the work of the heavenly Father and then again in 12:32, where Jesus promises, "And I, when I am lifted up from the earth, will *draw* all people to myself." Thus, what happens in John 21:1–14 may be seen as Jesus "fishing and hauling" through the hand of his disciples, who would not be capable of doing it without him (15:5). Nevertheless, they are invited to contribute from their catch to the breakfast, which Jesus then gives to them (21:13), just as he had earlier given fish to the multitude (6:11).

John 21:15–23: Peter and the Beloved Disciple

When the Fourth Gospel was published, the Beloved Disciple and Peter were no longer merely characters linked to the historical Jesus. As time passed, both of them had become authorities to which certain groups within emerging Christianity felt affinity even after their deaths, which seem to have occurred at the time when John 21:19, 23 was written. While the Beloved Disciple was part of the community behind the Gospel and Letters of John, the apostle Peter had followers in Jerusalem (Acts 1:15; cf. Gal 1:18), in Syrian Antioch (Gal 2:11), in a faction of the Corinthian church (1 Cor 1:12), and, according to the tradition of the early church, especially in Rome (see 1 Pet 5:13). Thus, his influence was present in almost every important center of early Christianity. If James Dunn is correct, "it was Peter who became the focal point of unity in the great Church. For *Peter was probably in fact and effect the bridgeman* (pontifex maximus!) *who did more than any other to hold together the diversity of first-century Christianity*" (2006, 403). Consequently, any other movement within emerging Christianity had to relate itself to this apostle and his followers. But how should the Johannine community relate itself to Peter and his adherents, a question that was left open at the end of John 20?

Peter and the Beloved Disciple appear side by side throughout FG. In John 13:23, the disciple whom Jesus loved is reclining next to Jesus at the Last Supper. Peter is obviously farther away, not only in terms of space but also regarding his personal relationship to Jesus. Thus, Peter does not address Jesus directly to receive more detailed information regarding the identity of the betrayer but instead tries to employ the Beloved Disciple as an intermediary (13:24). Only one of these outstanding disciples is portrayed as Jesus' intimate. Accordingly, at the crucifixion Jesus entrusts his mother to the Beloved Disciple (19:26–27), while Peter obviously did not succeed in following Jesus up to this hour. Although Peter and "another disciple," who is very likely to be identified with the Beloved Disciple, "were following Jesus" to the place of his trial before the high priest (18:15), only one of them remains true to his calling. Peter betrays Jesus three times (John 18:17, 25–27), which surely brings him into discredit. One may even be surprised that Peter surfaces again at all in FG. After Mary Magdalene had informed the disciples that Jesus' tomb was empty, Peter and "the other disciple" ran to check this news (20:1–8). "The other disciple" outran Peter, reached the tomb first, and looked into it; Peter actually entered the tomb, but then "the other disciple" also went inside and "saw and believed." This is the last time these two disciples are singled out before the original ending of the Fourth Gospel (20:30–31). There can be no doubt that in FG "the other disciple" far surpasses Peter. Thus we may assume that early readers were puzzled upon reaching John 20:30. How should they relate to someone like Peter, who was in all respects second to the Beloved Disciple? How should they relate to a disciple who had, after all, betrayed Jesus?

John 21:15–23 provides a clear answer to these questions. Here Jesus asks Peter three times whether he loves him; each time Peter assures Jesus of his love and is then reinstated in his pastoral ministry (21:15–17). This narrative may therefore be seen as an attempt to enlist support for Peter. According to the recency effect, Peter will not be remembered as the one who betrayed Jesus but rather as the one to whom the risen Lord entrusted his followers. This is a remarkable shift in the perception of Peter in the eyes of the Johannine community. As Peter is now again held in high regard, what are the consequences for the Johannine community's view of the Beloved Disciple? For the first time, he seems to be portrayed as second to Peter. When Jesus and Peter are talking, "the disciple whom Jesus loved was following them" (John 21:20)—he is no longer closer to Jesus than Peter. Jesus' harsh response to Peter's question regarding the fate of the Beloved Disciple (21:21–22) clarifies that the recommissioning of the one is not meant to dishonor the other. As we know from the Corinthian correspondence of Paul, there were inclinations in certain Christian groups to favor one apostle over the other (1 Cor 1:12; 3:3–4). Accordingly, it seems reasonable to read this final exchange between Jesus and Peter in John 21 as a clear rejection of such all-too-human tendencies.

The History behind John 21 and the Johannine Epistles

Thus far I have shown that John 1–20 may be read in light of John 21. What does such a reading say about the historical setting of the chapter? We began our study by referring to John A. T. Robinson's statement regarding the historical connection between John 21 and the situation behind 1, 2, and 3 John. As we have seen, John 21 provides necessary corrections and reinterpretations of what has been said earlier in the narrative. Viewed from this perspective, we may affirm Robinson's reading by noting that John 21 may serve the same purpose as the Johannine Epistles.

But against Robinson's reading, the historical situation of the Epistles seems to be far more concrete than that of John 21. The background of 1 John is marked by the experience of a schism (see esp. 1 John 2:18–20). Consequently, as 2 and 3 John indicate, topics such as brotherly love (2 John 4–6; cf. "love" or "beloved" in 3 John 1, 2, 5, 6, 11) and the attempt to define the Christology of the community over against that of the heretics (2 John 10–11; cf. "truth" in 3 John 1, 3, 4, 8, 12) are very prominent. Contra Robinson's reading, it no longer seems possible to define these heretics as "a gnosticizing movement within Greek-speaking Diaspora Judaism" (1965, 138).

The final chapter of John shows a small, leftover number of disciples who hope for the blessing of the Lord for their ministry. In this respect, to a certain degree it is possible to identify similar circumstances behind John 21 and the Epistles: the groups behind both texts seem to be considerably decimated in number, although of course the historical situation behind 1 John is rather different from the post-Easter experience represented in John 21. Could this reduction in numbers have led the remaining factions in both cases to the conviction that, having lost so many members of their community (perhaps not true believers in the first place; see 6:64), they were no longer numerous enough to follow Jesus' commission? The rehabilitation of Peter may support the view that the community behind John 21 was attempting to relate to other Christian groups now that their leader had passed away (John 21:23). There is, however, no indication in the Johannine Epistles that the community was inclined to move in the direction of some sort of Petrine group within early Christianity, as may be indicated by the rehabilitation of Peter in John 21.

Thus, in general, a synchronic reading of John 21 within the context of the larger narrative of FG cannot support Robinson's claim that the final chapter of FG and the Johannine Epistles reflect the same historical context. Both texts, however, surely served the purpose of providing hermeneutical guidance to a Johannine community whose situation, as represented by the understanding of the topic of discipleship, may have changed considerably. When the Gospel of John was finally published, perhaps many years after

John 1–20 was written, a reinterpretation and authorization of FG by the identification of the Beloved Disciple as the author of the text seemed necessary (see John 21:24). Ultimately, however, unlike the Johannine Epistles, the historical situation behind John 21 remains largely unknown.

Sources in the Shadows: John 13 and the Johannine Community

Mary L. Coloe

> "In John we are dealing with a man who is not piecing together written sources but placing his stamp upon the oral tradition of his community with a sovereign freedom. Indeed he *is* his own tradition. As Menoud puts it, it is as if he is saying to us from beginning to end: 'La tradition, c'est moi!' " (Robinson 1962b, 97–98)

The above quotation from John A. T. Robinson's "The New Look on the Fourth Gospel" reflects in part the trajectory of my own research and writing at the turn of the twenty-first century. If indeed it is possible to speak of a "source" for the Fourth Gospel, I look to the Johannine community as the primary *Ur*-text. But even in this pursuit, the questions of today are no longer the same historical-critical questions of a previous generation, since a new methodology, loosely called "literary criticism," has opened up a range of different approaches not only to the written text of the Gospel of John but also to understanding the processes that gave rise to that text.

The Fourth Gospel as we now have it is the narrative formulation of one community's insight into the person and ministry of Jesus. This theology developed over several decades of oral teaching, Spirit-guided recollection, and ongoing community praxis in changing historical circumstances. Underlying the theology that determined the particular narrative shape of the Fourth Gospel was a community's experience of the living presence of Jesus, mediated now through "another Paraclete" (John 14:16). In the words of Sandra Schneiders, "it was a particular *lived experience* of union with God in the risen Jesus through his gift of the Spirit/Paraclete within the

---

I am grateful for the support of the Australian Research Council, which provided a grant enabling time to pursue research for this essay.

believing community (spirituality) that gave rise gradually to a particular articulated *understanding* of Christian faith (theology). This theology was encoded in the Gospel text, and through it we gain access to the experience, the spirituality, that gives this gospel its unique character" (Schneiders 1999, 48).

Reading the Fourth Gospel, alert to its nuances and subtle forms of intra- and intertextuality, my research set out to discover aspects of the text's theology and then to ask what would be the living "spirituality," or sense of religious identity, of a community that would articulate its theology in this manner? *God Dwells with Us* (Coloe 2001) was the fruit of such an approach. In this book I traced the way the temple functions across the text of the Fourth Gospel and came to the conclusion that the temple was not only the major thematic image of the person and mission of Jesus but also an image of the identity and mission of the Johannine community.

A key text in the transformation of the temple symbol from the person of Jesus to the community of believers is the statement at the beginning of John 14, "In my Father's house are many dwellings (*monai*)" (14:2). The chapter then describes these "many dwellings": the Father dwelling (*menōn*) in Jesus (14:10); the Paraclete, who now dwells (*menei*) with believers and in the future will dwell in them (14:17); the Father and Jesus, who will make their dwelling (*monēn*) with believers (14:23); and Jesus, who dwells with the disciples (14:25). In other words, John 14 describes the divine indwellings in the Christian community, which can accurately be called a "living temple" or, in the terminology of the Fourth Gospel, can be named by Jesus as "My Father's household" (*oikiai tou patros mou*).

A second key text in appreciating the temple symbolism in the Gospel of John is the title applied to Jesus in his "lifting up" on the cross: "Jesus the Nazarene, the King of the Jews."[1] Three times the Gospel of John identifies Jesus as "the Nazarene' (18:5, 7; 19:19), and John alone refers to the designation on the cross as a "title" (*titlon*). In Mark and Luke these words are termed an "inscription" (*epigraphē*; Luke 23:38; Mark 15:25), while Matthew calls them a "charge" (*aitian*; Matt 27:37). The background for the title "the Nazarene" can be found in two texts that were readily connected through first-century Jewish exegetical methods. Isaiah 11:1 identifies the future branch of Jesse as a *nēṣer*, which is the root word behind the name "Nazareth," and Zech 6:12 identifies the future temple builder as a man called "Branch" (*ṣemaḥ*). According to rabbinic exegetical methods, it was acceptable practice to interchange two similar words in their interpretation

---

[1]. A detailed discussion of these two points can be found in Coloe 2000, 47–58.

of a passage.[2] Evidence from Qumran (4Q161; 4QpIsa[a] line 18) shows that *ṣemaḥ* and *nēṣer* were interchanged in a messianic interpretation in which the Davidic *nēṣer* was to be the builder of a new temple, the *ṣemaḥ* of Zech 6 (Coloe 2001, 171–74). The unique way in which the Fourth Gospel uses "the Nazarene," the fact that this designation is called a "title," and the consistent use of temple imagery indicates that Johannine Christology presents Jesus as the Nazarene temple builder of Zech 6:12.

From the cross, Jesus' role as the temple builder is completed when he raises up the new temple in the scene where the relationship between his mother and the Beloved Disciple are changed (John 19:25b–27). In this moment the disciple becomes son to the mother of Jesus and thus brother to Jesus and child of God. The risen Jesus confirms this new identity when he commissions Mary Magdalene, "Go to *my brothers and sisters* (*tous adelphous mou*) and say to them, 'I am ascending to my father and *your father*, to my God and your God' " (20:17). On the cross, the words of Jesus in chapter 2 are realized: "Destroy this temple, and in three days I will raise it up" (2:21).

This extremely brief description of some of the arguments presented in *God Dwells with Us* shows the steps I have taken in an attempt to discover the spirituality of the Johannine community, that is, the *Ur*-text or source behind the Fourth Gospel. Step one represents careful narrative-critical exegesis of those texts in the Gospel of John that focus on the temple. Step two is the formulation of a Christology coherent with the findings of the textual analysis, namely, that God has entered into historical experience through the humanity of Jesus. Jesus was the dwelling place of God (see esp. John 1:14; 2:19, 21). Step three is the articulation of the community experiences that lay behind the Fourth Gospel's particular theology and the narrative symbology of Jesus as the dwelling place/temple of the divine presence.

By the end of *God Dwells with Us* I concluded that the Johannine community saw itself as a living temple, participating in Jesus' divine filiation. But there was a problem. While the Fourth Gospel's narrative could express its theology through the symbol of the temple, in the post-70 C.E. experience of the Johannine community the temple was no longer appropriate as a means of expressing its "self-identity." The temple, along with its elaborate cult, no longer existed, nor were Christians identified as "Judeans" either by Rome or by emergent rabbinic Judaism. In this historical context another terminology was needed to describe the emergence of the community's new self-identity.

---

2. This method, based on similar, not necessarily identical terms, is known as *kayotse bo bemaqom aher*. For further details of rabbinic exegesis, see Manns 1991, 306–19; Scott 1995, 127–33; Hauser and Watson 2003.

In the Hebrew Bible the most frequent name for the Jerusalem temple was "the house of God" (*bêt yhwh*), and it was appropriately furnished.

> All of them [the temple furnishings] are shaped as furniture of a dwelling-place and testify that the house is really arranged as a habitation: the lamps for light, the tables for bread, the small altar for incense (an item which was not lacking in any luxurious residence in antiquity), the altars bearing the epithet of God's tables (Ezek 41:22; 44:16; Mal 1:7), the sacrifices being called God's bread (Lev 21:21–22; Num 28:2), the typical image of the gods as eating the fat of the sacrifices and drinking the libations of wine (Deut 32:38) and the like. (Haran 1969, 255)

When the Johannine Jesus calls Israel's house of God "my Father's house" (John 2:16; 14:2), he is speaking not only of a building in Jerusalem. In the Hebrew Bible, the expression "my father's house" never refers to a building but rather to those people considered part of the household group, those whom we would today call "the family" and even future descendants (see Gen 24:38; 28:21; 46:31; Josh 2:13). So the expression *en tēi oikiai tou patros mou* (14:2) takes on a personal sense and can more accurately be translated, "in my Father's household." Rather than a self-perception as "temple," with all that this implies (such as sacrifices, cult, and a priestly hierarchy), I formed the hypothesis that the term "household of God" better expressed the self-understanding of the Johannine community.

In order to test this hypothesis—that the phrase "household of God" expressed the Johannine community's self-identity—my recent work has examined the "household" scenes within the Fourth Gospel (Coloe 2000; 2004). Is it possible to detect in these scenes any hints that we are dealing not only with "time past" (i.e., the time of Jesus) but also with "time present" (i.e., the time of the Johannine community)? Is the living "household of God" casting its shadow on those scenes in the Fourth Gospel where Jesus gathers his own? In these shadows, can we discover the real "sources" of this fascinating and elusive text? The rest of this essay will seek to answer these questions by examining John 13, the footwashing. Within the aims and the limitations of this essay I will focus on two aspects of John 13: (1) the act of footwashing within its first-century social and religious context; (2) what might lie behind the description of the footwashing as a *hypodeigma* ("model, example").

The Footwashing Narrative

One of the critical tools used in recent narrative approaches is the attention given to the actual structuring of the narrative, with an awareness of some common narrative techniques used in ancient writing, both biblical and classical Greek and Roman. My discussion here will be based on a proposed outline of John 13 that relies on antithetic parallelism in the discourse material (13:6–38) that follows the brief description of Jesus' act of footwashing (13:4–5). Since chapter 13 introduces the second major section of the Gospel of John—the "hour" of Jesus (chs. 13–20 [21]) and, in particular, his final meal with the disciples (chs. 13 –17)—the footwashing story begins with a "mini-prologue" that recapitulates a number of themes present in the opening Prologue of chapter 1 (1:1–18). I have indicated references to these themes in italics in the outline below.

1. Before the feast of the Passover (13:1)
   Jesus, *knowing* that his hour had come to depart from this *world to the Father*, having *loved* his own, those in the *world*, he *loved* them to the end.
2. During the supper (13:2–3)
   The devil had already made up his mind that Judas Iscariot son of Simon should betray him. Jesus, *knowing* that everything had been given into his hands by the Father and that he came from God and was going *to God*....

Notably, several of these themes reappear in the closing verses of the Farewell Discourse at 17:25–26:

> O righteous *Father*, the *world* has not *known* thee, but I have *known* thee; and these *know* that thou hast sent me. I made *known* to them thy name and I will make it *known* that the *love* with which thou hast *loved* me may be in them and I in them.

After this mini-prologue there is a very brief description of the footwashing (13:4–5), and the discourse and dialogue that follows (13:6–38) interpret the meaning of this action for the disciples. In this discourse/dialogue material there are two major sections, 13:6–20 and 21–38, with the first section moving from Peter to Judas and the second section moving in reverse from Judas to Peter. Central to both sections is Jesus' teaching and "gifts" of a model and a new commandment for the disciples. The passage may be outlined as follows.

    A. Dialogue with Peter (13:6–11)
       B. Teaching and "gift" (13:12–15)
          C. The betrayer (13:16–20)
          C'. The betrayer (13:21–30)
       B'. Teaching and "gift" (13:31–35)
    A'. Dialogue with Peter (13:36–38)

While most scholars conclude the footwashing story with the departure of Judas at verse 30, there are sound structural and thematic reasons for including verses 31–38 within the footwashing pericope. The departure of Judas makes a break between verses 21–30 and what follows, but this break simply concludes the subunit (C' on the outline above). Judas's departure sets in process Jesus' arrest and crucifixion, which the Fourth Gospel presents as the "hour" of Jesus' glorification (12:23). Judas's departure is thus the catalyst for Jesus' exultant cry to the Father, "Now is glorified the Son of Man, and God is glorified in him" (13:31). It follows that Jesus' words to the Father, with their theme of glorification, are necessarily linked to Judas's betrayal and its consequences. Further, the discussion with Peter (13:36–38), where he queries Jesus' statement about "following" him, parallels the discussion in verses 6–11, where Peter queries Jesus' action in washing his feet. The language of "giving" a commandment (13:34) recalls the language of "giving" a model (*hypodeigma*; 13:15). Frederic Manns also argues for the unity of the entire chapter on the basis of the *inclusio* formed by the occurrence of *tithēmi* in 13:4 and 38 (Manns 1981, 151). The above structural reasons situate verses 31–38 within the footwashing narrative and make them the conclusion of the scene. Where verses 31–38 look back to the footwashing, 14:1 forms an *inclusio* with what follows, as marked by the repetition of the phrase, "Let not your hearts be troubled" (14:1, 27). Even though there is no change in scene, time or characters, 14:1 marks the beginning of a new stage in the discourse.

Structurally, the entire chapter can be outlined as follows:[3]

> Prologue to the hour (13:1–3).
> Washing of the feet: welcome to the final meal (13:4–5)
> A. Peter's objection (13:6–11)
>   B. Teaching and "gift" (13:12–15)
>   C. The betrayer (13:16–20)
>   C'. The betrayer (13:21–30)
>   B'. Teaching and "gift" (13:31–35)
> A'. Peter's objection (13:36–38)

Ancient Footwashing

Footwashing was a common practice in ancient Mediterranean cultures as "(1) a part of daily cleansing, (2) an act of hospitality (washing the feet of guests), and (3) in various cultic settings" (Hultgren 1982, 541). According to Manns, footwashing had a particular significance within Judaism, as it recalled the hospitality shown by Abraham in welcoming his divine guests

---

[3]. For detailed arguments supporting this structure, see Coloe 2004, 401–6.

under the oaks of Mamre (Gen 18:4; Manns 1981, 160). While the original Hebrew text portrayed Abraham merely providing water for his guests to wash their own feet, the LXX suggests that someone else washed their feet (Thomas 1991, 35), and by the first century C.E. this tradition had developed to present Abraham himself washing the feet of the guests as an act of gracious hospitality. The table below illustrates the development of this theme.

Masoretic Text	Septuagint	*Testament of Abraham*
"Let a little water be brought to wash your feet, and rest yourselves under the tree" (Gen 18:4).[4]	"Let some water be brought and your feet be washed, and make yourselves cool under the tree" (Gen 18:4).[5]	"Then Abraham went forward and washed the feet of the commander-in-chief, Michael. Abraham's heart was moved, and he wept over the stranger" (*T. Ab.* 2:9).

Manns argues that *Targum Neofiti* has the same tradition as the *Testament of Abraham*, where Abraham is the one who fetches water and washes the feet, while the strangers are only the active subjects of the following verb "to rest" (Manns 1981, 160). His rendition of *Neofiti* reads, "I will go and get some water in order to wash your feet." Philo also notes an ambiguity about who does the footwashing in his comments on Gen 18: "Wherefore he [Abraham] does not give a command like a lord and master, nor does he presume to offer washing of the feet to freemen or servants but (regards) Him who has made Himself directly visible as the one who gives commands, saying, 'Let water be taken,' and does not add by whom. And again (in saying) 'Let them wash (your) feet,' he does not make clear whom nor make it known exactly" (*QG* 1.4.5). While the targumic evidence may not be conclusive because of difficulties in dating, with the support of Philo and the *Testament of Abraham* (75–125 C.E.) there is evidence of this reading of the Abraham tradition within Judaism contemporary with the Johannine community.[6]

---

4. While the MT uses second-person plural imperative "you (pl.) wash," the consonantal text can also be read as a third-person plural (see Wevers 1993, 247). The third person would continue the sense of the first verb, as in the above translation (see Westermann 1985, 273). Both Westermann and von Rad note that Abraham's speech uses the third person, avoiding the use of "I," thus showing profound respect for his visitors (see von Rad 1972, 206).

5. In this version the first two verbs are in the third-person imperative form (*lēmphthētō*; *nipsatōsan*) and only *katapsuxate* is in the second person, suggesting that the bringing of water and washing of feet be carried out by a third person. For further discussion of the text in its Masoretic and Septuagint form and also the *Testament of Abraham*, see Thomas 1991, 35–36.

6. For discussion of this dating, see Charlesworth 1985, 1:875.

These texts show that by the first century c.e. Abraham and his personal gesture of footwashing were established in Jewish tradition as the epitome of hospitality (Fitzgerald 2000, 522). Even though there is no explicit mention of Abraham in the Johannine footwashing story, there may be clues to indicate that there are intertextual echoes from Gen 18.[7] Both Genesis and the Gospel of John describe the host offering a small piece of bread, frequently translated as a "morsel": at Gen 18:5, Abraham says, "I will fetch a morsel of bread"; at John 13:26, following the footwashing, Jesus offers Judas a "morsel" (*psōmion*). The word *psōmion* is unique in the New Testament to the Fourth Gospel, where it appears four times in this brief unit (13:26–30) and may have been used deliberately because of its aural similarity with the verb for "take" at Gen 18:4 (*lēpsomai*, Gen 18:5 LXX). Further, both Genesis and John use the language of "master/Lord" and "servant" (Gen 18:3; John 13:16). Although the Targumim have dating difficulties and cannot provide conclusive evidence, *Neofiti* gives this scene a possible Passover context, as Sarah is told to make unleavened bread: "Hurry and take three seahs of fine flour, spread it and make unleavened bread" (*Tg. Neof.* Gen 18:6; see McNamara 1992, 104). The Passover setting of Jesus' final meal is clear from John 13:1. Culturally, and within Jewish religious traditions about Abraham, there is evidence to suggest that a first-century community would understand the Johannine footwashing primarily as a gesture of hospitality and welcome.

Footwashing also had a cultic purpose in Judaism, for it was necessary to wash one's feet before entering the precincts of the temple. The Mishnah records, "[A man] … may not enter into the Temple Mount with his staff or his sandal or his wallet, or with the dust upon his feet" (*m. Ber.* 9:5). This cultic purpose predates the compilation of the Mishnah, for the first-century Jewish philosopher Philo offers a number of comments on the practice of footwashing prior to entering the presence of God. In commenting on Exod 12:3 and 6, Philo states, "he who was about to offer sacrifice should first prepare his soul and body … for, according to the saying, one should not enter with unwashed feet on the pavement of the Temple of God" (*QE* 2.1.2;

---

7. In examining the possible scriptural echoes in the Pauline literature, Richard Hays (1989, 29–32) proposes seven criteria to test the likelihood that the author is using such a technique: availability, volume, recurrence, thematic coherence, historical plausibility, history of interpretation, and satisfaction. Five of these seven criteria are satisfied in trying to assess if John 13 has possible echoes of Gen 18. The text was available; there are other points of contact with the Abraham scene; there is coherence and satisfaction in understanding the footwashing as a gesture of hospitality; and it is plausible that first-century readers would understand it in this way.

similarly *Spec. Laws* 1.207).[8] Philo's remarks indicate that footwashing was a customary gesture in the first century prior to entering the temple, as the Mishnah would later encode. This same conclusion is reached by Weiss with regard both to Hellenistic synagogue practice and also the Jerusalem temple: "the notion that in order to walk on the pavement of the temple disciples were supposed to have washed their feet was a well established and recognised one in the Judaism of the second temple" (1979, 305). The precedent for washing one's feet prior to entering the temple was established in Moses' instructions that Aaron and his sons should wash their hands and feet prior to entering the tent of meeting or approaching the altar (Exod 30:17–21; cf. 2 Chr 4:6; Ps 25:6).

In discussing footwashing as both a gesture of welcome into a house and also as the prelude to entering the temple, the artistry of the Fourth Evangelist is apparent, for these two aspects of "house" and "temple" come together in Johannine theology. As noted above, in *God Dwells with Us: Temple Symbolism in the Fourth Gospel* I examined the symbolism of the temple across the Johannine narrative. I argued that the temple is the major christological symbol within the Fourth Gospel, as it is identified with the person and ministry of Jesus (1:14; 2:19, 21). Not only does the temple function as a symbol of Jesus as "the dwelling place of God," but this meaning is transferred to the disciples, who, at the cross, are drawn into the household of God. In John 14:2, the expression "In my Father's house are many dwellings" introduces a description of God's dwelling within the disciples, enabling the community to be a living temple, or, in the language of the Fourth Gospel, to be formed into "my Father's house." Fittingly, before the disciples enter the Father's house (14:2), they are welcomed with the traditional gesture of having their feet washed (13:4–5).

In chapter 13, in his gesture of washing the disciples' feet, Jesus acts as the one sent and authorized by the Father to welcome his disciples into "my Father's house" (John 14:2). Since the term "my Father's house" carries the earlier sense of "temple" from 2:16, it is doubly appropriate that the disciples' feet are washed prior to entry, for they are being welcomed into the Father's household and so to become the living temple of God.

---

8. "By the washing of the feet is meant that his steps should be no longer on earth but tread the upper air. For the soul of the lover of God does in truth leap from earth to heaven and wing its way on high, eager to take its place in the ranks and share the ordered march of sun and moon and the all-holy, all-harmonious host of the other stars" (*Spec. Laws* 1.207).

Footwashing as a *Hypodeigma*

Peter initially objects to having his feet washed because he perceives this to be a degrading act for Jesus to perform (John 13:6–11). It is important to note that this is Peter's perception, not necessarily the perception of Jesus. While Peter understands the footwashing as an act of servitude, the Gospel of John frequently uses misunderstanding as a literary device; the reader should therefore be cautious before accepting Peter's view. Jesus even states explicitly that this action will not be understood until a later time (13:7). The following verses (13:12–15) develop a deeper understanding of the meaning of Jesus' action by describing it as a "model" for the disciples (*hypodeigma*). The term *hypodeigma* is rare in the New Testament and is only found here (John 13) and in Hebrews (4:11; 8:6; 9:23), 2 Peter (2:6), and James (5:10). In these other texts the term is usually translated "example" and is commonly understood in ethical terms as a good example of humility. Culpepper examines the use of *hypodeigma* in the Septuagint and relates it to the example of the martyr's death, which in turn links Jesus' "example" (the footwashing) with his subsequent death (1991, 143). I do not disagree with Culpepper on this link, but I wish to add a further element to understanding why the Fourth Gospel uses this term to describe Jesus' action. What is meant by saying, "I have given you a *hypodeigma*"?

In looking to the Old Testament background, it appears that *paradeigma* and *hypodeigma* are interchangeable (Schlier 1964, 74, 33). In the Septuagint we find *para/hypodeigma* used in two senses. First, these terms can be used to describe human behavior. Thus, Enoch is presented as an example of repentance (Sir 44:16); similarly, the Maccabean martyrs are held up as examples in their fidelity unto death (2 Macc 6:28, 31; 3 Macc 2:5; 4 Macc 6:19; 17:23). This is the meaning discussed by Culpepper. A similar sense relating to human behavior is found in Jer 8:2 and Nah 3:6, where the term is used in the sense of public shame or exposure. Second, *para/hypodeigma* can be used in the sense of a physical model or prototype from which something is to be copied. Thus, Moses is shown the "pattern" of the heavenly tabernacle: "In accordance with all that I show you concerning the pattern (*hypodeigma*) of the tabernacle and of all its furniture, so you shall make it" (Exod 25:9). Similarly, David gives Solomon the "plan" of the temple that he is to build: "Then David gave his son Solomon the plan (*hypodeigma*) of the vestibule of the temple, and of its houses, its treasuries, its upper rooms, and its inner chambers, and of the room for the mercy seat" (1 Chr 28:11; cf. 28:12, 18, 19). Ezekiel is shown a vision of the temple as the "model" of the new house of God: "When he had finished measuring the interior of the temple area, he led me out by the gate that faces east, and measured the temple area (*to hypodeigma tou oikou*) all around" (Ezek 42:15).

I believe it is this latter meaning of *hypodeigma* as a prototype or model of the tabernacle and temple that lies behind the Johannine use of the term. Very early in the narrative Jesus describes his death as the destruction and raising up of a new temple (John 2:19, 21). These words of the divine Logos must be taken seriously. As the story develops, the symbol and rituals of the temple are part of the narrative flow, especially across chapters 7–10. It is within the context of the Feast of Tabernacles that Jesus reveals himself as the good shepherd who is able to lay down his life (John 10:11–18). The narrative of the footwashing recalls these words as Jesus lays aside and takes up his garments (13:12–14). Through these intertextual links the footwashing emerges as a symbolic anticipation of the crucifixion. This is why it is so critical that Peter, in spite of his objections, needs to have his feet washed by Jesus: "Unless I wash you, you can have no part (*meros*) with me" (13:8). According to Brown, the term *meros* "means to be drawn into my destiny," "share in my inheritance" (Brown 1966–70, 2:565). Footwashing is thus an invitation to the disciples to participate in Jesus' "hour."

The hour of Jesus in which the disciples may participate is an expression of the fullness of divine life. The cross will reveal that he loved his own to the end (*eis telos*; 13:1). The Fourth Gospel does not propose a theology of atonement, reconciliation, or forgiveness as its theological explanation of the cross. Consistently in the Fourth Gospel, Jesus' death is explained as a gift of love: "For God so loved the world he gave his son" (3:14); "greater love has no one than that he lay down his life for his friends" (15:13). As Dorothy Lee notes, "This love is the reason for the sending and dying of the Son: it is an act of self-giving love by the Father, whose will draws the world to its eschatological destiny, manifest in the restoration of the divine image. The language of love intensifies at the Last Supper, where it undergirds the meaning of the footwashing (13:1), the significance of Jesus' death and the vibrant centre of the believing community (13:34–35)" (Lee 2002, 100). In my proposed outline of John 13 (above), the gift of a *hypodeigma* in verses 12–15 (B) is reflected in the parallel unit at verses 31–35 (B'). Here Jesus "gives" (*didōmi*) the disciples a new commandment of love. The love Jesus enacts is the model of love he proposes for his disciples: "love each other as I have loved" (13:35). The footwashing, understood as a symbol of his self-giving death, is but another way of demonstrating "love as I have loved." This is why the footwashing can be called a *hypodeigma*: not because it is a "good example of humility" but because it symbolically expresses Jesus' self-gift of love, which will be revealed on the cross. It is Jesus' total self-giving on the cross that is the paradigm of the love that is to exist in his Father's household. So the two expressions parallel each other: "wash each other's feet, as I have done" (13:14); "love each other as I have loved" (13:35).

Following the footwashing Jesus calls his disciples "little children" (13:33), recalling the promise from the Prologue that those who do believe will become "children of God" (John 1:13). The footwashing is already taking effect as the disciples take on a new identity as children of the Father. For these disciples, footwashing is a proleptic experience of the welcome into the Father's household, which will be accomplished at the cross.

John 13 symbolically anticipates the crucifixion, where one temple, that of Jesus' body, is destroyed, and a new temple, the household of the Father, is created. What is acted out in symbol in John 13 is realized at the cross. In his life and death, Jesus is the temple of his Father's presence (1:14; 2:21). After the resurrection, the disciples, as children of the Father, continue to be the dwelling place of God in history. What Jesus is *now*—the incarnation of the divine indwelling—the disciples will be *later*. This is why Jesus' act of footwashing can be described as the *hypodeigma* or "paradigm" of the future temple/house/hold of God. In welcoming disciples into his Father's household, Jesus proleptically draws them into his own divine sonship.

Sources in the Shadows

From the above analysis, I propose that the narrative of the footwashing is based on the living experience of the Johannine community, which understood itself to be God's household. This lived sense of community identity leaves traces in the text in the sustained metaphor of the disciples as "children of God."[9] Such a spirituality of temple/household gives rise to the unique Johannine language of mutual indwelling, where the Father, Jesus, and the Spirit dwell with/in believers (ch. 14) and believers dwell in Jesus (ch. 15) and participate in his filial relationship with God. The community's spirituality is therefore the primary "source" of this Johannine text. While previous generations of scholars have looked for the Fourth Gospel's documentary sources in earlier lost Gospels, the Synoptics, or gnostic writings (Robinson 1962b, 96–97), the rise of narrative criticism has led to a deeper sensitivity to the nuances of the text in its language, structure, symbols, and characterizations. In choosing the literary form of a narrative Gospel that focuses on telling Jesus' story, traces of the community, living some sixty years after the nar-

---

9. The metaphor of disciples as children in God's family is developed in detail in van der Watt 2000. I prefer the language of "household" rather than "family" primarily because the narrative itself speaks of "my Father's house/hold" (John 2:16; 14:2) and also because recent studies of first-century family structures point out that a twenty-first-century Western understanding of "family" and kinship is very different from first-century notions of "family" (see Balch and Osiek 2003; Hellerman 2001).

rated events, are necessarily faint, like a background wash across the canvas of a watercolor. The Fourth Gospel places in the foreground the figure of Jesus, his disciples, and a particular understanding of Jesus' ministry. But the community's spirituality—living as children in the Father's household—does cast its own shadow across the text, as I have shown in my analysis of John 13.

While the present essay has taken up the issue of the Fourth Gospel's sources, there are two other points raised by Robinson that are also evidenced in the above discussion of the footwashing. As my work has shown, "the background of the Evangelist and his tradition … is not to be sought among the Gnostics or the Greeks" (Robinson 1962b, 98). Rather, the Gospel of John is thoroughly grounded in the theological traditions of Second Temple Judaism and in the same exegetical methods found in the Dead Sea Scrolls and the early rabbinic writings.[10] In a very distinctive manner, the Fourth Evangelist has written into the tragedy of 70 C.E., when Israel's temple was destroyed. He has developed his own Christology and ecclesiology by drawing on the meaning the temple held for Israel. While the rabbis were recasting their own traditions to reflect the loss of the temple and its sacrificial system, this Evangelist was recasting the Jesus story in the light of his absence but with the affirmation that God still dwells in the Christian community, for a new *bêt ĕlōhîm* ("house of God") has been raised up as disciples are born into the household of God.

Robinson's comments about the Fourth Gospel as a reliable witness to the historical Jesus, particularly in relation to John the Baptizer, have also been vindicated in recent scholarship (Brown 1979, 29, 69–71). The work of Christopher Niemand takes the proposal of Raymond Brown regarding the Fourth Gospel's polemic against disciples of John the Baptist even further. Niemand suggests that the narrative of the footwashing may well have been used as a means of initiating disciples of the Baptizer into the Johannine community (1993, 404–11). If so, this ritual accords honor to the Baptizer in recognizing the validity of his baptism so that his disciples need not undergo a second immersion. The Fourth Gospel therefore not only evidences the conflictual situation between disciples of Jesus and disciples of John in the time of Jesus (1:6–9, 19–34; 3:25–30), but in chapter 13 it may also offer a glimpse of the later history of a Johannine community still grappling with this conflict and working toward a resolution.

Writing almost fifty years ago, John A. T. Robinson identified five significant presuppositions of previous Johannine scholarship that his con-

---

10. For an example of a commentary which emphasizes John's relationship to Judaism, see Manns 1991.

temporaries were calling into question. Scholars of the past five decades have fought against the "critical orthodoxy" expressed in the five presuppositions Robinson described, successfully opening the way for a new generation of scholars to address new issues and to employ new methodologies. This is not to say that earlier questions have been answered but rather to acknowledge that greater truth may be found by working within a horizon that allows uncertainty and with the realization that all our historical suppositions arise from our own reconstructions. By shifting the focus from the world behind the text to the world within the text and the world in front of the text, new landscapes have emerged for a new generation of scholars to explore.

"Salvation Is from the Jews": Judaism in the Gospel of John

Brian D. Johnson

Jesus' comment to the Samaritan woman in John 4:22, "Salvation is from the Jews," seems to be a positive reflection upon "the Jews" (*hoi Ioudaioi*). Coming from the lips of the main character of the Gospel of John, this sentence seems to suggest that the viewpoint of the Gospel of John toward "the Jews" specifically and Judaism in general is not entirely negative. There are other statements within the Gospel of John that also suggest a more positive portrayal of "the Jews" (Keener 2003, 217). However, the presentation of "the Jews" in the Gospel of John is commonly understood as almost entirely antagonistic. The present essay will consider two questions relating to this issue. First, is it *necessary* to see the Gospel of John within a context of stiff dissension with "the Jews"? While the number of studies that take this approach might suggest that it is necessary, I will suggest that it is possible to imagine a more positive appropriation of the themes and symbols of Judaism. Second, how does the author utilize the practices, stories, and beliefs of Judaism within his presentation? I will attempt to show that these various Jewish themes are focused upon the person of Jesus. Of course, one might expect that a composition that explicitly seeks to inform about the person of Jesus and to engender belief that he is "the Christ" (John 20:30–31) would focus its major themes on him. However, it is less often noted that John's use of themes from Judaism is almost entirely positive. While some might immediately think that the appropriation of the language, symbols, and so forth of one group by another could arise *only* from a conflict between those two groups, I would argue that it is also possible to imagine a use of these same themes to present a particular interpretation of their properly understood focus. This essay, then, will examine the use of the themes of Judaism within the Gospel of John in order to understand if they can be seen positively rather than negatively.

"The 'Wind' Blows Where It Wills"

In an article that developed from a paper originally delivered in 1957, John A. T. Robinson (1962b) remarked on significant changes in the presuppositions of scholars on the Gospel of John. This paradigm shift included several elements, but the one that makes Robinson seem most prescient is his observation that scholars were beginning to turn toward Judaism in order to explain the background of the Gospel of John. Robinson admits he is doing nothing more than "trying to assess straws in the wind" (Robinson 1962b, 94). In other words, Robinson estimated there had been a change in the weather: the winds had shifted when they previously had been blowing in another direction. I contend that we are in the midst of another shift in wind direction. Like Robinson, however, I can only attempt to discern which way the wind is blowing, and like a weatherman on the evening news, whether I have identified a squall line forming or simply the whistle in my own ears will become obvious only when the storm breaks or fails to do so.

What Robinson detected was actually a shift back to an earlier conclusion. At the turn of the twentieth century, aside from a few dissenting breezes (Neill and Wright 1988, 339), the wind was blowing steadily toward a Hellenistic understanding of the background of the Gospel of John. Robinson detected that scholars were now beginning to turn to Judaism in order to understand the background of the Gospel of John. It is interesting and important to note how Robinson phrased his understanding of the Jewish background of the Gospel of John. He argued that the thought world of the Evangelist is not at a distance to the thought world of the setting of the Gospel of John itself, but instead the setting of the narrative and its background seem to be very close, or even one and the same. It is this perception of similarity that led Robinson and others to suggest a Jewish background for understanding the Gospel of John. They suggested that the Fourth Evangelist was much closer to the events he records than the consensus view of Robinson's day suggested (Robinson 1962b, 98).

One cannot doubt that the Jewish understanding of the background of the Gospel of John has become the predominant paradigm. For example, Visotzky writes in a recent essay, "I do not think that one can study the Gospel of John without regular recourse to the literatures and artifacts of first-century Judaism" (2005, 92). However, with the publication of J. Louis Martyn's *History and Theology in the Fourth Gospel* in 1968, this focus on the Jewish background of the Gospel of John has taken a trajectory that was not anticipated in Robinson's study. Rather than understanding that a Jewish background brings the author of the Gospel of John closer to the events he narrates, this approach understands that the text was born out of a later conflict with the

Jewish community. In fact, this theory does not rely on a similarity between the thought world of the Evangelist and the background of the Gospel of John, such as Robinson suggested, but instead ironically *requires* that the Gospel of John must be seen as removed and distant from the time and setting that it narrates. So, while this theory builds upon Robinson's observations, it also directly contradicts Robinson's conclusion.

The conflict with Judaism that is central to Martyn's theory has led to a further hypothesis, that there was a new group born from this conflict: the "Johannine community." Important to Martyn's view are the Fourth Gospel's three uses of the word *aposynagōgos* ("put out of the synagogue"; John 9:22; 12:42; 16:2). Martyn argued that this term shows that the Gospel of John reflects a period marked by conflict with the Jews, a conflict that had resulted in expulsion from synagogues for those who held to the beliefs presented in the Gospel of John. Martyn cites a prayer from the Babylonian Talmud called the Eighteen Benedictions as evidence of this conflict and expulsion. The twelfth of these benedictions, also called the Birkat Haminim or "Benediction against the Heretics," is taken by Martyn to suggest just such an expulsion from the synagogues. Therefore, the Gospel of John should not be read as what it purports to be but rather as a two-level drama that projects this later period of conflict into a narrative of the life of Jesus.

Wayne Meeks is one of the many notable scholars who have built upon Martyn's hypothesis. Meeks, focusing on the social implications of Martyn's proposal, argued that the Gospel of John was written for sectarian purposes in the midst of this conflict and subsequent split with Judaism. Jesus is "alien from all men"; he is rejected by the Jews, "his own"; and he draws into an intimate relationship those who really understand his message. Thus, the Gospel of John may be "called an etiology of the Johannine group" (Meeks 1972, 69). Meeks's focus on the sociological aspect of the Gospel of John's relationship with Judaism became fertile soil for many commentators. Following his foundational study, commentaries began to spend significant space on the sociological elements of this split with Judaism and its effect on the Gospel of John's use of Jewish symbols and language. One dramatic example is Malina and Rohrbaugh's *Social-Language Commentary on the Gospel of John*. According to this commentary, the language of the Gospel of John suggests that the book was written "to an audience composed of individuals who emerged from and stand opposed to society and its competing groups" (Malina and Rohrbaugh 1998, 10). The work of Martyn, Meeks, and Malina and Rohrbaugh demonstrates that the "new look" emphasis on the Jewish background of the Gospel of John, which grew out of an initial observation of the close correspondence between the thought world of the author and that of the events he narrates, has actually resulted in a hypothesis that *depends upon* precisely the opposite conclusion: a separation between the Evangelist and his narrative.

The dominance of Martyn's paradigm in recent research on the Gospel of John is a given in Johannine studies. The Jewish background of the themes and language in the Gospel of John is frequently viewed against the backdrop of a sharp conflict with Jews that took place much later than the events recorded in the text. After surveying a number of studies since Martyn's book, Saeed Hamid-Khani writes, "All these studies are united in the conclusion that the enigmatic language of the Fourth Gospel reflects the reaction of a sectarian community experiencing alienation and hostility within its social context" (Hamid-Khani 2000, 17). This hypothesis has been so prolific and productive that it had been able to withstand serious criticisms that undermine the foundations of Martyn's original hypothesis. It is interesting to note, for example, Andrew Lincoln's recent evaluation: "It is generally agreed that Martyn has overestimated the importance of the benediction [against the heretics] for Jewish-Christian relations in general" (Lincoln 2000, 270). Despite this shortcoming, however, Lincoln continues to follow Martyn's hypothesis, later writing, "We can now return to Martyn's original hypothesis. Even if the earliest form of the Twelfth Benediction did not include Gentile Christians, this in itself would by no means undermine Martyn's argument. Neither the Fourth Gospel nor Martyn, in his attempt to link the Gospel's narrative with Jamnia, appear to have had Gentiles in view. Expulsion from the synagogue would primarily have affected Jews" (Lincoln 2000, 275). That Lincoln continues to appeal to the Twelfth Benediction despite his earlier assessment that Martyn overemphasized it demonstrates the pervasive effect of the Martyn hypothesis in recent Johannine scholarship.

While Martyn's hypothesis, and the subsequent work of other scholars who have built upon it, continues to loom large in Johannine scholarship, there is an increasing body of literature that is both undermining this hypothesis and suggesting another way to understand the historical situation that the Gospel of John addresses. This tendency is a shift back toward Robinson's "new look" in the sense that it follows from Robinson's conclusions regarding the closeness of the background of the Gospel of John to the events that it portrays. However, this emerging perspective could also be called a "newer look" than Robinson's because of its use of newer interpretive methods, such as narrative criticism, and because it necessarily addresses a new scholarly landscape.

I would argue that drawing on Robinson's earlier conclusions is valuable. Robinson's argument that the Fourth Evangelist's background is close to that of the events portrayed in the Gospel of John is often neglected in considerations of the connection between the Fourth Gospel and Judaism, but this insight can still prove helpful. I will continue this survey of literature by suggesting that opposition to Martyn's hypothesis has risen like a cloud the size of a man's hand on the horizon and that the number and diversity of these studies suggest the possibility of another storm brewing. While I do not wish to present an exhaustive survey of all criticisms of Martyn's hypothesis, I will suggest three areas where his approach is now being questioned: the historical evidence for a conflict between John and Judaism; the language of the Gospel of John; and the origins of the Gospel of John.

In terms of the historical evidence for a conflict between John and Judaism, several recent studies have questioned whether the Birkat Haminim could serve as an appropriate background for the Gospel of John, either because of its date and locale (van der Horst 1994, 367–68) or because links between this benediction and the Gospel of John appear tenuous (Keener 2003, 213). Daniel Boyarin has produced a forceful article that questions the notion of a linear development of early Judaism and Christianity that could account for the type of break necessary to produce Martyn's Johannine community. Boyarin says of "Martyn's reconstruction" that it "simply cannot stand because the historical foundations upon which it rests are so shaky that the edifice falls down" (Boyarin 2002, 218). Boyarin's critique has not yet been adequately addressed by those who wish to maintain the Martyn hypothesis. However, it does seem clear that some will continue to build upon Martyn's hypothesis despite its loss of this major brace.

Scholars have also recently questioned Martyn's understanding of the language of the Gospel of John. Francis Watson, in his article "Toward a Literal Reading of the Gospels," points out the allegorical nature of Martyn's two-level reading, and makes a case for taking seriously what the author claims to be doing (1998). Another important contribution is Stephen Motyer's book, *"Your Father the Devil?"* (1997). Motyer focuses on John 8:44 ("your [the Jews'] father is of/from the devil"), the statement in John's Gospel that seems to reflect most blatantly the sort of sharp disagreement and social division necessary for the viability of Martyn's hypothesis. Motyer instead proposes a different context, understanding, and purpose for John's Gospel, arguing that this statement and the argument of the Gospel of John should be understood as a polemic *within* Judaism. Finally, Peter Philips has questioned the way that Johannine scholars have used sociolinguistics to make a case for the "antilanguage" of the Gospel of John. By examining the subject of sociolinguistics more widely and through careful analysis of the specific interdisciplinary theories used by Johannine scholars who take an antilanguage approach, Philips adeptly shows that scholars such as Malina have used these sociolinguistic categories in a way that is inconsistent with their actual claims. Philips argues that the Gospel of John is structured in such a way that it can invite "fascination," making the text open to "outsiders." Philips further suggests that within

Meeks's own work "there is a seed of ambiguity sown ... [in this] article as to how closed this [Johannine] community really is" (Philips 2004, 57). Finally, Adele Reinhartz has criticized Martyn's hypothesis because of his focus upon particular statements within the Gospel of John to the exclusion of others (Reinhartz 2001, 45). Reinhartz points out important statements within the narrative that would suggest an ecclesiological situation far different than that proposed by Martyn. Her careful analysis, and the other studies cited above, suggest that it is possible to read the language John's Gospel differently than Martyn has suggested.

Finally, some have questioned Martyn's understanding on the basis of new approaches to the origins of the Gospel of John. Martin Hengel's *The Johannine Question* (1989) marks an important turning point in the discussion. Hengel questions the legitimacy of views of the origin of John's Gospel that depend on the existence of a "Johannine community." Other studies have built on Hengel's work and show the viability of his approach. As one example, Richard Bauckham's article and later book entitled *The Gospels for All Christians* (1998) suggest that the Gospel of John was not narrowly sectarian but was written to a much wider audience. Other works, such as Craig Blomberg's *The Historical Reliability of John's Gospel* (2001) and Köstenberger's *Encountering John* (1999), have been influenced by Hengel and Bauckham. These studies have proposed an origin of the Gospel of John that does not rely upon a conflict with Judaism and the birth of a Johannine community.

This "newer look" understands the Jewish background of the Fourth Gospel not as a dramatic separation between synagogue and church that develops a Johannine community but rather in terms of the Fourth Evangelist's intentional use of the language of Judaism to achieve his purposes. In reference to Martyn's hypothesis, Stephen Motyer concludes, "I think this consensus needs seriously to be challenged.... Far from reinforcing Christian sectarianism, *the Fourth Gospel is deeply aware of the traumas and needs of late first-century Judaism, and seeks to address them not as a fugitive from the fold, but as a member of the flock.*" (Motyer 1997, xii). Is it possible to understand the Gospel of John in this way? In light of the edifice that has been built on Martyn's foundation, is it possible to dissent? I suspect so, and I have tried to demonstrate that there are signs this is the case. I have cited a few of these breezes above. That they come from the variety of approaches and backgrounds is suggestive as well. I am *not* trying to suggest that there is some single, monolithic, or even consistent approach to the question of Judaism within the Fourth Gospel that opposes Martyn's hypothesis. I am suggesting, rather, that these approaches, when taken together, demonstrate that the Martyn hypothesis must be reevaluated. I would further suggest that the conclusions of Johannine scholars over the next fifty years may be more significantly influenced by the dissenting voices than by Martyn's hypothesis. Without accepting the particulars of each of the studies mentioned above, it is still possible, as Robinson did a half-century ago, to detect a change in the weather. When we add to this shift the intense study currently being applied to the numerous expressions of Judaism that existed in the first century, it is clear that the time is ripe for a reevaluation of the author of the Gospel of John's approach to Judaism. This reevaluation will require a much more nuanced approach to these various forms of Judaism and their relationships with various early Christian groups. Perhaps an approach more similar to Robinson's "new look" will emerge to guide discussion of these questions in the future.

I want to be clear that the way one answers the question of the relationship between the Gospel of John and Judaism is not of little consequence. Instead, as can be seen from the survey of scholarship above, this question is central to the way one understands the Gospel of John as a whole. Until an alternative paradigm to Martyn's is shown to be productive, however, the consensus paradigm will stand. It will stand, not because it is an inherently superior way of explaining John's Gospel (although it may well be), but simply because an alternative paradigm will not be accepted until it is shown to have explanatory power (Johnson 1998, 269–70; also Wright 1992, 104–20; Meyer 1994, 40–58). The present essay alone cannot accomplish this, but it is hoped that it will point the way toward at least one area of study that will show that the Gospel of John's presentation of the themes Judaism can be understood as more positive than is often suggested.

"Salvation Is from the Jews"

The use of the language, symbols, and themes of Judaism is widespread within the Gospel of John. This section will survey briefly three of these areas in order to understand how the Gospel of John uses this language. One area that has received a good deal of attention lately is the temple theme in the Gospel of John. This theme will be examined first, then titles used for Jesus will be examined, and finally the Jewish feasts. I would argue that the Gospel of John is primarily concerned with the *identity* of Jesus and that the author's primary way of exegeting Jesus' identity is through the *systematic* and *systemic* use of the language, symbols, stories, and beliefs of Judaism, including John's appropriation of the Jewish temple, titles, and feasts (Wright 1992, 122–26).

The Temple

The temple theme is prominent in the Gospel of John and provides an excellent starting point in considering the author's use of Jewish symbols in his presentation of Jesus. We can find in this theme evidence of John's positive use of Jewish symbols to construct his image of Jesus. The use of the temple in John's Gospel has received significant treatment recently. Particularly, two excellent monographs have traced the temple theme (Coloe 2001; Kerr 2002).

The theme of the temple is perhaps most clearly seen early in John's account of the temple incident (John 2:13-25). Here, in a context of conflict with "the Jews," Jesus presents himself as the temple. He takes on the role of this symbol that is central to Judaism's identity and praxis. The narrator makes Jesus' intention clear in John 2:21 ("He spoke this regarding the temple of his body"). The author explicitly shows that Jesus' statement regarding the destruction and rebuilding of the temple is pointing to what he will accomplish in his death. The author of the Gospel of John may have moved this account to the beginning of his narrative to highlight this theme (cf. Mark 11:1-19), which is then carried through much of the rest of the book.

In John 7 we find Jesus entering the temple courts at the high point of the Feast of Tabernacles. There he makes a strong statement regarding his identity: "If anyone thirsts, let him come to me. And let him drink, the one believing in me. As the Scriptures said, 'Rivers of living water will flow from within him'" (7:37-38). Most Johannine scholars understand this passage to be focusing upon Jesus and the rivers of living water flowing from within him. The Scripture Jesus cites is unclear but may be a reference to Zech 14:8, where it is said that "living water" will flow from Jerusalem and perhaps more particularly from the temple (see Joel 3:18; Ezek 47:1-7; also Kerr 2002, 239-41). This backdrop may also explain John's emphasis upon the flow of blood and *water* from Jesus' side after he dies on the cross: here is the water flowing from within the temple of Jesus' body (John 19:34; Kerr 2002, 241-43).

Perhaps the highpoint of the temple theme in John's Gospel is found in John 14:1-4, where both the phrase "my Father's house" and the repeated word "place" could perhaps be best understood in reference to the temple (Kerr 2002, 275-78). If this is the case, Jesus is suggesting that where he is going (that is, to the cross) is where he will prepare a "place"—that is, a "place of worship"—for his disciples. Through his death Jesus will become the place that is symbolic both of God's presence and of the way in which one draws near to God. The symbolic role that the temple building had in Judaism now is to be understood in relationship to Jesus, who fulfills the role of the temple for his followers.

Jesus is systematically shown throughout the Gospel of John to be taking upon himself the purpose and role of the temple. He does what the temple was to do and at times was unable to do. In the accounts where the temple is explicitly mentioned, there is often conflict. The conflict always centers on Jesus' identity.

Jewish Titles

Another way the author of John's Gospel develops Jesus' identity is through the use of titles. These titles all seem to have meaning only in the context of Jewish tradition. We can begin with the various titles applied to Jesus by considering John 1:35–49. Here, as we are first introduced to Jesus, a significant number of Jewish titles are immediately applied to him, including "Lamb of God," "rabbi," "Messiah," "Son of God," and "King of Israel." The sheer number of these titles leads Koester to conclude that "Jewish Christians were almost certainly at the center of the audience for which John's Gospel was written. The opening scenes present Jesus as a rabbi and as the Messiah or 'Christ' foretold in the Jewish Scriptures. The titles 'Son of God' and 'King of Israel,' which appear on the lips of Nathanael, also recall Jewish tradition (1:35–51)" (Koester 2003, 19–20). One sign that these titles seem to be most closely attached to a Jewish context is that it is necessary for the narrator to translate them into Greek for readers who may be unfamiliar with the terms. In this section I will show that all five of these titles identify Christ through a positive interaction with Jewish tradition.

"Lamb of God" is the first major title applied to Jesus after the Prologue (John 1:1–18). Jesus is called "the Lamb of God" only twice in the Fourth Gospel, both times by John the Baptist in the first chapter (1:26, 29). This title can be understood in connection with the Johannine passion narrative and may refer to Jesus fulfilling his role as the Lamb of God in connection with the Passover. Keener, for example, states that, "in having Jesus killed, they were slaying the new Passover lamb" (Keener 2003, 1100). However, even if a connection between John's passion narrative and the Passover lamb is rejected, other suggestions are typically made from within Jewish tradition (Skinner 2004, 89–102). In the discussion of the Passover below I will offer reasons for understanding the reference to Jesus as the Passover lamb. It should be noted here, however, that the overlap between categories such as these and their close connection show that the symbols and language of Judaism serve an integral role in John's narrative. The comprehensive nature of these themes argues for the intentional use of Judaism to present Jesus' identity. In this particular instance, the author makes no attempt to explain this connection with Judaism away, nor does there seem to be an attempt to distance Jesus from this Jewish context. Therefore, the identification of Jesus as the Lamb of God probably should be understood as a positive interaction with Judaism.

Nathaniel describes Jesus as "King of Israel" in John 1:49. Though Nathanael does not call Jesus "Christ" or "Messiah," the term "King of Israel" expresses a messianic expectation. The depiction of Jesus' triumphal entry into Jerusalem in John 12:12–15 shows this same expectation applied to Jesus both symbolically, through the waving of palm branches, and in terms of belief, through the great crowd's exclamations and the narrator's quotation from Zech 9:9. John's use of the titles "King" and "King of Israel" are important, however, not only because of their messianic significance. First, although Jesus is identified in John's Gospel with great figures from Israel's history—most notably Moses and Abraham—David is mentioned only once in the Gospel of John (7:42). Additionally, David is mentioned only in a context where people are asking about prophecies that assert that the Christ should come from David's family and hometown. The author likely intends the crowd's questions to be taken ironically by readers who were familiar with the outlines of the Synoptic traditions about Jesus' birth in Bethlehem, the "City of David." While those in the narrative who debate if Jesus is the Christ do not understand, the informed reader knows that Jesus had come from David's town and lineage. John's Gospel uses the title "King of Israel" in a way that is similar to references to Jesus as David's son as found in tradition that appears in the Synoptics. Second, Jesus' understanding of himself as the King of Israel in the Gospel of John seems to contrast the popular understanding. In 6:15 Jesus withdraws because they are coming to make him king by force. Also, when Pilate asks Jesus bluntly "Are you the king of the Jews?" Jesus cannot answer with a simple yes or no. Jesus clearly affirms that he is a king, but he is just as emphatic that he is the King of an "otherworldly" kingdom. While the author seems to suggest that some have misunderstood how to apply this title to Jesus, "King of Israel" is a title that the author is saying well expresses part of his understanding of Jesus' identity. That this Jewish title is applied to Jesus within the narrative is another example of the positive way the author uses the beliefs and terms of Judaism to describe Jesus positively.

Another of the terms applied to Jesus in John 1 is "rabbi." The two disciples in 1:38 who are exemplary in following Jesus from the beginning to the end (21:2) of his ministry call him "rabbi." Nathanael calls Jesus "rabbi" before piling two more significant titles onto him, "Son of God" and "King of Israel." Collectively, Jesus' disciples call him "rabbi" in 4:31; 6:25; 9:2; and 11:8. When Mary recognizes Jesus in the garden, she calls him *rabbouni*. Brown suggests that this variation is perhaps a form of affection (Brown 1966–70, 2:991–92), but it may be better understood as intensification, or simply a variation in spelling (perhaps better explaining its only other New Testament usage in Mark 10:51). Either way, it seems to be a title clearly related to rabbi (BDAG, 902). The only person other than Jesus who is called "rabbi" in John's Gospel is John the Baptist (3:2), in a context where he is asserting to his own disciples Jesus' superiority. Perhaps this term is not yet being used technically as "an honorary title for outstanding teachers of the law" (BDAG, 902). However, it is derived from Hebrew and is translated with the Greek "teacher" (*didas-*

kalos) by John. This certainly indicates a Jewish context as well as a title of respect (Riesner 1992, 807–11). In John 13:13–14 Jesus commends his disciples for calling him "teacher" (*didaskolos*) and Lord (*kyrios*). As for Jesus doing what a rabbi does, the Gospel of John shows him both collecting disciples and teaching. There is an interesting concentration of forms of the verb "teach" (*didaskō*) in chapter 7. Jesus is described only once in the narrative of John's Gospel as teaching in synagogues (6:59) and once as teaching in the temple, yet at his trial Jesus offers the defense that he always (*pantote*) taught in the synagogues (18:20).

After examining the use of "rabbi" as a title for Jesus, Andreas Köstenberger suggests that this term, along with "teacher" (*didaskalos*) and "Lord/Master" (*kyrios*), are the ways that Jesus is typically addressed in John's Gospel. He further suggests that these three titles are "largely synonymous in John" and that we can see Jesus filling the role of rabbi in a "customary teacher-disciple relationship in first-century Judaism." Köstenberger's careful examination of the Gospel of John carries out his conclusion that Jesus is portrayed in John's Gospel as being "perceived by his contemporaries primarily as a Jewish religious teacher" (Köstenberger 1999, 100–101). If this is true, the title "rabbi," understood within a context of Judaism, shows a positive application of a Jewish term to Jesus. Perhaps particularly important here, the author makes no attempt to distance Jesus from a term that would have portrayed him as "a Jewish religious teacher."

Jesus is first identified in the Gospel of John as the "Son of God" by John the Baptist in 1:32–34. This is done in connection with John the Baptist's testimony regarding Jesus' baptism. Nathanael calls Jesus "Son of God" in connection with the title "King of Israel" (1:49). The next use in 3:18 is either from Jesus or the narrator, depending on where we see Jesus' remarks ending and the narrator's comments beginning. This occurrence is somewhat ambiguous, but the use of "Son of God" elsewhere in Jesus' teaching will shed light on this instance. In Jesus' answers to the Jews in 5:25 and 10:36 he refers to the "Son of God," and in 10:36 he makes clear that he is referring to himself with this title. Twice the title "Son of God" appears in the Lazarus account: once from Jesus, when he speaks of the Son of God being glorified (11:4); and once by Martha (11:27), when she affirms her belief that Jesus is the "Christ," a term that is then set in apposition to "the Son of God." The penultimate use of this term is when the Jews are before Pilate and bring the accusation that Jesus deserves death because "he made himself the Son of God" (19:7). Finally, in the purpose statement of John's Gospel (20:31) we find "Son of God" once again paralleled with "Christ."

"Son of God" is perhaps the title that is most difficult to associate immediately with a Jewish background. There are at least two areas of consideration, however, that show that it should be understood in just this way. First, in view of the other phrases and terms with which "Son of God" is associated, it seems that the author intends this title to be understood within a Jewish context. Twice "Son of God" is coupled with "Christ" and once with "King of Israel." Larry Hurtado notes the use of "Messiah" and "Son of God" in John 20:30–31, suggesting that these titles "reflect a provenance in Jewish and biblical traditions" (Hurtado 2003, 358). Additionally, when we consider the way John the Baptist uses this title, it seems intended to identify Jesus as the one sent from God. Second, John's frequent use of the language of "Father and Son" could be an indication of how "Son of God" is to be understood in the Fourth Gospel. The language of the Father and Son seems to suggest the strong relationship between Jesus and God, but also their continuity in action. It is this element that seems to make the title "Son of God" a particular source of conflict between Jesus and the Jews.

Finally, in contrast to the Synoptics, we find the title "Christ" applied to Jesus throughout the Gospel of John. One of the two disciples of John the Baptist who begin to follow Jesus is identified as Andrew, who goes and tells his brother Peter, "We have found the Messiah," which is then translated "Christ" (1:41). What a contrast to the account of Mark, where Peter's "discovery" of this reality serves in some sense as the high point of the narrative (Mark 8:27–30)! Peter's confession in John is that Jesus is the "Holy One of God." Two times "Christ" is given as the translation of "Messiah." A number of times this title is used in a context where people are speculating whether Jesus can indeed be the Christ. There is a collection of these uses in chapter 7, which shows the expectation of the people in regard to the Christ: that he would be the one to do wonders and who would be from David's city. The compound use "Jesus Christ" is used twice: once at 1:17 and again at 17:3. Perhaps the most important use of this title is in 20:31, where the author states that his purpose in writing was to engender belief that the Messiah is Jesus.

THE JEWISH FEASTS

That the author of the Gospel of John makes different use of the Jewish feasts than do the Synoptics cannot be doubted. Two obvious examples are the three separate incidents at Passover in John's Gospel, as opposed to only one in the Synoptics, and the closer connection in John between the feasts and Jesus' activities and teachings. Feasts such as Dedication, which are absent from the Synoptics, receive mention in the Gospel of John as well. Motyer points out in connection with the temple theme that, in John, "the festivals are closely woven into the structure of the Gospel" (1997, 36). Gale Yee's *Jewish Feasts and the Gospel of John* (1989) remains the most comprehensive study to date of the Jewish festivals in the Fourth Gospel; more recently, Alan Kerr devotes a chapter of his book on the temple in John to Jewish festivals (Kerr 2002, ch. 7). The emphasis that the author of the Gospel of John places upon the feasts is another example of his use of Jewish practices to discuss Jesus' identity. The author does not distance Jesus from the feasts but instead seems intentionally to connect important statements about actions of Jesus with the feasts. As will be seen in the survey below, this connection seems to be more than simply using the feasts as a narrative backdrop.

Certainly Passover is the most important feast in the Gospel of John. The author refers to three separate Passover feasts. The emphasis in the first seems to be on the temple (John 2:13, 23), as Jesus replaces the place where one comes to celebrate the Passover (Saldarini 1998, 87). During the second Passover, we find a close connection between Jesus and Moses and between Jesus as the bread of life and the manna that God provided in the wilderness (6:4). Perhaps here we see an emphasis upon Jesus' role over that of the one who brought God's redemption to Israel in the exodus event. In the third occasion of the Passover, the focus becomes the observance of the Passover itself (13:1; 18:28, 39; 19:14). Here Jesus is identified with the lamb offered in the Passover feast and becomes the "Lamb of God" that takes away the sins of the world. Many have suggested that John intentionally promotes this understanding by adjusting the timing of Jesus' crucifixion, but Craig Blomberg's careful discussion has recently shown that this is not the only way, and probably not the best way, of understanding the "day of preparation" at John 19:14, 31 (2001, 246–47). The specific timing of Jesus' death, however, is not essential, as there are two other very strong indicators that Jesus is presented as the Passover lamb in John's passion. First, there is the use of hyssop, which is connected with the Passover event at Exod 12:22. In John 19:29 hyssop is used to lift vinegar to Jesus as he hangs on the cross. Hyssop is rarely mentioned in the New Testament, the only other occurrence being Heb 9:19. It seems as though the author has chosen to use this word in order to draw our attention to something about the significance of this event within the context of Passover. Another telling sign of this emphasis can be seen in John's description of the *crurifragium* (breaking the legs of those on the cross; John 19:31–37). John alone refers to the *crurifragium* and specifically indicates the significance of Jesus' legs not being broken by drawing attention to the "prophecy" of Exod 12:46. Here in the midst of the exodus event, and in God's giving of the Passover regulation, the author of the Gospel of John presents Jesus as the Passover lamb.

The connection between the Feast of Tabernacles and the fulfillment of Old Testament prophecies of the messianic age has been discussed widely by Johannine scholars. I have suggested above in the section on the temple that a translation of John 7:38 that focuses upon Jesus ("from his/Jesus' body will flow rivers of living water") is to be preferred. Taken this way, this text shows Jesus claiming for himself the role of the temple, but an additional dimension of his activity here should be noted: Jesus' dramatic use of language draws attention to his activity. Phrases such as "the greatest day of the feast" and "shouting with a loud voice" both call attention to this account. Jesus, through his words on this feast day, calls to mind the prophecies of Joel 3:18; Ezek 47:1–7; and Zech 14:8, all of which refer to a messianic age. These prophecies suggest that a fountain will flow from the temple that will cause the land to be fertile. The Ezekiel passage suggests that even the waters of the Dead Sea would be fresh when this river flows into it. In John 7 Jesus claims that he is the source of this "living water." This feast then becomes focused again on the identity of Jesus. Gale Yee summarizes, "As he did with the feasts of Sabbath and Passover, John exploits the rich symbols of the feast of Tabernacles to articulate his own theology of the person of Jesus" (Yee 1989, 82).

The connection between the Feast of Dedication and John's presentation of Jesus' identity is not nearly as clear, and not as much has been written on this as on the other feasts. For example, Yee's discussion of Dedication is the least satisfying part of her otherwise excellent treatment. The lack of clear reference is likely the reason for this paucity of scholarly suggestions. However, if the other feasts are understood as connecting directly to Jesus' actions and words, then it is at least possible, if not likely, that there should be a connection here as well. James VanderKam has suggested interesting parallels of language between John 10:22–39 and the Jewish accounts of Antiochus IV Epiphanes and Dan 7; 8; and 11 (VanderKam 1990, 212). He concludes, "It seems no accident that John dated Jesus' assertion of his divinity to the festival of Hanukkah when the blasphemies of Antiochus IV, the self-proclaimed god manifest, were remembered" (VanderKam 1990, 213). So, Jesus is portrayed as legitimately claiming for himself, according to VanderKam, what Antiochus IV had illegitimately claimed. It is perhaps more likely, however, that the focus in John 10 is upon the Maccabean rulers themselves, whose cleansing of the temple was celebrated in this feast. It is possible that Jesus is claiming to be a "good shepherd" (10:11) in contrast to those "who came before" (10:8). Shepherds often are used as metaphors for the rulers of the people. What those who came before—the Maccabees—had failed to be, Jesus now claims for himself. Understood in this way, this becomes another instance where John presents Jesus as the true King for the people. However, Jesus' references here show that his rule is different. Whereas the Maccabees ruled because of their political power and the military force they could control, Jesus becomes the true shepherd of the people by laying down his life. This reading is similar to VanderKam's suggestion in that it has Jesus arguing for legitimacy over against illegitimacy, but in this case it would perhaps be in comparison to the Maccabees rather than to Antiochus. The Maccabees would be the group remembered more positively by the Jewish people during the Feast of Dedication.

Overall, within the Gospel of John the feasts form a systematic presentation. They also seem to serve a role deeper than simply providing a background for Jesus' activities. Jesus' actions and words are presented in a way that seems to interact directly with the practices and interpretation of these feasts. In all of these accounts, the reader is shown the connection between the person and identify of Jesus with the feast in question. Particularly, the elements of the feasts that would have been known and revered by Jews are reinterpreted in reference to Jesus. His identity is presented positively in connection with these feasts.

"Are You the King of the Jews?"

It will be obvious to students of the Gospel of John that I have not yet discussed an extremely important element in any consideration of John's relationship with Judaism: the identification and function of the *Ioudaioi*, "the Jews," in the Fourth Gospel. This has been intentional, insofar as I wanted to approach the Gospel of John's use of Jewish themes without prejudging the stance the Evangelist is taking in regard to Judaism. From the survey above it can be seen that the author regularly uses terms, practices, and symbols to identify Jesus that only have meaning within a Jewish context. If this is the case, is it necessary for the Johannine scholar to understand this thoroughgoing use to be the result of an antagonistic division with a Jewish group? I think at least we can say that it is not *necessary* to conclude that this is the case. Without prejudging the question of the development of "Johannine Christianity," one could see that John's appropriation of these Jewish categories is more positive than is usually portrayed.

When all the evidence above of the author's *intentional* portrayal of Jesus within the framework of Judaism is piled up, it raises the question, In what sense can John be understood to be "anti-Jewish"? Or, perhaps, why would someone who is to be understood as "anti-Jewish" intentionally portray his protagonist in Jewish terms? Is a theory of "antilanguage" and/or the assumption of a conflict between the "Johannine community" and Jews sufficient to explain the fact that the author does not disparage these Jewish elements? In only one case, or perhaps two, does John modify the meaning of the Jewish elements he incorporates. Instead, he presents Jesus as the true fulfillment or the correct interpretation of these symbols. Jesus is the one who properly wears the Jewish titles, who takes the place of the temple as the place of worship and as the one dwelling with his disciples. If the author decides to portray his hero so thoroughly in light of these symbols, practices, stories, and beliefs, it must be asked, Why? Why does he choose this as his preferred paradigm? If it is understood that the *Ioudaioi* are representative of opposition in John's Gospel, this must be balanced with the clear indication that, rather than rejecting Judaism outright, the author uses Judaism positively and as the chief strategy for achieving his purpose: to identify the protagonist of his account, Jesus. Understood in this way, it can be seen that we should not take too hasty a leap in immediately identifying the *Ioudaioi* or in simplifying the function of this group within the narrative world of the Gospel of John.

The author of the Gospel of John certainly reappropriates elements of Judaism, but with the apparent desired effect of showing that Jesus is that which gives Judaism meaning. As Hamid-Khani writes, "the essential function of John's language is wedded to his purpose—a steadfast conviction that Jesus is the embodiment of the saving self-revelation of God according to the witness of Israel's Scriptures. For John, above all else, Jesus is the Promised One because the Scriptures anticipate him, speak of him and find their supreme realization in him" (2000, 230).

Hamid-Khani's observation leads to my first major conclusion. The relationship between John and Judaism is not one of outright rejection; instead, it is both acceptance and rejection. Or, to use the language of sociolinguistics, it is both *convergence* ("the intentional strategy to secure good will by adapting speech to coincide with those with whom you are communicating") and *divergence* ("deliberately choos[ing] a language, or dialect, which is not used by the receiver"; Philips 2004, 68). After analyzing the Johannine use of language, Peter Philips concludes that those responsible for the Gospel of John are "willing to engage with the world around it rather than choosing to be excluded and disengaged from it" (Philips 2004, 71). While John rejects the particular Jewish understanding of the Jewish institutions, he accepts the institutions themselves. In particular, he understands these Jewish institutions as the appropriate way to describe the identity of Jesus. Furthermore, these Jewish themes are interwoven and interlocked with Jesus' identity to such an extent that one must conclude that this is an intimate part of the author's way of thinking.

Second, Judaism within the Gospel of John is not a one-dimensional "theme." Because of the pervasiveness of John's use of these elements of Judaism and because of their interconnection, to single out one element alone is illegitimate and potentially misleading. One example of this problem would be those studies that pick up on the Jewish juridical language in the Gospel of John and use this as an interpretive paradigm for the entire book. I would suggest that the Fourth Gospel gives us a glimpse into a thought world that is thoroughly steeped in Judaism. This is again a return to Robinson across the divide of Martyn. As Robinson argued, the thought world of the Evangelist is much closer to the thought world of the events that he narrates. Any attempt to isolate any one theme, such as the temple or the Jewish juridical language, will be necessarily incomplete. While these studies might, in one sense, be said to have "gotten it right" in that they recognize one aspect of Judaism in John's Gospel, they have made only one thin tracing in what is a three-dimensional object. Or, to use a different metaphor, these studies have seen a single, solitary reflection off of a multifaceted gem. Tracing one theme may prove useful in understanding the Gospel of John as a whole, but no one theme within Judaism is capable of doing justice to the way this author has interwoven several elements of Judaism and has presented Jesus as the answer to them all. This again shows the need for a larger, more comprehensive study of the way the author interacts with the thought world of first-century Judaism.

Third, if it is proper to look at the "matrix" of the author's thought world, rather than at the development of the Johannine community, to explain different and disparate elements within John's narrative, then the complex culture in which the author finds himself and to which he is addressing his message about Jesus should be the focus of our study. Again, I would suggest a return to Robinson here. However, I would modify Robinson's "new look" to a "newer look" by suggesting that perhaps Judaism alone might not fully explain Johannine thought. Even as first-century Palestine was a mixture of Judaism and Hellenism, the background against which the Gospel of John must be understood is just such a matrix. This is certainly not a simple picture but a very complex and demanding one for the student of the Gospel of John. That having been said, however, such an approach is certainly more plausible and subject to more concrete controls than a sociological analysis of an unknown, and possibly nonexistent, Johannine community.

This goes precisely to my view that the Gospel of John is concerned with a particular way of being a first-century Jew, namely, a Jew who understands Jesus to be the Christ, who sees Jesus as fulfilling both the place and function of the temple and the feasts and who is significantly superior to the prophets, Moses, Jacob, and the other heroes of Israel's history. As our understanding of first-century Judaism grows, it is clear there was variety in understanding what it meant to be a Jew. I would argue that the thought world of the Gospel of John fits well within the context of interpretive variety within first-century Judaism.

Another Look: Johannine "Subordinationist Christology" and the Roman Family

Beth M. Sheppard

Since John A. T. Robinson published *Twelve New Testament Studies* in 1962, the tools and techniques available for executing scholarly research and exchange have shifted dramatically. For instance, paper indexes and abstracts, the treasure trove of libraries just a few decades ago, have been replaced by computerized databases. In addition, the advent of e-mail programs, satellites, instant messaging, and video conferencing have simplified the ability of scholars to share ideas with colleagues and students anywhere in the world. These technological changes have sensitized the current generation of scholars to the ease with which not only ideas and knowledge but also other aspects of culture may be transmitted. Indeed, today's American and European students, who have been raised with "live satellite news links" on BBC and CNN, are not necessarily surprised to see photos in which bedouin tents located a half-day's bus trip from Jerusalem are graced with television antennas. Likewise, they readily accept that Coca Cola, with labels imprinted in Arabic on one side and Hebrew on the other, are available in shops in Israel.

"Globalization" is the term used to articulate the tendency for humans to engage in cultural exchange, be it an exchange of ideas or the pervasiveness of products such as Coca Cola in foreign countries. Popularized by such books as *Jihad vs. McWorld* (Barber 1996), globalization is characterized by the understanding that no single nation can exist in isolation from others and that each individual culture, though retaining unique characteristics that may make it identifiable, contains elements adopted from other countries and societies. While technological advances since the 1960s have helped to speed the effects of globalization and make it easier to perceive, globalization is not a new phenomenon. Cultural exchange and interaction is as old as humanity itself. This renewed interest in globalization, however, has opened doors for scholars since the time of Robinson to take another look at the wide variety of cultures that intersected in the world of the Fourth Gospel (FG). Hence it is becoming increasingly popular to explore not only Jewish and Greek (Hellenistic) contexts for this text but Roman and others as well. The wide variety of cultures that were at play in the ancient world precludes the possibility of an extended discussion about each one in the space of a single essay. In order to do justice to a single topic, the place of Roman culture in the Johannine literature will take center stage in the next pages.

Robinson himself said very little concerning Rome in the four survey essays that were included in his *Twelve New Testament Studies* collection (1962b). What he did offer was a mix of essays on the Fourth Gospel. Two of these addressed theoretical concerns, and two provided, as the subtitle of one indicates, a "test of exegetical method." This combination of design and experiment provides an excellent balance that may be readily adapted for the following discussion. The first two sections below will focus on theoretical concerns relating to the exploration of Roman culture in the Fourth Gospel. The last half of the essay will provide a "test" in which the Fourth Gospel's father-son motif is examined within the context of Roman family structures. The goal is to determine whether an explication of the Roman family sheds light on a puzzling phenomenon concerning the relationship between Jesus and God. More specifically, in the Fourth Gospel Jesus sometimes appears equal with God the Father, while in other cases Jesus appears to be subordinate to the Father's will. I will argue that this apparent theological tension may be resolved by viewing the Fourth Gospel against the backdrop of Roman society.

Robinson and the Myth of the "Pure" Culture

Although Robinson does not use the term "globalization" in his essays, he reveals some sensitivity to the variety of traditions that make up of the Fourth Gospel. Yet this is only because Hellenistic acculturation, in Robinson's framework, is subsequent to the original "Southern Palestinian" milieu of the story (1962a, 116). His concern is linked to his affirmation that the Fourth Gospel is not merely a product of late first-century Christianity but that it instead represents an accurate witness to the historical Jesus. In service of this agenda, Robinson tends to draw a sharp distinction between the Hellenism that characterizes the environment in which the text was published and the Palestinian Jewish society of the Jesus tradition that underlies the text (see 1962b, 98). For instance, in an exegetical survey of the parable of the Good Shepherd (John 10:1–5), Robinson takes great pains to point out "the parable is 'clean' " of the influence of the church's situation in the Hellenistic world. Instead, he comments, it is likely "a genuine parable drawn from life in Palestine" (1962c, 75, 69). The underlying assumption is that the context of first-century Judea was thoroughly Palestinian with little or no Hellenistic or Roman cultural interplay. In essence, Robinson sets up a dichotomy between the Hellenistic world and the Palestinian world that is a bit too simplistic.

Twenty-first-century scholars who are aware of globalization might be less prone than Robinson to think that terms such as "Jewish," "Hellenistic," or "Roman" represent isolated, homogenous, cultures when applied to the first-century world. For example, classicists such as Seth Schwartz demonstrate this newer understanding. He observes that Herodian Jerusalem was "a city whose public spaces featured the best that Italian and imperial Greek architecture had to offer, and whose elites gloried in their friendships with local dynasts and Roman grandees" (Schwartz 1991, 335). Schwartz continues, however, with the acknowledgment that the Jewish temple precinct dominated the city. The Jewish aspect was also evident in local housing. The very same dwellings that were decorated with Greco-Roman frescos were, unlike their counterparts in Pompeii, unique in the fact that depictions of human figures and animals were absent. In essence, Jerusalem freely borrowed from the Greco-Roman culture but still retained its Jewish ethos. Ramsey MacMullen also points out that Palestine in the time of Jesus' birth was an amalgamation of cultural influences. He notes that Herod established a temple to Jupiter in Heliopolis that was constructed in accordance with Roman design preferences (MacMullen 2000, 20) and that Herod's other cities contained features such as Roman baths, sewers, and aqueducts. Furthermore, MacMullen emphasizes the contact between Hellenistic, Roman, and Palestinian culture in his discussion of a legal inscription that was uncovered in Palestine. The stone carving dates from the time of the Roman emperor Augustus and records an edict that prohibited grave robbing. The mix of cultures was evident in the fact that the law was promulgated in the land of the Jews and was expressed "partly in Roman, partly in Hellenistic terms" (MacMullen 2000, 11). Robinson's simplistic formulation, in which Hellenism or even the Roman world is associated with the early church and serves as the context for the Fourth Gospel's reception rather than the historical period that encompassed the years of Jesus' life and ministry (1962b, 100), does not account for factors such as the cultural exchange represented in the architecture and inscriptions of Palestine. Further, Robinson would be hard pressed to point to a particular date in first-century history where Palestinian Judaism ended and influences due to Hellenism or Romanization took off. Historically speaking, there is no such date, and, as Robinson's contemporary Ethelbert Stauffer quipped, by the time of the defeat of Cleopatra by Augustus, three decades before the birth of Jesus, "the Mediterranean was a Roman lake" (Stauffer 1955, 80).

This is not to say that Palestine's culture, as conceived by Robinson, was absent from Judea in the time of Jesus or in the era when the Fourth Gospel was written. Rather, the Holy Land stood at a crossroads where its culture was flavored by interactions with the wider Mediterranean world. The central shift in understanding from the time of Robinson to the present day is not that the Fourth Gospel is a product of a larger culture. Indeed, Robinson conceded that Hellenistic influences were present in the years when the Fourth Evangelist was writing his book. Rather, the post-Robinson understanding is that Jesus himself lived within the realities of the Hellenized Eastern portion of the Roman Empire and that Roman elements too are an essential ingredient for illuminating both the text and the life of Jesus.

The move toward understanding the cultural interplay that was extant in the time of the New Testament has been the subject of recent scholarly interest. George Riley, for instance, in his very accessible book *The River of God*, uses the analogy of a river into which flows tributaries of various national and cultural influences (2001, 9–10). He writes that "Christianity cannot in fact be derived from the Old Testament or Jewish tradition alone," and further comments, "If Judaism is the mother of Christianity, then the Greco-Roman world is the father, not merely the context" (Riley 2001, 15, 7). During the late 1990s, a few years prior to the publication of Riley's work, a number of biblical scholars began to examine ways that Roman traditions, legal conventions, and culture impacted the lives of residents of Judea. Tal Ilan, for example, follows classicists and ancient historians in situating the role of Jewish women during the Second Temple period within the context of both Judaism and Greco-Roman family constructs (1995, 7). She discovered that at times, despite legislated Jewish ideals, Jewish couples actually resorted to Greek customs in marital practices (Ilan 1995, 227). Further, she observes that Roman inheritance law appears to have colored how some Jewish women came into possession of property at the death of family members (Ilan 1995, 167–68). Another researcher, James S. Jeffers, also recognized the interplay of cultural influences that impacted the first-century residents of Jerusalem. He describes the land as "an amazing patchwork quilt of cultural and political influences" and asserts that an understanding of the Roman people is integral to an understanding of the world of the New Testament (Jeffers 1999, 14–16, quote 14).

A ROMAN LENS PROVIDES "ANOTHER LOOK" AT THE FOURTH GOSPEL

At approximately the same time that Jeffers and Ilan were beginning to explore the relationship of the Greco-Roman world in a way that took into consideration a number of biblical books, Richard J. Cassidy (1992) was blazing a new trail that specifically addressed the Johannine writings. He situated the Fourth Gospel squarely within the Roman Empire and employed Pliny's correspondence with Trajan as the touchstone for his thesis that FG reflects struggles with the cult of the emperor and Roman authorities. Unlike Robinson, who was concerned with the historical Jesus, Cassidy is primarily interested in the Roman influences that were present at the time the Fourth Evangelist was setting down his account of Jesus' ministry. Nevertheless, Cassidy's insights were significant in that for the first time the Fourth Gospel as a whole was being viewed, not from the perspective of Hellenism, Judaism, or Gnosticism, but rather from a Roman angle.

The collective effect of the scholarship of the 1990s, produced by scholars such as Jeffers, Ilan, Riley, and Cassidy, is that a new appreciation for the role of Rome during the New Testament period is becoming firmly established. That scholars are moving in the direction of examining the Fourth Gospel within a Greco-Roman context was even obvious at the Society of Biblical Literature 2003 Annual Meeting in Atlanta. During the open session of the Johannine Literature Section, three of the four presenters sought to come to grips with various Roman aspects of the Fourth Gospel. Evidence that interest in Roman influences on the New Testament period is a trend that has a firm foothold within the Society is indicated in a variety of quarters. For instance, during the 2004 Annual Meeting, scholars in the Social History of Formative Christianity and Judaism section were struggling with methodological issues related to the need to define terms such as "Hellenized" and "Romanized." Participants in that session also explored the extent to which questions relating to ethnicity must take into account regional variations in degrees of acculturation (Chancey 2004). Arriving at an accord regarding issues such as these may take some time, but efforts in this vein will provide the means for deeper research into the Roman situation of the first century.

How far this new interest in the Roman environment will progress in relation to Johannine studies in particular is dependent upon four factors. First, the understanding must be clear that the focus of an individual essay, chapter, or book on Hellenistic or Roman elements of the Fourth Gospel does not depreciate the text's Jewishness. Jerusalem at the time of Jesus was a cultural crossroad where Roman, Jewish, Hellenistic, and other Mediterranean influences converged. Dialogue will be entirely unproductive if scholars divide into camps that make claims that the Gospel of John is exclusively Jewish or Greek or Roman or some other single cultural aspect. The realities of ethnic diversity, acculturation, and assimilation, to which consciousness of globalization has sensitized today's researchers, make acknowledgment of the complexity of the first-century situation in the Mediterranean region a necessity. Just because a scholar specializes in authoring essays that focus on one particular cultural strand of the Fourth Gospel, however, does not mean that he or she automatically denies the presence of others. Craig Keener's outstanding contribution illustrates this point. Keener, like Robinson, concentrates on the Fourth Gospel's Jewish context. In his two-volume commentary, Keener writes, "Many scholars now acknowledge that the thought-world of John is thoroughly Jewish." He recognizes that this movement within Johannine studies may be largely attributed to Robinson, who "followed Lightfoot in regarding this Gospel as the most Hebraic book in the NT after Revelation" (Keener 2003, 171). Keener posits a Diaspora Jewish setting for the Fourth Gospel, although he demonstrates that Roman sources as well as rabbinic texts, the Dead Sea Scrolls, Greek resources, and a host of other ancient writings and inscriptions all may be drawn into service to elucidate aspects of the text. Hence, Horace's satire on wealth and influence, which contains mention of a client knocking at a door for legal advice at the break of dawn (Horace, *Sat.* 1.9–10) is cited as background for John 18:28, a verse that mentions that Jesus was led to the praetorium at an early hour (Keener 2003, 1098). Thus, while Keener clearly sets the Johannine Jesus within the framework of Judaism, he is also free to use Roman sources, among others, to flesh out the world in which Jesus lived and moved.

The approach of consulting Roman sources and customs may prove to be particularly worthwhile in regard to a number of Johannine passages and motifs that are obscure or for which no academic consensus has emerged. It is quite possible that at these junctures, despite the general Jewishness of the Fourth Gospel, what is reflected is a glimmer of the Roman world. In other words, taking another look at these passages through a Roman lens might help to shed new clarity on the issues. This hypothesis will be tested later in this essay when the question of Jesus' subordination to God the Father is explored in relation to Roman family structures and practices. In any case, the main point of the discussion thus far is this: a key factor in how scholars in the current century will examine the Fourth Gospel involves the assumption that this text is a part of a milieu that included a wide array of cultural influences, including Roman as well as Greek, Jewish, and even others such as Egyptian and Persian.

This brings to mind the second factor that is drawn into the examination of the Fourth Gospel against a Roman backdrop. In order for scholars to follow the lead of Keener and others who consult Roman sources, Latin must take its place with Hebrew, Greek, and Aramaic as a biblical language in the tool kit of the new generation of biblical scholars. Robinson himself had a solid grasp of Latin, although he did not explore Roman texts in relation to the Fourth Gospel to a great extent. To accept the premise that Latin is as valuable as Greek or Hebrew, one must caution against the untutored view of biblical languages that entry-level Bible students often harbor. Although the Fourth Gospel is written in Greek, to suppose that its content might represent "Hellenized Jewish" but not "Romanized Jewish" thought merely on the basis of its language of composition is shortsighted. In some sense, Greek was as much a language of the Roman Empire in the first century as was Latin. Educated Romans, such as the Emperor Hadrian, sometimes spoke Greek more readily than the official language of the capital city from which he ruled (Goldhill 2001, 12). That Greek was commonplace in Rome is clear from Horace. The poet, though admitting to once writing verse in Greek himself (Horace, *Sat.* 1.10.31), pens a satire in which he derides the poet Lucilius for what might be analogous to our modern "Spanglish," for in Horace's words Lucilius "*quod verbis Graeca Latinis miscuit*" ("mixes Latin and Greek words"; Horace, *Sat.* 1.10.20). Latin-Greek bilingualism was a recognized phenomenon in the Roman world, and although Roman elites would have been formally educated in the language of the Hellenes, "the Roman world was so thoroughly steeped in Hellenism that even someone who had not learnt Greek would still have been able to understand and deploy a whole host of Greek words and a number of commonly used phrases" (Biville 2002, 84). Indeed, even in Rome itself the public library known as the *Porticus Octavie* contained both Latin and Greek scrolls (Kilgour 1998, 45). In the eastern provinces in particular, Roman citizens and businessmen, many of whom spoke Greek, were among the first waves of settlers and may even have been descendants of Greek slaves who had been freed (MacMullen 2000, 1–3). Furthermore, the value of both languages was demonstrated in the day-to-day administration of the provinces. Legal edicts and public notices were, according to Ulpian, published in the languages most accessible to provincial populations (Ulpian in Justinian, *Dig.* 14.3.11.3). In the eastern empire, this frequently meant Greek and perhaps a local language. Clifford Ando, a classicist, remarks that Pilate's placard upon Jesus' cross—inscribed with the phrase "King of the Jews" in Hebrew, Greek, and Latin (John 19:19–20)—is a paradigmatic example of Roman publication of key information for consumption by provincial citizens (Ando 2000, 96).

Simply put, Roman society was a multilingual society. So, the fact that the Gospel of John was written in Greek does not imply that it is devoid of Roman cultural influences. To access the Roman culture that was part of the matrix in which this text evolved, the ability to consult both Latin and Greek sources is helpful. Mastery of Latin is not requisite for every New Testament scholar. It is, however, imperative for those who want to investigate the Roman context for the Fourth Gospel. Exploring Roman aspects does not supplant studies focused upon Jewish and Hellenistic influences on first-century Christianity. Rather, familiarity with Romanized culture and Latin is simply another lens for examining the text.

Just as those who take "another look" at the Fourth Gospel employ Latin and recognize the value of exploring Roman sources for insight to John's

Gospel, the third factor that marks this approach is a willingness to dialog with those outside the discipline of biblical studies. Classicists and ancient historians have produced a tremendous body of very accessible literature on Roman imperialism, economics, and culture that provides fodder for research. Similar to the way in which globalization represents the permeability of boundaries between countries, so too do advances in electronic database technology and information resources herald an era in which lines between academic disciplines are no longer inviolate. A glance at the notes pages of James Jeffers's book *The Greco-Roman World of the New Testament* illustrates this point beautifully. Jeffers cites information from well-known biblical scholars such as Wayne A. Meeks and F. F. Bruce, yet he also consults the works of secular historians such as Richard Saller and Suzanne Dixon (Jeffers 1999, 330–37). Accessibility to research and information beyond the traditional confines of the field of biblical studies, then, is the third element that marks this emerging trend in Johannine studies.

Dialogue with classicists and historians of the ancient world serves another function. Conversation helps biblical scholars to develop a historiographical perspective, a new philosophy of history, that is a necessary ingredient for examining the cultural interplay in the Fourth Gospel. In addition to contributing to the store of knowledge about the Roman imperial period, discourse with secular historians only emphasizes the large number of methodological approaches and subdisciplines that mark the field of history. For instance, there is economic history, legal history, political history, national history, and social history, to name just a few. Philosophical approaches are also numerous and include, but are not limited to, scientific objectivity, determinism, skepticism, and now, according to Joyce Appleby, Lynn Hunt, and Margaret Jacob, practical realism or qualified objectivity (1995, 247).

In his "new look" article Robinson was primarily concerned about issues of historiography and the question of whether the Fourth Evangelist might be regarded as a trustworthy historian for the ministry of Jesus. As he points out, "The decisive question is the status and origin of the Johannine tradition. Did this come out of the blue round about the year A.D. 100? Or is there a real continuity, not merely in the memory of one old man, but in the life of an ongoing community, with the earliest days of Christianity?" (Robinson 1962b, 106). Robinson believed that "in the Johannine tradition we may at points be as near to the Jesus of history as in the Synoptic Gospels" (1962b, 100). Robinson was writing at a time during which the philosophical underpinnings of the field of history were being shaken to their core. History in the early 1960s was still largely influenced by scientific method and the presupposition that, once facts were identified, they might be distilled into a knowable truth. Following in the wake of postmodernism, however, the premise concerning a historian's ability to know truth objectively was questioned. Essentially, every query that a historian raises is relative to his or her perspective. As a result of this new idea, there has emerged a stance known as "qualified objectivism." This is the position, as articulated by Hunt, Appleby, and Jacob, that "history" involves the interpretation of facts. Consequently, the same collection of data by multiple investigators may result in differing portraits of events based on each interpreter's motivations, values, and other factors. Nevertheless, there is still "the viability of stable bodies of knowledge that can be communicated, built upon, and subjected to testing" (Hunt, Appleby, and Jacob 1995, 254). Craig Blomberg appears to accept this understanding of history when he describes what is "historical" within the Johannine narrative as "factually accurate within the range of literary and historiographical freedom recognized in the ancient Mediterranean world" (Blomberg 2001, 66).

The author of the Fourth Gospel, whether one accedes that he is an eyewitness or not, is a historian. As such, he is an interpreter of the events he is recording. Similarly, the modern scholar who examines the Fourth Gospel within a particular historical context, such as Roman culture, Jewish culture, or even Hellenistic culture, is offering an interpretive framework for understanding the text. In essence, then, the historian who takes account of evidence and seeks to offer a cogent and accurate explanation of how those pieces of evidence may be combined is offering a portrait of the event or text that is "true." Qualified objectivism, in that case, serves as the last of the four factors that characterizes the research of those taking another look at the Forth Gospel's cultural context.

"Another Look" at the Fourth Gospel	
A New Assumption:	The Gospel of John is part of a milieu that includes Roman as well as Jewish, Hellenistic, and other Mediterranean influences.
New Tools:	Latin joins other biblical languages.
New Dialogue Partners:	Classicists and historians of the ancient world
A New Philosophy of History:	Qualified objectivism

Before jumping into the Johannine text to explore how this new scheme might be tested on the subordinationism that is intertwined with the father-son motif of the Fourth Gospel, a recap of some of the key elements that comprise the approach associated with what has been termed here "another look" at the Fourth Gospel is in order. The modern preoccupation with globalization was employed to highlight the idea that awareness of cultural exchange is sensitizing scholars to realities of assimilation and acculturation, not only in the modern world, but within the ancient world as well. While Robinson advanced the field of Johannine scholarship by stressing the insight that Jesus lived within the larger cultural context of southern Palestine, subsequent scholars have built upon the notion that Jesus and the Fourth Evangelist existed within a rich mix of ethnic and cultural influences. It was then pointed out that during the 1990s and early twenty-first century a growing body of literature emerged that marked an interest in considering the Roman background, in addition to the Jewish, Greek, and others, of biblical texts. These scholars evidence not only a willingness to consider Roman influences at the time of Christ and the era in which the Evangelist was writing but also enthusiasm for using Latin to access Roman sources, dialogue with classicists, and a view of history that may be described as "qualified objectivism."

Robinson was fond of applying his theoretical musings to actual Johannine passages as test exercises or experiments (1962b, 61, 67). In the spirit of historical inquiry, then, the remainder of this essay will turn to an investigation of the father-son motif of the Fourth Gospel and ask, as Robinson might put it, a "naïve" question: Might some of the elements that are described either as "subordinationism" or an "exalted Christology" in the Johannine father-son imagery be reflections of Roman family structures during the first century?

The Father-Son Motif and Subordinationist Christology

A brief description of what is understood by the descriptor "subordinationist Christology" will serve as a good starting point before turning to a sketch of some of the key elements of the Roman family. One of the significant issues in examining the Christology of the Fourth Gospel is the difficulty that arises from the Evangelist's portrait of the bond between Jesus and God. The primary vehicle employed to describe this relationship is the father-son motif that is introduced in John 1:14. In that verse, the "Word" is described as the "only born Son" of the Father. The family theme pervades virtually every chapter of the Gospel of John and continues through 20:31, where Jesus is declared to be the Christ, the "Son of God." The paradox concerning the father-son image emerges throughout the course of the narrative because, as Marinus de Jonge points out, "[N]ot for a single moment is the reader allowed to forget that the Word/the Son is identical with *and yet subordinate to* the Father (1988, 147; emphasis original). For instance, at John 14:10 Jesus says that he does not speak on his own authority, yet in 14:11 there is an equality implicit in the statement that Jesus is in the Father and the Father is in him. Thus, in the space of two short verses the Johannine Jesus describes himself both as dependent upon the Father and equal to him. Paul Anderson describes this phenomenon as a christological tension that includes both "subordinationist" and "elevated" elements (1996, 3). Subordinationist elements are associated with passages that center either on Jesus' dependence on the Father or some aspect of Jesus' human nature. By contrast, the elements of the Fourth Gospel that involve an "exalted Christology" include, among other aspects, Jesus' actions as works commissioned by the Father and passages that stress that Jesus and God are one. Anderson provides an excellent set of appendices that detail the various verses and literary motifs that constitute each of these apparently contradictory Christologies (1996, 266–267).

While there is no room to repeat Anderson's comprehensive treatment here, the framework that he develops to categorize approaches to the riddle of the tension inherent in the Christology of the Fourth Gospel bears summarizing. Essentially, there are three major approaches. In the first, the friction between the elevation of Jesus and his subordination is either harmonized or relegated to the realm of the text's mystical aspect. In a second track, the contradictions are explained in terms of multiple sources or redactors. The input of this collective during the Fourth Gospel's composition resulted in multiple strands of interpretive traditions that are evident in the contradictory elements of the text. In the last category proposed by Anderson, the tension within the author's Christology is inherent in the Evangelist himself and is a reflection of the Evangelist's dialogue with his own historical situation and/or that of his community (Anderson 1996, 2–15).

Interpretations that reflect the new sensitivity to globalism and acculturation and that draw on Hellenistic, Jewish, or Roman contexts to explicate the father-son motif would, consequently, best fit within Anderson's last category. The Roman context, however, has not yet been fully explored. Jewish backgrounds have been investigated, for example, by John Ashton and by Anderson himself. Ashton advances a hypothesis that Johannine Christology is marked by Jewish traditions. Further, references to Old Testamental and pseudepigraphical angelology assist in illuminating the tension occasioned by the equality or ditheism between Jesus and God. For Ashton, just as angels are messengers, so too is the Son frequently depicted as an emissary of God in the Fourth Gospel (1994, 71–89). Along similar lines, Anderson also posits a Jewish context for the father-son motif by linking the agency element inherent in God sending Jesus as his envoy with Jewish tradition. Rather than angelology, though, Anderson connects the messenger functions of the Son with the figure of the "prophet like Moses" in Deut 18:15–22 (1999, 36–40).

Branching away from solely Jewish contexts on the grounds that the "fourth evangelist's understanding is consistent both with Jewish and non-Jewish authors in the first-century Greco-Roman world," Adele Reinhartz situates the Johannine father-son motif within the framework of an Aristotelian (Hellenistic) concept of procreation known as *epigenesis* (1999, 84). In Aristotle's scheme, the seed of the father is the determining element not only for the sex of a child but also for its physical and personality traits. The stronger the seed, the more the child resembles his father than his mother (Reinhartz 1999, 90). Although Reinhartz does not use "subordination" or "equality" terminology per se, she does sketch a portrait of Jesus as unique among humans as "the only one in the human or indeed divine realms who has come forth from, or been generated directly by, the divine seed" (1999, 94). As a result, Jesus' uniformity with the father might be attributed to the idea that the very essence of the father dwells within Jesus, while his subordination is a natural outcome of the parent-child relationship.

On the Roman side of the first-century cultural polyhedron, Mary Rose D'Angelo also struggles with the "subordinationist" elements of Johannine Christology. She recognizes the Roman patriarchal ideology and subordinationistic element inherent in the term "father," but she does not explore Roman family structures to the extent that she explicates the "ditheistic" elements in FG, points where Jesus and God are portrayed as equals. D'Angelo merely cautions that the "social arrangements of ancient patriarchy are refracted through the complex imagery in John in ways that are diffuse and diverse" (1999, 61).

In essence, looking more closely at a Roman context for father-son relationships in the world of Jesus might shed light on why some Johannine passages appear to depict a low Christology while others portray Jesus as God's peer. In actuality, Roman family structures included numerous subtle conventions in which sons were both equal and yet subordinate to their fathers. Of particular interest, the concept of *patria potestas,* or a father's authority, the *peculium,* the role of mothers, and even Roman inheritance law, may be used to illustrate the possibility that some aspects of the subordinationist/exalted Christology conundrum may simply be points at which Roman culture has impacted first-century views of the father-son relationship. Three issues in particular will be discussed in regard to Jesus' perplexing relationship with the divine: Jesus' remarks in John 17 concerning his and God's co-ownership of property; the inconsistency of Jesus' ready acknowledgment of his mother despite his reticence to mention his human father; and, finally, the matter of "christological exclusivism," in which recognition of Jesus is required as the sole means for achieving eternal life.

JOHN 17 AND OWNERSHIP ISSUES

In the first part of this essay, the assertion was made that, just as globalism was sensitizing scholars to the blurring of cultures, so too was technology enabling easier access to works written on the classics and history. An examination of the Roman context for the question of family property and ownership in John 17 must rely on sketches of the Roman family provided by scholars in these other disciplines. The late 1980s and early 1990s was an era in which classicists were interested in social history, particularly that of the family (e.g., Bradley 1991; Dixon 1992; Rawson 1986). Their description of the Roman kinship unit reveals an institution that included some conventions quite different from those of today's American family. For instance, rather than the primary family unit of husband-wife-children being determined by genetics, in the Roman view the family was a legal construct that involved relationships of power and dependency that did not require consanguinity. The key concept was that of *patria potestas*, usually the authority of the oldest male progenitor, who was known as the *paterfamilias*. The *paterfamilias* was *sui iuris*, or independent of any older male's authority. All the children of the *paterfamilias*, whether naturally conceived within a legal marriage or adopted, and his children's children were under his power until his death, unless he had emancipated them (Gaius, *Inst.* 1.127). He also had authority over all property and slaves belonging to the family, whether such property was his own or that of his dependent adult children.

This brief portrait of the Roman family and the father's control of property within the family unit might provide a key for comprehending John 17:9–10. In this pericope Jesus prays for those who had followed him, describing his disciples with the enigmatic comment that they have been given to Jesus by God yet still to some degree belong to the Father. This theme begins with a comment in 17:6 to the effect that Jesus' followers were God's and have been assigned to Jesus. The implication here is that Jesus has a power over these followers that is equal to that of God. However, in verses 9 and 10 Jesus affirms that he was praying for "those whom you have given to me, for they are yours. All of mine are yours and yours are mine." If everything that Jesus possesses is the father's, then to some extent he might be conceived to be subordinate to the father. As has already been mentioned in the discussion concerning the work of Anderson, Jesus' relationship with the Father is sometimes described in terms of an "agency" in which Jesus serves as God's emissary. But the concept of a sort of quasi-joint ownership like that mentioned in this passage does not fit neatly into the motif of prophetic agency established in Deut 18:15–22 nor into the angelology of Ashton. Perhaps for this reason, neither Anderson (1999) nor Ashton (1994) make mention of John 17:9–10.

In any event, John 17:9–10 is explicable in terms of the conventions for handling property/possessions within the Roman family unit. A household contained both things, *rei*, and individuals, *personae*, all of which were subject to the authority of the *paterfamilias*. Since the *paterfamilias* had lifelong power even over adult sons and all of the items and children that those sons possessed, the result was that a fully grown son might have legal possession of nothing (Gaius, *Inst.* 2.86–87). In the words of J. A. Crook, this was "the most astonishing and anomalous aspect of *patria potestas* ... [that] adult, married *filii familias*, who had held the highest offices in the state, who clearly had their separate domicile and conjugal family, could yet own not a penny and could acquire only for [the] *pater*" (1967, 119). This custom for property ownership was a thoroughly Roman practice and one that the Greeks did not observe (Veyne 1987, 27). Rather than adult sons living under the *patria potestas* of their fathers until their fathers' deaths, Greek males were only under parental authority until the age of eighteen or when their names were entered into the public register (Eyben 1991, 115). Yet the Roman structure was not as confining as the Greeks might have imagined. The Romans devised a unique legal loophole to provide adult sons with a measure of autonomy over property and financial affairs: the *peculium*. The *peculium*, rather than a simple allowance, was a substantial amount of property, slaves, and/or funds that were placed under the son's jurisdiction by the *paterfamilias*. While still technically remaining within the auspices of the *paterfamilias* as part of his estate, the *peculium* was essentially "owned" and managed independently by the son. Given this dynamic, Jesus' statements in John 17 accord well with the understanding that God functions as Jesus' *paterfamilias* and that Jesus' followers were essentially a *peculium* that had been entrusted to Jesus' direction and oversight by his Father. Consequently, the statement that Jesus' followers might be simultaneously possessions of both Jesus and the Father is simply another aspect of Jesus' divine sonship that would make perfect sense from a Roman point of view. Whether the passage represents a subordinationist Christology or an exalted Christology is not as important as the fact that Jesus' relationship to his father and his understanding of his followers as "possessions" clearly follows the pattern of property ownership within Roman families. With regard to his concern for his followers, which are also God's own, Jesus is simply filling the role of God's Son.

THE MOTHER OF JESUS

Just as recourse to Roman family practices illuminates the riddle of John 17:9–10, an understanding of the role of women within the Roman family helps to shed light on Jesus' relationship with his mother (John 2:1–5; 19:25–27), a very human aspect of Jesus that might be described as part of the Johannine subordinationist Christology.

Jesus' interactions with his mother are, in a sense, a foil for the Johannine father-son imagery. The emphasis on God as Jesus' father resonates with a high Christology, but at first glance Jesus' interactions with his mother tend to emphasize his human aspect and, as such, might be construed as part of the subordinationist Christology. Nevertheless, from a Roman cultural context, Jesus' recognition of his mother would not factor into a low Christology at all, because in Roman eyes the maternal relationship had no impact on an individual's lineage. In particular, it was a surprising feature of the Roman family that, during the imperial period, a wife, married *sine manu*, did not fall under the authority of her husband's or her husband's *paterfamilias*. Instead, she remained under the authority of the *paterfamilias* of her birth family (Saller 1994, 76). This created the peculiar situation of a mother not necessarily belonging to the same family as her children, even through she resided in the same domicile. Against the backdrop of a Roman understanding of mothers, one may recognize that Jesus might interact with his human mother without depreciating his relationship with God the Father. In other words, the bond between Jesus and his mother would not adversely affect his divinity, the source of which would be God the Father.

It is perhaps due to considerations such as these that the narrator of FG does not endorse any association of Jesus with Joseph, whom some Johannine characters regard as Jesus' human progenitor. From the perspective of Roman culture, this is an understandable omission, given the Fourth Evangelist's desire to emphasize Jesus' divine sonship. Jesus' human parentage, though, was obviously known to his Jewish opponents, who countered his claims of a heavenly origin by noting that Jesus was the son of Joseph (John 6:38–42; see 1:45). Their query, "Is this not Jesus, the son of Joseph, whose father and mother we know?" echoes Horace's words that whenever a man is elected to the senate or comes to public notice, he hears the question *"Quis homo hic est? Quo patre natus?"* ("Which man is this? Of which father is he born?" [*Sat.* 1.6.28–29]). The key difference between the Roman formulation and the Jewish version of the question at John 6:42 is the role of the mother. For "the Jews" who point out Jesus' parentage at 6:42, maternal lineage as well as paternal is apparently key to a person's identity. Information about maternal kinship was important in Jewish-Palestinian culture (Destro and Pesce 1995, 270–71). By contrast, for Horace and other Romans at the time of Jesus, only a man's paternity was of import. Horace stresses this point later in his satire by remarking that a freeborn person should be relieved not to descend from the senatorial rank and its burdens of ambition: *"His me consolor victurum suavius ac si quaestor avus pater atque meus patruusque fuissent"* ("It seems to me that I comport myself more happily because my grandfather had been a quaestor and my father and my uncle, too" [Horace, *Sat.* 1.6.130–

131]). According to Horace, it is one's relationship with the paternal line that determined Roman identity. The Roman jurists affirmed this concept. For instance, from a legal standpoint, women could not possess *patria potestas*. If a freeborn woman had a male child outside of marriage, that infant was by definition a *paterfamilias*, for while he had no legal father, likewise he did not fall under the legal authority of the mother (Gaius, *Inst.* 1.64). Furthermore, the Roman conventions of adoption and emancipation provided the means for men to change their *paterfamilias*, the person to whom they owed filial duty. This new *paterfamilias* exercised *patria potestas*, or authority, over their lives. If Jesus was under the *patria potestas* of God, then his relationship to his mother really did not depreciate or contradict the divinity implicit in his bond with God the father or the activities that he undertook as part of his duty to his father (5:36).

Just as the ownership issue of John 17 may not involve a tension between high and low Christology, but rather function as an outgrowth of the metaphor of Jesus as God's divine Son, so too does a Roman perspective mitigate the "low christological" elements inherent in the "human" side of Jesus' relationship with his mother. In a Roman context, the father alone was necessary for understanding relationships of kinship, authority, and loyalty. Suzanne Dixon summarizes the insignificant role of mothers in kin relationships thus: "[A] woman was the beginning and end of her own *familia,* apparently meaning that she could not pass on to her children her family name or her sacral and inheritance rights as a man could his" (1992, 2). In short, true fatherhood in the Fourth Gospel exists only when the children or descendants recognize and live within the *patria potestas* of their *paterfamilias*. Jesus' penultimate authority is God; therefore, Jesus has no interaction with his earthly father in the Fourth Gospel. Mary, by contrast, appears quite frequently. She is present at the wedding in Cana and at the foot of the cross, in attendance for the beginning of Jesus' earthly ministry and its final seconds. Since, however, women were not able to hold *patria potestas*, her role in Jesus' life was no bar to Jesus' filial relationship with God. As Robert Nisbet comments in relation to Roman family structures, "The organization of Roman society would have been disrupted if men had claimed relationship to their mother's blood relatives. For then a person would have fallen under more than one *patria potestas*" (1964, 259–60). Jesus' primary relationship, despite the mention of his mother in the text, is with his heavenly Father.

THE WAY TO THE FATHER AND INHERITANCE LAW

When taking "another look" at the Gospel of John, Roman family structures and the *peculium* have been employed as a point of reference for interpreting 17:9–10. After that, a brief examination of the legal status of women in the family was used as a backdrop to explicate why the Fourth Evangelist might be reticent to explore Jesus' relationship with Joseph but does not demur from including scenes in the narrative in which Jesus' mother figures prominently. An additional aspect of the Fourth Gospel that resonates with a Roman context is the Johannine theme that Alan Culpepper terms "christological exclusivism," the Fourth Evangelist's claim that salvation is accessible only through the expedient of faith in Jesus Christ (2002, 95, 97). An example of "christological exclusivism" is reflected in John 14:6, where Jesus declares, "I am the way, and the truth, and the life. No one comes to the Father except through me." Perhaps not surprisingly, Anderson includes this verse in his list of passages that indicate an exalted Christology (1996, 266).

This type of exclusivism may be interpreted against the framework of Roman inheritance law. Estate planning in Rome was built on the premise that a father's duty was to pass a patrimony to his son intact (White 2003, 458). Essentially, a father was to serve as a "trustee" for future generations (Justinian, *Dig.* 28.2.11). Thus, even to some extent during a father's lifetime, a father and son were "considered to be joint owners of the estate" (Gaius, *Inst.* 2.156). Stemming from this concept of practical, if not legal, co-ownership, sons, whether adopted or blood kin, were considered to be "necessary heirs." Thus, if a father died intestate (without a will), the son would inherit his father's possessions. Even if the father made out a legal estate-planning document that neglected to mention the son, the male offspring who had been under his *potestas* would acquire the father's property automatically (Gaius, *Inst.* 2.127). In particular, there were two requirements for necessary heirs: one had to be a "son," either born or adopted of the father; and one also had to be under the father's authority. Jesus, as described in the Fourth Gospel, meets both criteria for serving as a "necessary heir" of God. First, Jesus' relationship to God is made clear early in the story, as he is designated the *monogenēs*, the only born Son of the Father (John 1:18; 3:16). Second, Jesus readily demonstrates the second requirement, that of serving under the *potestas* or authority of his heavenly Father. For instance, at 5:30 Jesus comments, "I can do nothing on my own.... I seek to do not my own will but the will of him who sent me."

In a Roman scheme, then, verses such as John 5:30 and 1:18 function in relation to the metaphor of Jesus' relationship to God. Theologically speaking, however, they have been on opposite sides of the subordinationist/high Christology issue. That is, John 5:30 is generally associated with a subordinated Christology, while 1:18 is often related to a high Christology. But setting questions of Christology aside for the moment, not only is Jesus portrayed in the Fourth Gospel in ways that match that of "necessary heirs" in the Roman world, but also Jesus' uniqueness as the *monogenēs*, the sole "necessary heir," is stressed. Marianne Meye Thompson has picked up on the proprietary aspect of Jesus' relationship to the Father. She observes that the Johannine Jesus, unlike the presentation in the Synoptics, never refers to God as "our Father" in a way that includes the disciples (Thompson 1999, 19–20). Claiming paternity of the deity is a prerogative exclusively ascribed to Jesus in FG. Only once, and then after the resurrection, does Jesus acknowledge a relationship between God and one of his followers. This occurs when he remarks that God is Mary Magdalene's Father as well as his own (John 20:17), a statement that does not depreciate his own status as the "necessary heir." Although females might serve as beneficiaries of wills in the Roman world, they could not function as "necessary heirs"—more precisely, that status was reserved for sons. Thus, while Jesus himself is the son (*huios*) of God (John 20:31), and while it is only through belief in the name of Jesus that others might become "little ones" (*tekna*) of God (John 1:12), a kin relationship with the divine is uniquely reserved for Jesus, God's "only-begotten."

Within the structures of Roman inheritance law, the status of being a necessary heir, and, indeed, the sole necessary heir, afforded a son a special position in relation to other beneficiaries of an estate. This unique role resonates with the "christological exclusivism" of the Fourth Gospel. For instance, the Evangelist's assertion at John 3:16, "God so loved the world that he gave his only Son, that whoever believes in him will not perish but have eternal life," may reflect a situation similar to that in which there are multiple beneficiaries of a will in addition to the necessary heir. Distant kin, friends, clients, and even slaves might receive legacies from an estate. The son, or necessary heir, however, served as the executor or the administrator of the property. He was the individual whom all of the other beneficiaries were required to acknowledge and from whom they needed consent as a prerequisite for gaining control of their own portions of the estate (Gaius, *Inst.* 2.200; 2.213–214). Failure to recognize the heir resulted in the legatee going away empty-handed (Justinian, *Dig.* 43.3.1.12; 43.3.1.2). Belief in Jesus as the son of God as the means to gaining eternal life as one's portion from God (17:2–3), or christological exclusivism, accordingly correlates well with Roman conventions for the role of a necessary heir and such an heir's interactions with his father's other beneficiaries.

The benefits that accrue to believers through the living God in the Fourth Gospel are staggering. What is at stake is no less than eternal life (John 17:2–3). This is a life that is available to all believers through Jesus, God's Son. After all, he is the Savior of the world (John 4:42). When the christological exclusivism of the Fourth Gospel is examined against the context of Roman inheritance law, issues concerning whether 1:18 and 5:30 represent high or subordinationist Christology subsequently dissipate. An alternate interpretation is that, rather than offering contradictory portraits of Christology, either low or high, some of the verses that are associated with the christological paradox of the Fourth Gospel are really outgrowths of a Roman concept of the family motif that is used extensively in the narrative. Just as the ownership issues of the John 17 and the ready acknowledgment of Mary's role in the life of Jesus do not depreciate the key theological issue that Jesus is God's Son, verses that stress that belief in Jesus is the key to salvation make the same point.

Conclusion

When Robinson penned his "new look" paper in 1957, he was aware that, while the Gospel of John was Jewish, the Fourth Evangelist was also part of a larger framework, that of the Hellenistic world. In recent decades, a flurry of scholarly activity, prompted by new experiences with globalization, is giving impetus to studies that recognize not only Greek but also other cultural strands within the New Testament. For the sake of brevity, the focus in this chapter was on Roman contexts for the Fourth Gospel. Indeed, studies on Roman aspects of the first-century world are needed to complement the work being done by those who are unearthing Jewish and Greek backgrounds for the text. Those undertaking this task not only embrace the presupposition that the Mediterranean region of which Israel was a part was a melting pot that included many cultural influences, Roman as well as others, but they are also willing to interact with classicists and historians in fleshing out historical contexts for the first century. In service of this agenda, familiarity with Latin as a tool for biblical studies and acceptance of a new philosophy of history, described here as "qualified objectivism," all play a role. As an example of the type of information that might prove of interest from this interpretive perspective, the hypothesis was tendered that some elements of the father-son motif of the Fourth Gospel, and the closely related issue of the apparent inconsistency of Jesus making himself "equal with God" at some points in the Fourth Gospel while at the same time "subordinating" himself to his father's will, are explicable in terms of Roman understandings of the family. In particular, a Roman context was proposed for clarifying aspects of Jesus' co-ownership of what belongs to the Father (John 17:9–10), the Fourth Evangelist's willingness to portray Jesus' relationship with his mother but not a human father, and the "christological exclusivism" that requires believers to acknowledge Jesus' relationship to the Father in order to receive eternal life. The Gospel of John is the product of an era in which Jewish, Greek, and Roman influences converged. There is now room for new interpretations of the mosaic.

Part 2
The New Current of Readers and Readings

JOHN 2:12–25:
A NARRATIVE READING

Armand Barus

Differing with E. P. Sanders (1985), who argues that the temple incident is a symbolic prophecy of the destruction of the temple, and Richard Bauckham (1988), who argues that it is a symbolic "attack on the financial arrangements for the sacrificial system," this essay will propose that the central message of the Johannine temple incident is the universality of the body of Christ as God's new temple in which Jews and Gentiles are united. A narrative-critical reading will be employed to produce a fresh interpretation of the temple incident. This means that the various narrative features of John 2:12–25 will be explored in order to reveal the central message of the text.

John's Narrative of the Temple Incident

Narrative-critical readings explore a theme by analyzing the content of a story (characters/characterization, plot) in its textual and narrative contexts (intratextual links, setting), considering how the story is told (narrator and point of view, literary devices) by analyzing it on two levels (story and discourse) in its readers' context. The characters, which are the focus of narrative analysis, are the carriers of the narrative themes. The characters who populate the narrative world have been chosen by the implied author to convey messages to the implied reader. What is more, the selection of characters in the narrative world could be seen as a reflection of the implied author's theological conception in dealing with the implied reader's pastoral needs, since the characters are constructs of the implied author. The following analysis will consider seven intertwined dimensions of the Fourth Gospel's presentation of the temple incident: intratextual links; literary design; setting; narrator and point of view; characters and characterization; plot; literary devices. A consideration of these elements will offer clues to the major themes of the narrative.

Intratextual Links

John 2:12-25 forms a cohesive, close-knit unit. The evidence to support this observation may be outlined as follows. (1) John 2:23-25 serves as a summary statement. The Fourth Gospel (FG) explicitly expresses its purpose in 20:31: "But these are written so that you may come to believe that Jesus is the Messiah, the Son of God, and that through believing you may have life in his name" (unless noted, all quotes are from the NRSV). The stated purpose serves as the conclusion of the book and provides a clue for determining the contours of the narrative. The narrator summarizes the narrative, as it were, with the responses of the characters to the protagonist. Similarly, the summary at 2:23-25 indicates the ending of a smaller narrative unit. The references to "faith" in 2:11 and 2:23-25, which are voiced by the narrator, serve as a boundary, making 2:12-25 a coherent narrative unit. The strategic placement of the summary of the belief motif divides the Fourth Gospel into distinct units. Thus, the narrator signals the end of the entire narrative by references to faith, and a reference to faith appears in the concluding section of each smaller narrative unit.

(2) The phrase translated "after this" (John 2:12), which occurs also in 11:7, 11 and 19:28, should be distinguished from "after these," which occurs at 3:22; 5:1, 14; 6:1; 7:1; 13:7; 19:38; and 21:1. The former ("after this") indicates both chronological and narrative sequence, whereas the latter ("after these") denotes only narrative sequence. Thus the phrase "after this" at 2:12 not only indicates a new scene but also joins this unit with the preceding one.

(3) The setting changes from Cana to Capernaum. Changed setting is accompanied by changing narrative mood, from a joyous occasion at the wedding at Cana to the conflict environment that is overshadowed by the protagonist's death. The spatial setting of Capernaum and the temporal setting of the Passover festival indicate a new narrative section.

(4) The plot, as discussed below, underscores the coherence of the unit.

The passage forms a cohesive unit but is closely linked to the preceding narrative by common motifs (faith, witness, *sēmeia*) and characters (Jesus, the disciples, Jesus' family, and the religious leaders). Although the chronological link between John 2:23-25 and 3:1 is not clear, the faith motif, the protagonist (Jesus), and the disciples tie both narrative units together. Thus, the belief motif coupled with the christological motif weave these three narrative units (1:19-2:11; 2:12-25; 3:1-4:54) together. Within the larger context of FG, this complex of units functions as a key to open a larger room where the ontological and functional nature of the protagonist are displayed in order to elicit faith in Jesus and to deepen and enrich the believers' relationship with him. In and through words and deeds, the protagonist fulfills his mission to exegete the nature of himself and the Father (1:18) so that people might believe in him. In 1:19–2:11, the protagonist starts his witnessing with a speech, but in 2:12–25 he begins with an action followed by a speech. Both witnessing activities (deeds and words) reveal the protagonist's nature.

Literary Design

The protagonist's witnessing activities, through both deeds and words, receive two opposing responses from various group characters embedded in the narrative world of John 2:12–25. These responses, which differ from those in 1:35–51, are communal in nature. The communal dimension of the faith motif condensed in 1:12 is dramatized by the appearance of the various group characters embedded in the narrative world. The design of the narrative in relating the various responses that Jesus receives is as follows:

(1) John 2:12: the response of the disciples and Jesus' family
(2) John 2:13–22: the response of the religious leaders at the temple
(3) John 2:23–25: the response of the people

Moving from the family circle, the narrator brings the protagonist into the center of Jewish civilization. The temple incident sets the protagonist's public ministry in a festive environment in the center of the social, political, and religious life of the Jews. The narrator artfully designs the beginning and end of the protagonist's public witnessing in the context of the Passover (John 2:13; 12:1) and the holy city of Jerusalem, creating an *inclusio* in the larger narrative. The protagonist's public witnessing activities in the temple courts produce three types of response: a silent response from his family, the sellers, and the money changers; a rejecting response from the religious leaders; and a believing response from the disciples and the crowds. The narrator basically provides both unrecorded responses and recorded responses. In the first scene (2:12), the narrator says nothing of what had happened in Capernaum or during the journey to Jerusalem, a trip that took approximately three days. In the second scene (2:13–22), two opposing responses to the protagonist's deeds and words are narrated. The narrator does not record the response from the sellers and the money changers. In the third scene (2:23–25), the festival crowd responds positively. These group responses highlight the communal aspect of the narrative texture, with its focus on 2:13–22.

Setting

The first scene in this episode (John 2:12) is located in Capernaum in a house. In Capernaum the protagonist, his family, and his disciples stay for a few days.

No definite days are given by the narrator because he intends to focus on the protagonist's public witnessing activities in Jerusalem.

The second scene is set in Jerusalem. The narrator brings the protagonist immediately to Jerusalem without mentioning the cities or villages passed through. These places are not important, since the focus of the setting is the Passover in Jerusalem. The protagonist's public ministry is located temporally just before the Passover festival and spatially in the temple, which is considered the center of the world (Ezek 5:5; 38:12; see Wright 1996, 406–12). A detailed spatial setting is given by mentioning different parts of the temple. The protagonist is in the court of the Gentiles (*hieros*) and proclaims the *hieros* as the *oikos tou patros* ("house of the Father"; John 2:16). For Jesus, there is no distinction between *hieros* and *naos*, a term that normally refers to the inner court of the temple. This clearly indicates that no distinction is made between Jews and Gentiles in Jesus' witnessing activities. In a similar tone, the narrator uses the terms *hieros*, *oikos* ("house"), and *naos* interchangeably. The religious leaders, by contrast, do not perceive the court of the Gentiles (*hieros*) as part of the temple and instead use *naos* to refer to the sanctuary, the inner court of the temple. They do not hesitate to transform the court of the Gentiles into a market for trading, a situation that makes it more difficult for the Gentiles to pray to God.

The narrator specifically modifies the term "Passover" with the attributive phrase "of the Jews" to indicate an implied Gentile readership, who otherwise might not understand Jewish customs and traditions. The narrator of FG mentions a total of three Passovers covering a period of at least two years (John 2:13; 6:4; 11:55), which together denote the macro-temporal setting of the protagonist in the narrative world. The framework of these three Passovers also creates a sense of dynamic and linear progress by indicating the beginning, middle, and end of the protagonist's public witnessing activities.

The third scene (John 2:23–25) takes place in Jerusalem during the Passover festival. The term "Passover festival" seems to refer here both to the Passover (14–15 Nissan) and to the seven-day Feast of Unleavened Bread that followed (15–21 Nissan). The narrator narrates this event, which is much longer than the time encompassed by the second scene, in a single sentence. The Passover festival is one of the major religious festivals for the Jews (Deut 16:16). It is understandable, therefore, that it might have been attended by Jews from Palestine (Judeans and Galileans) and the Diaspora and by Gentiles who were attracted to Judaism. The provision for exchanging currency proves that the people gathered in Jerusalem came from different parts of the world. In 12:20 the narrator explicitly reports that Greeks, who had become proselytes, attended the Passover festival. The international character of the pilgrims is also reported by Luke (Acts 8:27) and Josephus (*War* 6.427).

Although one cannot establish the exact number (the estimate of attendance given by Josephus is not accepted by modern scholars), at least one can affirm that a large number of people participated in the Passover festival in Jerusalem. One may reasonably state that the Passover festival was an international festival. The inclusiveness of the protagonist's witnessing activities is thus highlighted by the international nature of the festival pilgrims.

The setting of the Johannine temple incident emphasizes the communal, nondiscriminatory, and international nature of the protagonist's witnessing activities. While emphasis is placed more on the communal dimension and less on the nondiscriminatory and international dimensions, the blending of these three terms stresses the theme of the universal. The setting helps to intensify the universal texture of the narrative.

Narrator and Point of View

By way of comparison, the role of the narrator is more evident in the temple incident than in the preceding narrative unit (John 1:19–51). The story is told predominantly in the third person, rather than in direct speech. As a witness-observer, the narrator is absent from the narrative action (heterodiegetic narrator). The presence of dialogical discourse is minimal in the narrative world (2:16, 18, 19, 20). The narrator even considers the dialogue between characters unimportant, since the focus of the narration is on the protagonist. The characters embedded in the narrative world interact directly with the protagonist. The reliability of the narrator is portrayed when he acts as the authoritative interpreter of Jesus by explaining his enigmatic words (2:19, 21). The narrator-as-observer interrupts the narration at a critical moment by giving an inside view of the main character. This is possible because the narrator's position in the narrative world is between the implied author and the characters, enabling him to move dynamically to either pole.

The narrator presents an anisochronous narrative in which the story duration and text duration are varied. Events in Capernaum and during the journey to Jerusalem, which take place over a few days, are compressed into a very short textual space, a technique called "ellipsis." The narrator omits the events during the journey to Jerusalem and brings the protagonist right to the heart of Jewish civilization; there, an event that occurs in a relatively short story time—the expelling of the merchants and the money changers and the response of the religious leaders—receives more textual space. In literary terms, this phenomenon is called "deceleration." By contrast, the third scene (2:23–25), which happens over a relatively long period of time, is given a very short textual space. This shift in narrative speed is called "acceleration." Taken together, these two literary phenomena indicate importance and centrality:

an event that is more important and central is given more textual space. This indicates that the focus of the narration is on the second scene (2:13–22).

The second scene's (John 2:13–22) role as the focus of the narration is intensified by the repetition of references to an event that happens only once. The expelling of the merchants and the money changers (2:16) reappears in 2:17, and 2:22 recalls the dialogue between the protagonist and the Jewish leaders. The former repetition is called "analepsis," while the latter is referred to as "prolepsis." Analepsis repetition returns to a past event, hence revealing an omniscient narrator by taking the implied readers into the disciples' inner thoughts. Prolepsis repetition takes the implied readers into a future event, providing them with information about what is yet to happen in the narrative world that could not otherwise be available. Prolepsis creates a sense of anticipation and expectation in the reading process: suspense builds as the narrator informs the reader of the protagonist's impending death. Of particular importance here is the passive verb *emnēsthēsan* ("they remembered") in 2:17 and 22. Through this verb the omniscient narrator narrates retrospectively, enhanced by the writing formula in 2:17, from a postresurrection point of view. After the protagonist's resurrection the disciples will understand his witnessing activities in deed (expelling the merchants and the money changers) and word (dialogue with the religious leaders). The verb *emnēsthēsan* also demonstrates the fusion of two horizons: events from before and after the resurrection are merged into a single cohesive narration.

Characters and Characterization

Notably, all communications in the temple incident center on the protagonist. Differing from the preceding narrative unit (John 1:19–2:11), there is no interaction between one character and another. This clearly points to the centrality of the protagonist within the narrative world.

If in the preceding narrative the characters predominantly are individual (John, Andrew, an unnamed disciple, Peter, Philip, Nathanael, Jesus' mother), the characters in John 2:12–25 are communal, groups of people. There are five group characters present in this narrative who interact with the protagonist: Jesus' family; the disciples; the sellers and moneychangers; the religious leaders; and the people at the festival. Each of these group characters will be analyzed in the order of their appearance in the scene.

Jesus, the protagonist, is first mentioned in 2:12. Differing from the preceding narrative, Jesus begins his witnessing activities with action rather than speech. In the narrative, these two forms of witnessing communication (word and deed) are kept in balance. Word without work sends a weak and incomplete message, whereas deed without word creates ambiguity. Jesus' action in the court of the Gentiles cannot be regarded as inciting a riot, since he does not attract the attention of the Roman guards, nor does he cause any permanent loss of investment to the merchants or the money changers. Jesus simply expels, using a whip, the cattle, sheep, and doves that are used in the sacrificial worship from the court of the Gentiles and scatters the coins. Both animals and coins can be easily gathered again.

Jesus' witnessing activities in the court of the Gentiles, expelling the merchants and the money changers followed by dialogue with the religious leaders, are not understood by the disciples. Only after Jesus' resurrection from the dead do the disciples understand the meaning and purpose of Jesus' deed and words.

Jesus' seemingly outrageous deed in the temple is understood as an expression of zeal. Before the resurrection, the small number of disciples who accompany Jesus to Jerusalem view his deed as total devotion to the temple or a passionate commitment to God, not as an expression of opposition to animal sacrifice or the temple. Jesus' zeal forces him courageously to restore the court of the Gentiles from a place of trade to a place of prayer by driving the sellers out and hints at the universality of his witnessing activities. Jesus' action is not an attack on the sacrificial system. What Jesus strongly objects to is the use of the court of the Gentiles as a place for trading. This trading must be done elsewhere, not in the court of the Gentiles. The protagonist is, as the setting shows, in the court of the Gentiles (*hieros*). Jesus then calls the court of the Gentiles *ton oikon tou patros mou* ("the house of my Father"; 2:16). The house of the Father includes both the Gentiles and the Jews. Jesus comes not only for the Jews but also the Gentiles. His zeal costs him his life. Without Jesus' death, the unification of Jews and Gentiles into one community could not take place. Jesus' death is expressed proleptically by the quotation from Ps 68:10 (LXX), making it the announcement of Jesus' death. The disciples interpret this text christologically after Jesus' resurrection, which causes a change from the aorist *katephagen* ("consumed") to the future *kataphagetai* ("will consume"). This change, which creates a sense of prophecy in the narrative world, is necessary, since the narrator composes this significant event from a postresurrection point of view. The future tense in the narrative world points to Jesus' death. Jesus will die in order to build God's new temple where Jews and Gentiles perfectly meet and dwell.

Jesus' word to the religious leaders in the temple is understood by the disciples only after the resurrection. Only at that time will the disciples come to a new understanding of Jesus' witnessing activities in and through word, that the temple of God is the body of Christ (2:21). The body of Christ is the real temple where God perfectly dwells (1:14) and where God and human beings meet (1:51). The transformation from building to person demands the "consumption" of the protagonist's own body. Why did Jesus' resurrection transform the disciples' understanding of him? The explanation of Jesus' dramatic deed through the dialogue with the Jews depicts the ontological nature of the protagonist. The active verb *egerō* in 2:19 ("I will raise it up") indicates that the protagonist has the power of resurrection and that accordingly he himself is the source of life. Death cannot hold the giver of life. Jesus, the source of life, raises himself from the dead. His resurrection power does not depend on outside power. The implied reader who has read the Prologue is now enabled to understand more clearly the narrator's statement in 1:4, "In him was life." Jesus is God from whom life flows and by whom it is sustained. Moreover, the narrator speaks also of the resurrection of Jesus as the work of God by using the passive verb *ēgerthē* ("he was raised") in 2:22. Jesus not only raises himself but also is raised by God from the dead. Thus the resurrection of Jesus is the manifestation of the power of both Jesus and God.

The resurrection event opens the spiritual eyes of the disciples to see the Old Testament with new eyes and to understand the significance of Jesus' witnessing activities through deeds and words. Why? The resurrection reveals the protagonist's divinity. The resurrection intimates Jesus' witnessing activities as the image of the invisible God.

With this understanding in mind, the implied reader would not be surprised by the narrator's statements that many people in Jerusalem believe in Jesus (2:23) and that "Jesus knows what is in human beings" (2:25). Jesus is God, hence he is the object of faith; Jesus is God, hence he has complete knowledge of human beings' hearts. Jesus is characterized as the omniscient figure who knows comprehensively and profoundly what is inside the human heart. In Jewish literature, knowledge of the human heart is exclusive to God (*Mek.* Exod 15:32; *Gen. Rab.* 65; *Midr. Qoh.* 11:5; 1QS 4:25; 1QH 7:14–18; Gen 6:5; 1 Chr 28:9; Pss 7:10; 26:2; 44:21; Jer 11:20; 12:3; 17:10). Jesus' possession of divine knowledge demonstrates that he is not simply human but also divine. The implied reader who walks in the Jewish tradition and is exposed to the protagonist's divine knowledge is coerced to embrace Jesus' divinity wholeheartedly.

Jesus' family first appears in the scene at John 2:12, as Jesus, his mother, and his brothers stay for a few days in Capernaum. The narrator does not tell the implied reader what happened there. In view of the fact that the mother of Jesus had seen many of the signs that Jesus performed, the implied readers naturally expect her to believe in Jesus. But the narrator remains silent on this issue. There is also no indication that Jesus' brothers already believe in him. It is not clear whether Jesus' brothers accompany him before and during the Passover festival and hence see and hear his action in the court of the Gentiles, his dialogue with the Jews, and the manifestation of many *sēmeia* ("signs"). When they reappear in the narrative world (7:2–10) it is stated that they do not believe in him. This suggests that the events in Jerusalem have no immediate impact on their lives. In light of 2:11, one might reasonably assume that the relationship between Jesus and his family is still undecided. Moreover, the narration about Jesus' family, which is textually short, indicates the narrator's intention to suggest that Jesus' "family" is not confined to blood relations.

The resurrection of Jesus radically transformed a second group character in the narrative, *the disciples*. Before the resurrection they did not fully understand the significance of Jesus' action and dialogue in the temple. The disciples mentioned in John 2:11–12 are obviously not the twelve. The chronological sequence "after this," as discussed above, affirms that "the disciples" mentioned at 2:11 are Andrew, the unnamed disciple, Philip, Peter, and Nathanael. They are the first people who receive and believe in him. The disciples' presence in the temple to celebrate the Passover as pious Jews is presupposed by the language of "going down" (2:12) and "going up" to Jerusalem (2:13). Despite seeing Jesus' deed in the court of the Gentiles, the disciples seem unaware of the universality of the protagonist's mission, which includes both the Jews and the Gentiles. Although they hear Jesus' words in the temple, they seem to miss the manifestation of his glory as God's presence on earth. But the resurrection event opens their eyes and ears. With the narrative being composed from a postresurrection perspective, the remembrance motif (*emnēsthēsan*) inevitably appears (2:17, 22), suggesting that the disciples in 2:17, 22 are greater than the number mentioned in 2:12. These postresurrection disciples are Johannine communities. What happens to them? Johannine communities are reminded of Jesus' witnessing activities in deeds and words. Verse 17 becomes a moment for the communities to see clearly the significance of Jesus' deeds, and verse 22 is the moment when they perceive the meaning of Jesus' words. The passive verb *emnēsthēsan* ("they were reminded") indicates that the communities are being reminded. By whom? The remembrance motif corresponds with Jesus' promise concerning the work of the Holy Spirit in the disciples' lives after his ascension (7:39; 14:26). The Holy Spirit helps the communities to remember Jesus' deeds and words and enables them to theologize Christ's events meaningfully. The resurrection of Jesus opens the communities' eyes to see the Old Testament christologically and to understand more deeply Jesus' words and deeds as portraying God's presence on earth. Through these means, the Johannine communities are enabled to grasp deeply who Jesus is ontologically and functionally.

The narrator states that Johannine communities understand the body of Jesus as God's temple after the resurrection. Jesus does not replace or even destroy the temple but rather personalizes it. The temple in Jerusalem is only a shadow of the real and perfect temple. Jesus is the real temple where God perfectly dwells (John 1:14). With this understanding, Jesus' witnessing activity through deed in the court of the Gentiles proclaims that there are no walls separating Jews and Gentiles in Jesus-as-temple. The universality of the temple, which is the body of Christ, emerges as the important point of Jesus' witnessing activities.

Although the disciples are probably present during the Passover festival when Jesus performs many signs (2:23), the narrator does not record their explicit impact on the disciples' lives. If many people respond by believing in Jesus, the disciples are silent in seeing the *sēmeia*. The response from the disciples, as mentioned above, comes only after the resurrection. The disciples, as described by the narrator in 2:22, believe in Jesus. This is the moment not of the birth of the disciples' faith but rather of a developed understanding of faith. Reading the events of the temple incident in light of 2:11 and 20:30, it can reasonably be surmised that the disciples' faith deepens as they see many signs. It is not going too far to state that the remembrance motif helps the disciples to understand Jesus' witnessing activities during the Passover festival in Jerusalem (2:23).

The animal merchants and moneychangers, the third group character in the scene, use the court of the Gentiles (*hieros*), with permission from the religious leaders, as a market for trading. Their business practices hinder the Gentiles who come to pray to God. The Gentiles are distracted from their worship by the noise of commerce, the bellowing of cattle, and the bleating of sheep. As noted above, the coins of the money changers, although scattered, can easily be gathered together again later, and Jesus expels those selling doves without releasing the doves from the cages. Thus there is no intention to bring harm to the animals or to inflict loss on the merchants and the money changers. Had the merchants and money changers viewed Jesus' action as an act of violence, then a complaint would have been immediately submitted to the Roman garrison in the Antonia fortress. Jesus simply forbids them to use the place of prayer for all nations as a market for trading. Jesus' action vividly demonstrates that the court of the Gentiles is as important as the sanctuary proper; both are part of his Father's house. The merchants and money changers, by contrast, deprive people from all nations of their place for worshiping God. Their actions imply that the Gentiles are not God's people, but Jesus affirms that worship by people of all nations is as important as the worship of the Jews. Jesus also testifies to the merchants and money changers that he has a unique and personal relationship with God by calling God his "Father" (2:16). Clear and bold as the protagonist's witness is, the animal merchants and the money changers do not give any positive marked response. They could be labeled as people who do not believe because they do not grasp the significance of the *sēmeia*.

The immediate response to Jesus' zeal comes from *the religious leaders* (not from the Roman authorities), a group character who might fear the loss of financial income (Bauckham 1988, 72–89). They question the authority behind Jesus' action, an authority that can be proved only by performing a sign. The questioning of authority that takes the form of the demand for a sign shows that the religious leaders close their spiritual eyes to Jesus' witnessing activities in the court of the Gentiles. Although there is no clear indication of hostility expressed by the religious leaders, the fledgling conflict with the religious leaders emerges. The conflict arises not because Jesus has an antipriestly attitude or a plan to destroy the temple but rather because of their unbelief. The demand of the religious leaders for a sign is, in fact, granted immediately by Jesus in the form of a reference to his resurrection (2:19). Thus, the resurrection could be perceived as the supreme and climactic "sign" in FG. It is a sign of a consummated universal community in which Jews and Gentiles are united. These two separated ethnic groups are unified into one body of Jesus, which is the new temple. The resurrection is a "sign" in that it produces faith that Jesus is the Messiah, the Son of God.

But may one also think of Jesus' action in the temple precinct as itself a "sign"? It is indeed a sign, for four reasons. First, the action results in belief in Jesus (2:22). Jesus' action deepens the disciples' faith. Second, the remembrance motif (2:17, 22) has the effect of deepening faith and hence intimates that the action is a *sēmeion*. Third, John 4:48 and 6:30, among others, show that signs are capable of engendering faith. Finally, the closing statement of the narrative indicates that the "signs" included in FG are meant to elicit and edify faith in Jesus (20:30–31). The *sēmeia* are thus Jesus' witnessing activities in words and deeds that portray the image of God. This point will be discussed later.

The narrator does not detail Jesus' witnessing activities through which *many people*, the final group character mentioned in the episode, come to believe in him (2:23). Jesus' witnessing activities in Jerusalem during the Passover festival are summed up in the word *sēmeia* (plural): many people believe in Jesus as a result of seeing the signs. Although *polloi* ("many, crowds") is masculine, it seems inaccurate to view these great crowds as consisting of only men. It is important to notice that the narrator does not specify the nature of these signs or the background of the people believing in him. But as the Passover was an international festival, it might have been attended by people from different parts of the world. Therefore, it seems possible to argue that the term *polloi* involves a large number of people, international in nature.

The narrator reports in 4:45 that Galileans participated in the Passover festival in Jerusalem and saw all that Jesus had done in Jerusalem. But there is no explicit response of believing in Jesus. They simply welcome him enthusiastically. This is plausibly an indication of their perception that Jesus' prior action in the temple precinct, among other things, is a protest against the commercialization of the sacrificial system, a system that brings economic benefits to Jerusalem while becoming an oppressive financial burden on people from other regions (see Bauckham 1988, 78–79). The Galileans' warm reception when Jesus returns home is also a response of seeing and hearing Jesus' witness. They welcome Jesus but do not give him honor by believing in him. The exclusion of the Galileans from people who believe in Jesus further strengthens the international nature of the term *polloi*.

PLOT

The plot—the structuring or organizing line of the story—is forward-moving. This is the logic and the shaping force of the narrative. If the plot is the body of the narrative, the characters are the soul (Bar-Efrat 2000, 93). As Jesus bears witness, the characters react in two contrasting ways. The portrait of two diametrically opposite characters in the narrative (believers and unbelievers) clearly connects the series of events into a cohesive narrative unit. Further, the presence of both believers and unbelievers in the narrative world shows that the plot is propelled by conflict. The plot is built on the conflict of belief and unbelief. As noted above, characters who respond with unbelief include Jesus' brothers, the merchants and money changers, the religious leaders, and many people who do not believe. The disciples and other people who believe dramatize the believers. Many people start their relationship with Jesus, hence indicating the evangelistic purpose of his action, whereas the disciples deepen their relationship with Jesus, hence expressing the edificatory purpose. The characters embody the plot insofar as their response is either belief in Jesus or unbelief.

LITERARY DEVICES

In the communication process, messages are conveyed and received explicitly and implicitly. Often the implicit message is stronger than the explicit message. As far as John 2:12–25 is concerned, two types of implicit messages may be detected: symbol and misunderstanding. These literary devices appear in the focus of the narration, the second scene in the temple (2:13–22). Through these literary devices communication between the implied author and implied reader is established and sustained to persuade the implied reader of the purpose of the implied author's writing: to elicit and edify faith in Jesus.

A "symbol" uses earthly realities to point to other realities. The implied reader seeks to put together two realities into one meaning, a meaning of which the characters in the text may not have been aware. In the Hebrew Bible the temple symbolizes the presence of God. The narrator's intrusive comment in John 2:21 unifies the symbol and what is being symbolized. The temple as the symbol of God's earthly presence is no longer restricted to a particular building but rather to the consecrated Jesus. Jesus is God's earthly presence, since the Father has consecrated him to be the living temple. The idea of the personalization of the temple is not unknown outside the Fourth Gospel. The Qumran community believed that the presence of God was no longer bound to the temple in Jerusalem but to the pure Israel represented by the Qumran community. In their view, the temple in Jerusalem had been desecrated by the religious leaders and the people (see Gärtner 1965, 16–44).

The device of misunderstanding is related to symbol in that the characters fail to perceive symbols that are then clarified by the narrator. Misunderstanding occurs in the center of the narrative (John 2:13–22) in order to heighten the implied reader's attention to the protagonist. The dialogue between Jesus and the religious leaders creates total misunderstanding. In the religious leaders' perception, Jesus is demolishing the temple, whereas Jesus means the demolition of his body by the religious leaders, which he will then resurrect. The narrator is able to clarify the misunderstanding so that the implied reader will not fail to understand Jesus' words. Now the temple is the resurrected body of Jesus. The narrator magnificently guides the implied reader, who saw the destruction of the temple in 70 C.E., to the resurrected Jesus as the real temple and hence forces readers to reorient their attitude toward the temple. The new center of life and worship is not the temple but Jesus himself. Jesus-as-the-personalized-temple is now spiritually present among the believers' community. The new temple is no longer confined to a particular place or people. The new temple that is the body of Christ now becomes universal. Failure to understand Jesus' words may lead the implied reader to fall into the narrative's victimization of the religious leaders who do not believe in Jesus. The religious leaders are victimized by their own failure to understand. The implied readers, therefore, are encouraged to follow the steps of the disciples by reading the Scriptures christologically and by deepening their understanding of who Jesus is, as revealed through his deeds and words.

These two literary devices, symbol and misunderstanding, are located in the second scene (John 2:13–22), which is the focus of the narration. These devices endeavor to persuade the implied reader to identify with either the religious leaders or the disciples. The implied reader cannot but embrace the narrator's ideological perspective, which is stated in 20:31. The implied reader is invited to join the international community of believers. The overall effect created by the narrator through these devices is the universal significance of the protagonist's death and hence the internationalizing of the believing communities.

Signs and Faith

As noted above, the group characters embedded in John's narrative of the temple incident carry the narrative themes. Two such themes will be highlighted here: faith and universal community; and the relationship between faith and signs.

Faith and Universal Community

The interaction between Jesus and various group characters in John 2:12–25 explicates the communal aspect of faith. The interaction results in evoking and deepening communal belief, both edificatory faith and evangelistic faith.

Let us turn our attention first to *edificatory faith*. The disciples are portrayed as believers in 2:11, but they do not understand Jesus' deeds in the court of the Gentiles. However, the new perspective brought about by the resurrection of Jesus opens a new understanding as the Holy Spirit reminds them of the meaning and purpose of Jesus' words and deeds. The disciples therefore realize the universal nature of Jesus' witnessing activities. The Jews and the Gentiles are united into one body of Christ. The unification of Jews and Gentiles inevitably brings Jesus to the cross. Jesus' death on the cross demolishes the dividing wall of hostility between Jews and Gentiles. In the body of Christ as God's new temple, there no longer exists alienated and hostile races but rather a unified and reconciled people. All ethnic groups are in the same position before God. This new understanding of the disciples is expressed, as discussed above, in the quotation from Ps 69:9 in John 2:17. Uniting the Jews and the Gentiles into one people of God "consumes" Jesus' body. This motivation, dramatized in the temple incident, costs Jesus his life. By his death on the cross, Jesus unites both ethnic groups into one perfect temple, his body. It is clear, therefore, how the disciples' faith deepens communally. The disciples communally see Jesus with new eyes. But this growth does not stop. The disciples continue to build their faith by relating the body of Jesus and the resurrection event. The narrator's intrusive comment in 2:21 affirms that the body of Jesus is the perfect dwelling place of God. It is perfect because there is no alienation between Jews and Gentiles or alienation of either ethnic group from God. In the postresurrection era, the Holy Spirit helps the universal believing community to remember the dialogue between Jesus and the religious leaders, while at the same time illuminating its significance. The believing community begins to understand that from the beginning God's eternal purpose has been to unite the Jews and the Gentiles into one people.

Interpreting the dialogue between Jesus and the religious leaders from the resurrection perspective, the believing community now has a new relationship with the Old Testament. The believing community is enabled to read the Scriptures christologically. Jesus is the Messiah foretold in the Old Testament, and through him alone one has the key to open up its correct meaning. The Holy Spirit further helps the disciples to understand the significance of Jesus' words. From the resurrection point of view, the believing community begins to understand Jesus' words as portraying the presence of God. The new perspective brought about by the resurrection event opens new eyes. The believing community then has no ambivalence as to how to relate to the Old Testament and Jesus' words by placing them on the same platform. The believing community's faith is further strengthened by the role of the Holy Spirit as they read the Scriptures christologically and interpret Jesus' words theologically. Thus both the Old Testament and Jesus' words deepen communal faith.

The interactions between Jesus and various characters also function to deepen *evangelistic faith*. In John 1:35–51 individuals come to faith, but in the temple incident the narrator is concerned with the birth of faith communally. People come to faith in Jesus en masse. The signs in the court of the Gentiles and the resurrection event edify the disciples' faith, but the signs performed during the Passover festival cause many people to believe in him and imply that many people also do not believe in him. It can be surmised, therefore, that the many people who believe are an international community. As weak as the evidence may seem, a narrative-critical reading suggests that it is not unreasonable that the many people who believe dramatize the universality of Jesus' body.

Many people believe in Jesus, but Jesus did not entrust himself to them. Why? The narrator gives two reasons. First, Jesus knew all people immediately and simultaneously (2:24). Second, Jesus does not need any information concerning human nature and personality, since he knows profoundly the hearts of all (2:25). These two notes affirm that people who believe in Jesus en masse are not required to each introduce themselves personally to Jesus. Also, people who believe do not necessarily physically follow him. Jesus knows them all comprehensively and simultaneously. In other words, the narrator distinguishes the people who believe in 1:19–2:11 from those who believe in 2:12–25: in the former passage, the first disciples follow Jesus as rabbi; the new believers mentioned in the latter passage do not. If relating to Jesus does not mean following him physically wherever he goes, the question arises as to how the later believing community may develop their relationship with Jesus. Whether individually or in large numbers, the protagonist knows them all simultaneously and profoundly, a note that points to Jesus' spiritual presence among the believing community. That Jesus "did not entrust himself" to the believing community (2:24) means that Jesus does not relate physically to those who believe. Jesus needs no such kind of physical relationship, since he knows the universal believing community fully. The narrator does not refer to Jesus' physical proximity but to his spiritual relationship with believers communally. This point is explained in 6:56 and 10:14–16. Jesus' spiritual presence among the believing community further affirms that the relationship between Jesus and the believers traverses spatial and temporal barriers, hence denoting its universality.

But how do believers communally strengthen their faith without following Jesus physically? In this connection, the function of the Old Testament and Jesus' words play an important role, which explains the reason for including both in the narrative. Although Jesus did not entrust himself to the universal believing community—that is, does not relate physically to them—their faith can be deepened through exposure to the Old Testament and his words. Thus, many people en masse can relate to Jesus simultaneously, entering a community that is universal in nature. The relationship between Jesus and the universal community of believers, which is created by the death of Jesus, is sustained and strengthened by the Old Testament and his words and enlightened by the Holy Spirit.

Faith and Signs

While *sēmeia* are given to the merchants, the money changers, and the religious leaders, these characters do not see their significance and, as a result, do not believe in Jesus. Only after the resurrection is the meaning of the signs understood by the disciples, resulting in a deepening relationship with Jesus. The believing community clearly sees the temple incident as pointing to the universality of believers created by Jesus' death.

People in Jerusalem during the Passover festival come to believe in Jesus. Why? Seeing the signs that the narrator narrates causes many to believe in him. But what are "signs"? Most scholars view the Johannine *sēmeia* as miracles. Many scholars conclude that the kind of belief that is grounded on a miracle is considered inadequate in FG. Schnackenburg, like others who take this view, concludes that "the belief of the crowds 'in his name' [2:23] … is characterized as an inadequate belief attached to miracles, which Jesus deliberately rejects" (1968, 341, 358). Faith, according to Schnackenburg and others, must be grounded on Jesus' words alone, since the miracles as a proof are widely rejected, particularly after the Enlightenment. But does *sēmeia* mean "miracles"? The *sēmeia* in John are not necessarily miraculous deeds, since they can also be a proleptic word or an action. "Signs" are witnessing activities through words and deeds that reveal who Jesus is. Although the *sēmeia* mentioned in 2:23 do not necessarily refer to 2:18, it is clear that the *sēmeia* point to Jesus' words and deeds. Thus, Jesus' deeds in the court of the Gentiles and Jesus' resurrection are viewed as "signs." Signs in the narrative point to the universality of Christ's body. Interestingly, the narrator makes a distinction between *sēmeia* and *terata* ("miracles") in 4:48. These two terms represent two different types of phenomena. Moreover, in line with 20:30–31, the *sēmeia* in FG are intended primarily to lead people to believe in Jesus. They are closely connected with the belief motif. Therefore, it would seem misleading to state that faith produced by signs is inadequate. *Sēmeia* refers to both Jesus' words and deeds, either of which can create and strengthen faith.

The crowds who believe in Jesus' name have an adequate faith, though fledgling, based on the witness of Jesus himself. This faith, like the disciples' faith, needs to be deepened, but the adequacy of such faith is revealed in the fact that 2:23 uses the same grammatical construction as 1:12, where belief in Jesus' name grants one power to become a child of God. Schnackenburg's reading of 2:23 would counter 1:12, thus suggesting that the narrator is self-contradictory and unreliable. Jesus himself says clearly, "him who comes to me I will not cast out" (6:37). Thus, it is important to assert that the narrator does not portray Jesus' rejection of people's faith. Unlike the *sēmeia* in 2:11 that strengthen the faith of the believers, at 2:23 signs become the *basis* of belief. The signs in 2:11 are not given to all people, only to the believing community. Faith founded on the observation of signs is not inferior, since the narrator portrays that *sēmeia* function to create and strengthen faith.

Thus, for believers the signs function to strengthen faith, whereas for unbelievers they evoke belief in him. The *sēmeia* are connected with the dramatic action and with Jesus' miraculous deeds and resurrection. Signs signify who Jesus is and create, in effect, a dividing point in human lives at which some people come to believe in his name (John 4:53–54) while others refuse him (e.g., 11:47). The *sēmeia* signify divine presence on earth to all ethnic groups, the universality of Jesus' witnessing activities.

Conclusion

A narrative reading reveals that the universality of Jesus' body as the new temple in which the Jews and the Gentiles are united is the central message of John 2:12–25. This universality is enhanced by the texture of the text and the presence of the group characters embedded in the narrative world. The hostile wall separating two alienated ethnic groups is destroyed by the death and resurrection of Jesus. The universality of the believing community is further dramatized in 3:1–4:54 by selecting characters of different gender, social status, and ethnic background. When one believes in Jesus, one is attached to a community that is universal in nature. One's relationship with Jesus causes a believer to relate to this universal community of believers.

The above analysis of characters has also demonstrated that FG is composed both to initiate faith in Jesus (*Missionsschrift*) *and* to deepen the faith of the believing community (*Gemeindeschrift*). The characters embedded in the narrative world dramatize the evangelistic and edificatory aspects of faith. The narrative reading helps reveal, over and above the linguistic and historical readings, the dual purpose of FG as stated in 20:31. What does the term *evangelistic* mean? Was FG regarded simply as a religious tract? Was FG circulated freely among nonbelievers? One can only conjecture the answer. The more likely scenario is that FG was used in Christian worship where nonbelievers were present. Justin's *First Apology* describes regular Sunday worship by Christians in city or countryside (*1 Apol.* 67) and mentions Scripture reading, including "the memoirs of the apostles" (= the New Testament Gospels), as the focal point of the gatherings. The inclusiveness of the Christian gathering, which was attended by nonbelievers, is hinted at in Justin's writings (*1 Apol.* 66, 67); from an earlier era, the presence of nonbelievers at Christian gatherings is explicitly reported in 1 Cor 14:23–24. Thus, FG was likely read and used by Johannine communities where nonbelievers were present.

New Jewish Directions in the Study of the Fourth Gospel

Matthew Kraus

Unconstrained by the demand for a streamlined encapsulation of her work, Adele Reinhartz would have subtitled her fine book *Befriending the Beloved Disciple* as "Several Readings of the Gospel of John Attempted by One Jewish Reader" (2001). Such a work, which unabashedly and compellingly addresses New Testament scholars as well as committed Jews and Christians, would have seemed inconceivable when John A. T. Robinson published his seminal piece "The New Look on the Fourth Gospel." The academic guild of 1957 would hardly have tolerated such a blurring of "objective" and "subjective" scholarship.[1] Less obviously, Robinson does not consider the possibility of a literary reading of the Fourth Gospel, much less multiple readings.[2] In addition, the presence of a Jewish person, not to mention a Jewish woman, in the community of New Testament scholars reflects a demographic shift radically different from the academic world inhabited by Robinson.[3] What then, does Reinhartz have to do with Robinson?

Before addressing this question, I have to acknowledge the elephant in the room. What can be gained by examining Jewish scholarship on the Fourth Gospel? Does the profound demographic shift that has occurred in

---

1. Since anthropologists and sociologists such as Clifford Geertz (1973, 193–233) and Peter Berger (1969) have identified scholarship as an ideology-laden social phenomenon, we recognize that previous generations of scholarship were not as "ideologically free" as they claimed. For a particularly egregious example, see Susannah Heschel's discussion of Nazi theology (2003). It should be noted, however, that socially constructed knowledge need not necessarily be inaccurate. See here Jonathan Brumberg-Kraus (1997, 140), who also cites Berger (1969, 180).

2. On the explosion of literary readings of the Fourth Gospel, see Nielsen 1999.

3. On the demographic changes in American biblical scholarship, see Saunders 1982, 82–84, 101–2; Sperling 1992. On feminist biblical scholarship, see Schüssler Fiorenza 1992; Meyers, Craven, and Kraemer 2000.

the scholarly guild, particularly in North America, matter? Is it sufficient to suggest that today's global community of scholars simply reflects the commitment to diversity characteristic of North American culture, a world center of biblical scholarship (see Saunders 1982, 101–2)? If we understand scholarship as subject to sociological processes, then diversity should have an impact on academic culture. In the wake of the 350th anniversary of Jews in America (2005), it behooves us to reflect on the impact, if any, of Jewish scholars on New Testament studies, but this should not be viewed as some futile exercise in cultural triumphalism. The application of anthropological and sociological theory to the academic enterprise suggests that such an analysis would be fruitful, since sociologically defined groups reflect and promote ideologies (see Geertz 1973; Berger and Luckman 1980).

An examination of Jewish scholarship on the Gospel of John raises numerous difficult issues that typify any discussion of the sociological dimensions of scholarship. How do we define a scholar as "Jewish"? Should we differentiate between those who openly identify themselves as Jewish and those who do not? Moreover, how do we confront the varieties of Jewishness that characterize the Jewish community today? More specifically, how does the Jewishness of scholars impact on their work? Clearly, these are uncomfortable questions because they pit the ethos of scholarly objectivity against the intuitive likelihood of an ideologically induced subjectivity. Such discomfort dissipates, however, when we distinguish between the two primary tasks of scholarship.

The Twofold Tasks of Scholarship: Discovery and Transmission

The scholarly enterprise involves both the discovery and the transmission of the newest knowledge. Reflections on the impact of Jewishness on scholarship, however, tend to lump discovery and transmission together. For example, although Jonathan Brumberg-Kraus provides an excellent taxonomy and analysis of Jewish scholarship on the New Testament, he does not draw out the implications of a distinction between the two tasks of the scholar. As a result, the question of Jewishness becomes mired with the question of objectivity. According to Brumberg-Kraus, Jewish New Testament scholars claim to perform three roles: the defender of the faith; the explainer of Christianity to Jews; and the "objective" researcher (1997, 131–35). Adopting some or all of these roles, the Jewish New Testament scholar may jeopardize the objectivity of his or her scholarship. On the one hand, the Jewish New Testament scholar concentrates, or is expected to concentrate, on "Jewish" topics (the portrayal of Jews, the role of Jews in the passion, anti-Semitism and the New Testament, Jewish texts and early Christianity; see Cook 1987b, 183–99; 1988,

3–30). On the other hand, in order to enhance the impression of objectivity, some Jewish scholars intentionally avoid Jewish topics (Brumberg-Kraus 1997, 137–40).

Most Jewish scholars since Robinson have, for similar reasons, avoided the Gospel of John, which makes the work of Reinhartz all the more striking. Reinhartz ironically muses that a year or two of psychoanalysis might uncover the deep connections between her Jewishness and her interest in the New Testament (2001, 12), but she rightly implies that this does not undermine the quality of her enterprise. Even when we admit our tendencies (or perhaps because we do so), we can still make compelling arguments based on evidence. We still have a conundrum, however, because if Jewishness matters, how can Jewish New Testament scholarship still be considered "objective"? I believe that distinguishing between discovery and transmission (conventionally called "research" and "teaching," respectively) resolves the paradox. What Brumberg-Kraus, Reinhartz, and all Jewish scholars are essentially doing is defending the objectivity of their research. Ideological implications emerge primarily in the other aspect of scholarship, its transmission. Reinhartz's Jewishness manifests itself less in her analysis of the textual evidence than in the fact that she is the one presenting certain arguments.

The observation that Jewishness matters more in the presentation of research than in its content was compellingly demonstrated at a session of the Society of Biblical Literature's Annual Meeting in November 2004, which included a presentation by Pamela Eisenbaum and an ensuing discussion on Jews and the Study of the New Testament. Initially, Eisenbaum approached the topic of Jewish scholars on the New Testament with skepticism, because religious orientation seemed irrelevant to scholarly objectivity. But when she expanded her inquiry to consider the sociological dimensions of scholarship—that is, the various functions of scholars as teachers, panelists, authors, media experts, journal editors and reviewers, as well as researchers—Eisenbaum determined that Jewishness did matter. Essentially, the multiple social functions of the academic require the presence of Jewish scholars in the New Testament guild. Eisenbaum noted that the mere presence of Jews (as well as other historically nonrepresented groups) alters the discourse by providing a check on public pronouncements (2004). Rather than restricting objectivity, diversity among scholars enhances it: since the implications of research may have real implications for Jewish people, the standard of objectivity becomes that much higher. Moreover, Jewish scholars still play a valuable social role as explainers of Judaism to non-Jews and explainers of Christianity to Jewish people. At the risk of overpsychologizing, I would also suggest that, as the recent situation concerning Mel Gibson's film *The Passion* demonstrates, Jewish scholars of the New Testament find their profession particularly rewarding because it enables them to integrate their serious scholarship with meaningful contemporary issues outside of academia. The primary impact of Jewish scholars on the New Testament lies in the presentation of the New Testament in and outside of the academy.

Where have you gone, Mr. Robinson? In what follows, I will discuss four Jewish scholars who have worked with the Gospel of John and explore how each approaches the issue of Jewish scholarship on the New Testament.[4] I will show how their scholarship reflects trends articulated by Robinson in 1957 but also goes in directions he did not anticipate. While rejecting an essentialist notion of Judaism and Jewish readings, I will highlight how Jewishness appears more in the *how* than in the *what* Jewish scholars say about the Gospel of John. Then I will analyze the Nicodemus passages (John 3:1–21; 7:49–52; 19:38–42) in order to test any conclusions that might be programmatic for understanding Jewish scholarship on the New Testament. In a sense, accepting Reinhartz's characterization of her work as *a* Jewish reading of the Fourth Gospel, I want to explore what emerges from several Jewish readings of the Fourth Gospel.

Samuel Sandmel: Opening the Door to Jewish Readings of the Gospel of John

Since this volume focuses on recent trends in Johannine scholarship, I will pass over the important history of Jewish scholarship on the New Testament in Europe and North America, as well as Israel, during the nineteenth and early twentieth centuries (see Cook 2000, 95–112; Brumberg-Kraus 1997). Although Samuel Sandmel certainly was not the first Jewish scholar of the New Testament, his prominence as a member of the guild of New Testament scholars cannot be underestimated. Careful to separate his Jewishness from the character and quality of his scholarship, he nevertheless explicitly identified himself as both a Jew and a scholar in *A Jewish Understanding of the New Testament* (1956) and *We Jews and Jesus* (1965). Even before these

---

4. There are a number of Jewish scholars of the New Testament; the discussion here has been limited in view of space restrictions and in order to focus on major themes in Jewish scholarship on the Gospel of John. A more comprehensive study of Jewish scholarship on the New Testament would consider the work of Dan Cohn-Sherbok (1996), Michael J. Cook (1974; 1978; 1983; 1987b; 1988; 1996; 1999; 2000), David Daube (1984; 1987), Pamela Eisenbaum (1997), David Flusser (1992), David Frankfurter (2001), Amy-Jill Levine (1988), Joel Marcus (1992; 2000), Mark D. Nanos (1996; 2002), Jacob Neusner (1989), Alan F. Segal (1990), Claudia Setzer (2004), David Sperling (2001), and Geza Vermes (1981). For collections of essays by Jewish New Testament scholars, see Frymer-Kensky 2000; Greenspoon, Hamm, and LeBeau 2000; and Klenicki 1991. Jewish treatments of the Gospel of John are much more limited. In addition to those discussed here, see Cook 1987a; Lieu 1998 and 2001; Tanzer 1991; Wills 1997.

books were released, however, the fact that he taught at a rabbinical seminary clearly marked him as Jewish.[5] In both works, we see Sandmel as the objective scholar. Since he addresses himself at times specifically to Jews, however, the significance of his own Jewishness emerges most emphatically in the transmission of this new knowledge.

In *A Jewish Understanding of the New Testament*, Sandmel explains why Jews cannot accept Johannine Christology (1956, 266–86). Based on his assumption that the Gospel of John reacts to the Synoptics, he identifies the work as a spiritual Gospel. Sandmel then poses the question of why this most spiritual of the Gospels happens to be the most anti-Jewish. The answer lies in the opposition between the corporeal and spiritual that serves as a dominating theme in the Fourth Gospel (FG). In the discussions between Jews and Jesus in FG, Jews represent those concerned with material matters, while Jesus focuses on spiritual matters. Thus, Jews function in the narrative as a corporeal foil for the spiritual Jesus. To a certain extent, this lets Jews off the hook for the crucifixion, because Jesus' death is not entirely a tragedy in the Gospel of John (as the spiritual is released from the corporeal). To be sure, Jews are blamed for Jesus' death, but only to highlight the contrast between the material and the spiritual. The emphasis on the divine nature of Jesus sets the Gospel of John on "the threshold of the doctrine of the Trinity" (1956, 277). Although the idea of a Paraclete as a preexistent, defending intermediary coheres with rabbinic ideas, attributing this role to the Holy Spirit abrades Jewish notions of monotheism. Rabbis can accept miracles and holy men but not a Christology that attributes creation of the world to the Holy Spirit. Nevertheless, since Christians believed and argued that the doctrine of the Trinity does not contradict Old Testament monotheism, Jews unfairly criticize Christians for being polytheists. Rather, the heart of the disagreement lies in different and incompatible approaches to explaining the nature of the one God: "The Fourth Gospel portrays, in a Christian way, and through the medium of the Christ, conceptions about God which are paralleled and held as firmly and as warmly in Jewish tradition in the Jewish way. Scholars have pointed out that the rabbinic parallels to the Fourth Gospel consistently assign to God the role that the Gospel assigns to the Christ" (1956, 282). Thus, the basic message of the Fourth Gospel corresponds with rabbinic ideology: God

---

5. Born in 1911, Sandmel received his doctorate from Yale University in 1949. Professor of Bible and Hellenistic Literature at Hebrew Union College in 1952 for over thirty years, he was the Helen A. Regenstein Professor of Religion of the Chicago Divinity School when he died. In addition to publishing numerous books on the New Testament, Sandmel edited the Oxford Study Edition of the New English Bible and served as president of the Society of Biblical Literature. See *Encyclopedia Judaica Decennial Book, 1973–1982*, 544.

exists, God loves humanity, and God is humanity's guide, security, and assurance of eternal life. Nevertheless, the basic medium of this message, Christ, contradicts essential Jewish beliefs.

In *We Jews and Jesus* we find the clearest articulation of Sandmel's Jewishness, combined with his harshest critique of the Fourth Gospel. To be sure, Sandmel expresses profound respect for the Gospels and Christianity, although as a Jew he cannot regard Jesus as more than a human being, nor can he accept that Jesus' death atones for the sins of humanity (1965, vii). Utilizing literary criticism, however, Sandmel reaches the limit of respectful disagreement in the case of the Gospel of John.[6] He finds the literary approach particularly congenial to a Jewish reader because "[t]o us Jews the Gospels are not sacred." A course on " 'The Bible as Literature' ... sometimes ... is a 'nondenominational' way of letting students become acquainted with the content of Scripture while avoiding the difficulties inherent in the divergences of Christian-Jewish approaches" (1965, 118–19). Such an approach facilitates an objective analysis congruent with Jewish sensibilities, for Sandmel acknowledges that a literary evaluation of the Gospels allows for a negative assessment of their literary merit. He does this somewhat reluctantly in the case of the Gospel of John: "There is this risk in the approach of 'Bible as literature,' that a negative response is necessarily admissible. Such, in my reading, occurs in the Gospel According to John" (1965, 125). In Sandmel's view, if one of the Fourth Gospel's purposes is to make Jesus attractive to readers, it fails miserably as a work of literature. Assuming the presence of a predetermined timetable known only to him, Jesus' omniscience embodies an unappealing absence of modesty and humility. In addition, Sandmel finds offensive the repeated device of Jesus referring to misunderstandings "by people of that which seems crystal clear" (1965, 125). Sandmel, echoing ancient critiques, cites the Gospel of John as an extreme example of what he feels generally about the Gospels: they hardly rank as works of the highest literary quality, especially compared to Ruth, 4 Maccabees, Faust, and the like (1965, 126; cf. Augustine, *Conf.* 3.5.9).

In Sandmel's view, this negative assessment of the Gospels cannot be reduced to the critical cantankerousness typical of scholars. "To a Jew [who

---

6. As a historian, Sandmel considers the Gospel of John interesting and important for uncovering Christian origins but rejects the historicity of one feature particularly germane to the Jewish experience: John's portrayal of Jesus' opponents as "the Jews" rather than "the Pharisees and chief priests" (1965, 125). Thus, while Sandmel generally follows the "new look" premise that "in the Johannine tradition we may at points be as near to the Jesus of history as in the Synoptic Gospels" (Robinson 1962b, 100), he rejects the historicity of the Fourth Gospel's depiction of "the Jews."

is not a serious student], reading as sympathetically as he is able, the Gospels create a bewilderment, not an appreciation. I can report that many a Jew, prior to reading the Gospels, has an estimate of them which the actual reading reduces." Sandmel goes on to explain that each Gospel was written as a reactive attempt to replace the previous Gospel, thus clarifying why the literary quality of the Gospels might be lacking while their content remains of great interest to the scholar (1965, 122–27, quote 126–27). Regardless of the validity of these claims, Sandmel seems correct in the general tenor of his argument, namely, that the form and content of the Gospels emerged primarily from the internal and external historical matrix of early Christianity, while the myth of literary artistry developed many centuries later as a result of the canonical status of these texts. This is not to say that the Gospels completely lack literary artistry. Rather, Sandmel simply wishes to qualify the claim that these are the greatest works ever written and that their literary quality explains their popularity.

One would expect Sandmel, as "defender of the faith," to explain why Jews cannot accept the Fourth Evangelist's Christology and why they should not admire the Gospel of John. Surprisingly, however, Sandmel utilizes his literary critique of the Gospels to exhort Jews to learn about their own heritage. While ably performing the task of transmitting new research, Sandmel argues that a Jewish reading of the Fourth Gospel stimulates deeper knowledge of authentic Jewish traditions. He explains his rationale in *A Jewish Understanding of the New Testament*:

> It is only the Jew who does not know his own heritage who can join in some modern Christian appraisals of Jesus as the greatest teacher.... It is all too often the premise that the life of Jesus is "the greatest story ever told" which attributes to his words an eminence actually transcending them. It is not that these words, at their best, are poor or base; on the contrary, they are superb. But they are by no means unequaled either in clarity, in vigor, in perception, or in profundity in Jewish literature. (1956, 283)

Sandmel situates the contrast between the Fourth Gospel's outstanding reputation and the reality of its infelicitous literary style against the background of many Jewish people's ignorance of their own heritage. According to Sandmel, if Jews would read biographies of their own rabbis, they would not claim that Jesus was the greatest rabbi in the greatest story ever told. Through this striking move, Sandmel utilizes the New Testament to promote Judaism among his co-religionists.

Why, then, should Jews read the Gospel of John? Not for historical information (except for the date of the crucifixion). Rather, the Fourth Gospel underscores how Christianity and Judaism are akin to each other without being identical. Although Jesus shares some features of Judaism, he is unique in the combination of these features (1956, 281–84). As a whole, the portrayal of Jesus is completely alien to Jews, but God's love of humanity represents common ground. More profoundly, the binary opposition between Jews and Jesus fosters mutual misrepresentation. The Gospel of John portrays Jews as lacking a concept of divine grace and love, while Jews reading the Gospel of John claim that Christians idolatrously worship a man. How Jews and Christians relate to the Gospel of John can model how they relate to each other: profound disagreement coupled with profound respect. In *Judaism and Christian Beginnings*, Sandmel notes that it is easier for Christians to relate to the Jesus of the Fourth Gospel than the Jesus of the Synoptic Gospels, while, ironically, this Johannine Jesus is the one that Jews find most difficult to understand (1978, 390). In the 1950s and 1960s, only a Jewish scholar of the New Testament could transmit the idea that Jews should take an interest in the Fourth Gospel.

Daniel Boyarin: From a Jewish Jesus to a Jewish Trinity?

Daniel Boyarin goes much further than Sandmel by tracing Christian trinitarianism to Jewish roots. According to Boyarin, "[i]t is at least possible that the beginning of trinitarian reflection was precisely in non-Christian Jewish accounts of the second and visible God, variously the Logos (*Memra*), Wisdom, or even perhaps Son of God" (2001, 249). The possible Jewish sources are threefold: Philo, the Targumim, and wisdom literature. Philo's doctrine of the Logos has parallels in the Gospel of John: in each, the Logos is both part of God and with God and also actively interacts with the world (2001, 249–52).[7] But Boyarin's observation that the Fourth Gospel's Logos theology bears points of contact with Philo's Greek writings is not nearly as surprising as his attempt to identify this same type of thinking in a Semitic-speaking context. In a brilliant observation, Boyarin turns on its head the traditional idea that the use of *Memra* in the Targumim provides a buffer between biblical anthropomorphisms and divine transcendence. If the *Memra* is truly anthropomorphic, then by definition it is the entity that is

---

7. Boyarin addresses the question of Philo's Jewishness by provocatively suggesting that Middle Platonism is a form of Judaism and Christianity. Since the Logos as divine mediator is a central thesis of Middle Platonism, and since this concept emerged from the interaction between Platonism, Stoicism, and Torah, it is no less logical to label the idea "Jewish" or "Christian" than to call it "Middle Platonism." If, by definition, "Hellenistic culture" describes the fusion of ancient Greek and Eastern cultures, why should we call it "Hellenism" rather than "Judaism" or "Egyptianism" or "Persianism"?

both divine and "humanlike." Like a person, the *Memra* acts in the material world, but these actions of creating, appearing, supporting, and saving reflect a more than human power. Rather than reduce the *Memra* to a euphemism, Boyarin argues that it makes more sense to read it literally as "an actual divine entity or mediator." Even though the Gospel of John's Logos theology in all its fullness may have deeper parallels with the wisdom tradition, the linguistic parallels between the Fourth Gospel and the Targumim trump the systematic theological argument. Not only is *Memra* cognate with Logos, but it does exactly the same things in both the Gospel of John and the Targumim. Thus, Boyarin radically suggests that "the Gospel of John ... when taken together with Philo and with the Targum, provides further important evidence for Logos theology, used here as a general term for various closely related binitarian theologies, as the religious Koine of Jews in Palestine and the Diaspora" (2001, 260).

Boyarin acknowledges the influence of biblical wisdom literature on the Gospel of John, particularly on the Prologue (John 1:1–18), but disagrees that apparent similarities between wisdom hymns and the Prologue necessarily mean that the Prologue itself is a hymn. Rather, he argues that John's Prologue is a midrashic narrative of the first five verses of Genesis that serves to bridge the preexistent Logos with the incarnation (2001, 262–63, 67). The parallels with wisdom can be attributed to the midrashic technique of bringing in an intertext from the Prophets or the Writings to explicate verses from the Pentateuch. The advantage of this reading is threefold: first, chapter 1 of the Gospel of John becomes a coherent literary unit; second, rather than viewing the Prologue as a wisdom hymn to the Logos tacked on to the incarnation statement in 1:14, there is a chronological preparation for the incarnation; third, the Prologue theologically explains the incarnation on the grounds of previous failed interventions of the Logos. Thus, the uniqueness of the Gospel of John is not the Logos theology, which is, in fact, Jewish, but rather the incarnation of a Jewish Logos theology in Jesus.

Let us examine Boyarin as a Jewish reader of the Fourth Gospel. In fairness to him, he does not identify himself as Jewish. At issue for him are oversimplified and essentialist explanations for the so-called "parting of the ways" between Judaism and Christianity (Boyarin 2001, 243–45; also 1999; 2004). Logos theology is not a new path but part of the Jewish theological Koine; the difference between Judaism and Christianity resides in the substantiation of the Logos in the person of Jesus. In this respect, Boyarin shares common ground with Sandmel in reducing the essential difference between Judaism and Christianity to Jesus. However, unlike Sandmel, rather than arguing that Jews ignorant of later Christian theology misunderstand trinitarianism as polytheism, Boyarin claims that Jewish contemporaries of the

Gospel of John would understand trinitarianism as a logical extension of their own binitarianism. The Jewish objection to John's Christology would not be on theological grounds but rather on historical grounds, namely, that the Logos was not incarnated in Jesus (just as Jews accept the idea of a Messiah but reject the claim that Jesus was this Messiah). Jews do not have a problem with Christology as much as with Jesus Christology. Boyarin also differs from Sandmel in praising the literary quality of the Prologue. He does so, however, by describing it as a quintessential rabbinic form: midrash. This fits in Brumberg-Kraus's taxonomy of "we encompass you" and "Jesus was Jewish" (here more as "the Gospel of John was Jewish"). Needless to say, Boyarin takes as a given what Robinson identifies as the second major trend of the "new look": the reconnection of the Fourth Gospel to its historical and social background. To be sure, in connecting the Prologue to a Jewish Koine rather than the Dead Sea Scrolls, Boyarin has a broader notion of the text's Jewish background.

Although technically a reading by a Jewish scholar, Boyarin's analysis is not justly served by being reduced to a "Jewish interpretation." Nevertheless, his Jewishness does play a role in the task of the scholar as communicator. There are many features that might give contemporary Jews pause, such as the idea that Jews of antiquity had a binitarian God-concept. As a Jew, however, Boyarin could hardly be accused of promoting a supersessionist ideology when claiming that Christians properly inherited, understood, and developed a common Jewish theological precept. Sandmel studiously avoids anything that smacks of supersessionism. Nonetheless, Boyarin differs from Sandmel at a much deeper level. While Sandmel sees the Fourth Gospel as both a challenge and an opportunity for Jews and Christians to differentiate themselves and respect each other, Boyarin questions such a view by arguing that this most different of the Gospels may not be so alien to Judaism after all. Thus, Boyarin provides a postmodern critique of strict boundaries between Judaism and Christianity and speaks to contemporary Jews who casually toss around slogans such as "Christians believe in three gods."

Paula Fredriksen: Does Jewishness Matter? and Matters of Jewishness

While Boyarin blurs the distinction between the historical and theological elements of the Gospel of John by linking the Prologue to the history of Jewish theology, Fredriksen takes the Fourth Gospel as a key to understanding the historical Jesus, particularly the reasons for his crucifixion. According to Fredriksen, Jesus was killed by the Romans because he was fomenting rebellion and the Romans desperately wanted to preserve stability (2000, 33, 254–59). The Fourth Gospel plays a crucial role in Fredriksen's reading because it puts the temple incident at the beginning of the narrative as one of many trips that Jesus made to Jerusalem (2000, 30–31). Not only do the frequent trips back and forth between Galilee and Jerusalem seem more plausible, but John's presentation gives the temple a more symbolic than dramatic function. For example, in Mark the incident at the temple triggers Jesus' arrest and passion, while "[f]or John, the significance of the actual temple is subsumed utterly by its christological significance: the whole image of the destroyed temple signifies the Passion" (2000, 31). In the Synoptics, the temple incident sets off a chain of events that result in Jesus' death because of his messianic claims; in the Gospel of John, the messianic claims play a role in the speeches of Jesus rather than the narrative. Therefore, according to the Gospel of John, Jesus must be killed not because of his messianic claims but because his activities would jeopardize the temple.

Reminiscent of Sandmel, Fredriksen contrasts the Synoptics' portrait of Jesus' popular following in Judea and Galilee with the opaque character of his speeches in the Fourth Gospel. Such speeches would hardly generate such popularity. The Fourth Gospel's passion story, however, has much historicity, as has long been recognized; for example, John is likely correct to suggest that Jesus' trial took place on Thursday rather than during the Passover (see Fredriksen 2000, 222–23). Fredriksen reads the absence of a christological confession in the Gospel of John, as well as the absence of the charge of blasphemy and false witness, as far more likely than the Synoptics' version of Jesus' trial. For Fredriksen, there are three "facts" that require explanation: (1) Why is the punishment crucifixion? (2) Why was Jesus, but not his followers, crucified? (3) Why does the incident with the money changers in the temple not trigger the passion in the Gospel of John? Many scholars have noted that crucifixion is a Roman punishment but do not necessarily conclude from this that he was crucified for Roman reasons (see, e.g., Hengel 1977). If the Jewish authorities felt that the Jesus movement constituted a religious threat, why would they not ensure the death of his immediate followers as well (Fredriksen 2000, 9)? What concerned the Romans? Utilizing the architecture of the temple complex, Fredriksen ingeniously argues that the overturning of the tables would hardly cause a major stir among the Jewish populace crowded in the temple area. The Roman guards, however, stationed on a level overlooking the temple court, saw a much more disturbing picture (2000, 220–34). Well aware of the disruptions that occurred during pilgrimage festivals, when numerous Jews from all over Judea, Galilee, and abroad would congregate in the temple, the Romans would be particularly sensitive to an incendiary spark that might ignite a riot. The public nature of Jesus' crucifixion would discourage other individuals from upsetting the Roman peace.

Using the Gospel of John to attribute the primary responsibility of Jesus' death to the Romans may seem odd, since no one would dispute that it is the most anti-Jewish of the Gospels. Nevertheless, Fredriksen does not consider the bulk of the Gospel of John to be historical, but rather theological. These theological themes trump the historicity of the text, especially its presentation of "the Jews," who function in FG as theological foils. According to the Prologue, Jesus comes from above, descends into human history, is rejected by his people, and ascends to heaven, where he becomes the exclusive path to the Father. Those who recognize Jesus' true status become the children of God who receive salvation. The story plays out the theme of descent and ascent as well as the theme of ignorant nonbelievers and knowing believers. Since Jesus must ascend, it is not really that important who is responsible for crucifying him. The Jews are much more important to John as representatives of the rejecting nonbelievers. That the Gospel of John identifies the nonfollowers of Jesus primarily as "Jews" probably reflects the social circumstances of the Johannine community, who may have been expelled from the synagogue before FG was written. Thus, the Jews in the Gospel of John represent not the slayers of Jesus but rather all people who reject him, and Jews participate in the death of Jesus in the Gospel of John as a result of literary consistency rather than historical accuracy (Fredriksen 1988, 18–26). In short, since the "Jews" in the Gospel of John are ahistorical, anything they do must be considered "ahistorical."

Tempting as it would be to identify this exoneration of Jews as representative of Fredriksen's Jewishness, I would not be doing justice to a serious scholarly argument accepted by Jewish and non-Jewish scholars alike. One reviewer of Fredriksen's work sees her Jewishness emerging not in this attribution of Jesus' death to Roman interests but rather in her sensitivity to the Jewish background of Jesus (Lindbeck 2000, 46–48). Somehow, being Jewish gives Fredriksen a greater ability to humanize both Jesus and the Jews portrayed in the Gospels. I find Fredriksen particularly interesting because her work begs the question of the significance of a scholar's Jewishness. Certainly Fredriksen does not see her Judaism as relevant. In contrast to Daniel Boyarin, who is quite open about his Jewishness (see 1997c, xiii), Paula Fredriksen does not regularly identify herself as Jewish. Fredriksen certainly does not deny her Jewishness, and the interested person perhaps could determine her religious background. Even in the recent debate concerning Mel Gibson's movie *The Passion*, however, Fredriksen was rarely identified as Jewish.[8]

---

8. While some reviewers have identified Fredriksen as Jewish (see Lindbeck 2000; Boys 2003), others overlook, or seem unaware of, her Jewish identity. Brumberg-Kraus was originally unaware of Fredriksen's Jewishness (1997, 132 n. 68). Peter Boyer's review of *The Passion* in *New*

While one might assume that Fredriksen became involved in the controversy over this film because of her Jewishness, she herself attributes her reactions to her scholarship and Catholic upbringing. As a scholar, Fredriksen addressed Gibson's claims of historical accuracy, and as a former Catholic schoolgirl she calls attention to the violent infliction of pain throughout the film (see Fredriksen 2003; 2004). Despite such pronouncements, one cannot avoid assuming that, at the least, Fredriksen's Jewishness sensitized her to the movie's implications and motivated her to publicly criticize the film. In saying this, I do not mean to imply that only Jewish people could or did publicly oppose Mel Gibson, but rather simply to note that the simple fact of one's Jewishness would necessarily impact how one reacted to *The Passion*. Even for a scholar such as Fredriksen, who clearly and successfully distinguishes her research from her identity, Jewishness became relevant in the transmission of scholarship. In other words, Mel Gibson's movie forced a public debate in which (rightly or wrongly) the Jewishness of Fredriksen mattered. Nevertheless, Fredriksen does not fall into the same category as Sandmel, Brumberg-Kraus, Mark Nanos, and Adele Reinhartz, all of whom explicitly acknowledge their Jewishness (see Nanos 2000, 212).

Adele Reinhartz: From Objective Scholarship to Scholarly Subjectivity

Fredriksen reminds us that Jewish scholars have to negotiate the claims of their Jewishness with those of objective scholarship. One approach, like Fredriksen's, is to compartmentalize Jewishness and scholarship. Adele Reinhartz has adopted both approaches. After several years of distancing her Jewishness from her scholarship, she makes her Jewishness the center of her recent book on the Gospel of John, *Befriending the Beloved Disciple*.

A friend once related to me a story about an academic conference on family photography. All the scholars in the room happened to be Jewish, but none of them called attention to this fact. My friend astutely observed that the failure to mention this was in fact a very Jewish (I would add, Ameri-

---

Yorker magazine identifies Fredriksen as a Jesus scholar but not a Jewish scholar (2003), and another review by Michael Medved refers to "Paula Fredriksen of Boston University" while specifically introducing David Klinghoffer as an "orthodox Jewish scholar" (2004). Since Fredriksen refers to her Catholic upbringing in one review of the film, one might erroneously conclude that she has remained Catholic (2004). I found a rather dilettantish online discussion of whether Fredriksen is Jewish or a liberal Catholic, which at the least demonstrates that Fredriksen has successfully separated her Jewish identity from her scholarship. In any case, the absence of biographical detail reflects the view that such information is irrelevant to the character and quality of one's scholarship.

can Jewish) thing to do, namely, to believe that one's Jewishness is completely irrelevant to one's activity in the secular world. In *Befriending the Beloved Disciple: A Jewish Reading of the Gospel of John*, Adele Reinhartz notes that her involvement in feminist biblical studies led her "to recognize that the scholarly objectivity I thought I could achieve by bracketing my Jewish identity was an illusion. I became aware of the degree to which my own work as well as that of other interpreters is affected in ways both explicit and implicit by our identities and allegiances" (2001, 14). Reinhartz adopts the position that confronting and engaging one's identity produces more objective scholarship because it exposes any ideological baggage that might burden one's reading of the evidence. It should not be overlooked that, in her early work, Reinhartz studiously avoided "Jewish" topics related to the New Testament (2001, 12–13; similarly, Brumberg-Kraus 1997, 139). Confronted with the realization that scholarship and identity are deeply implicated with each other, rather than easing into the topic, Reinhartz confronts what is for Jews the most difficult of the Gospels, the Gospel of John. What makes Reinhartz's book so significant is that she addresses directly the Gospel that is most alien and offensive to Jews. Instead of characterizing the Gospel of John as a book of little interest to the average Jewish person (à la Sandmel), Reinhartz experiments with a direct and close Jewish reading of the Gospel of John. Reinhartz explores the extreme in order to define the middle: in effect, she claims that if Jews can read the Gospel of John, they can read any book of the New Testament. And she goes further by modeling how a Jewish person might approach this text.

Let me briefly summarize Reinhartz's rich book, highlighting what makes her reading Jewish. Applying a theoretical model of "reading as relationship," Reinhartz argues that the author of the Fourth Gospel establishes friendship with the reader by offering a gift. "The gift offered by the Beloved Disciple is the promise of eternal life, through faith in Jesus as the Christ and Son of God" (Reinhartz 2001, 24). Unlike modern novels, where the reader is more or less free to accept or reject the gift, the Beloved Disciple demands that the reader receive the gift for his or her own sake: those who reject the gift are defined as evil and will perish (2001, 24–25). In addition, this gift is universal, offered to all peoples. As a result, the binary opposition between good and evil, between life and death, between those who accept and those who reject the gift applies to all peoples at all times. The reader of FG can adopt four different postures toward this gift. The compliant reader accepts the gift, while the resistant reader rejects the gift (2001, 54–98). These two stances essentially reflect the options offered by the author of FG. The resistant reader, however, cast in the position of the Other, need not accept the assumption that Otherness constitutes evilness and death. Rather, assuming that Otherness is legitimate creates a reading strategy outside the framework of the approaches allowed by the text. This dynamic generates Reinhartz's third and fourth reading strategies: a sympathetic reading, in which the reader ignores the divisive aspects of FG and focuses on the common elements; and an engaged reading, in which irreconcilable difference is addressed, acknowledged, and accepted (2001, 99–159).[9] Reinhartz explores all four readings by examining three levels of the Fourth Gospel's narrative: the history of Jesus; the cosmological tale of the Logos coming to the world and departing from the world in order to save humanity; and the ecclesiological story of the Johannine community (2001, 32–53).

From a Jewish point of view, the compliant reading of FG is particularly problematic. The historical story encodes a binary opposition between Jesus and his opponents. Since those who reject the gift of eternal life are characterized for the most part as "the Jews," the compliant reader would have to view Jews as negative role models responsible for the death of Jesus (2001, 65–66). Similarly, in the cosmological tale of good versus evil, Jews represent the unbelieving world, who stand not only in opposition to Jesus as a historical figure but also to God as a cosmological force for good in the world (2001, 69–70). The ecclesiological tale generates more problems because the scanty evidence for the Johannine community makes it more difficult and speculative to read the Fourth Gospel as a response to communal challenges. Reinhartz basically argues that for some reason the Johannine community saw their opponents as the Jews. Either the Johannine community was expelled from the synagogue or there was an inner-Jewish "family feud" in which some marginal Jews irately referred to their co-religionists as "the Jews." Regardless of why the Beloved Disciple chose the Jews as the negative pole for the identity of the Johannine community, the ecclesiological tale establishes a binary distinction between the Johannine community and "the Jews," with deep ethical implications. In short, the compliant reader must view the Jews as the enemies of Jesus, God, and the church.

The resistant reading, not surprisingly, is more congenial to Jews, but at the expense of the ideology of the text. Reading against the grain of the text, Reinhartz argues that the Jews in FG can be understood as the victims (2001, 87). As in any conflict, there are two sides to a story, but the Jewish version does not receive adequate or fair "airtime" and is inaccurately characterized by the Fourth Evangelist. Since the Roman role in Jesus' death is attenuated in favor of Jewish culpability, the resistant reader could argue that FG provides a tendentious, self-serving account of a more complex conflict that unfairly pil-

---

9. In reality, the sympathetic approach unconsciously reinscribes the Other as illegitimate, because one looks to the Other to find support for one's own position. Therefore, in being accepted only in part, the Other, as a whole, is rejected.

lories Jews (2001, 86–87). Similarly, in the case of the cosmological tale, Jewish opposition to Johannine cosmology does not receive fair treatment. Rather, the Jews have a different cosmological story and therefore view Jesus as a false prophet promulgating a system that encourages people to desert Judaism in favor of a system at odds with Jewish monotheism. Thus, the resistant reader opposes to the Johannine version a Jewish cosmological tale unmediated by the Beloved Disciple (2001, 87–95). As for the ecclesiological tale, where the evidence is much scantier, Reinhartz offers (but does not directly endorse) the plausible alternative that the Johannine community intentionally withdrew themselves from the synagogue but then disingenuously claimed that they were forced out (2001, 96–97). In short, then, according to the resistant reading, Jesus and the church should be seen primarily as the active enemies of the Jews and of God. While this story may be conducive to a Jewish (particularly a Jewish apologetic) reading, it reinscribes the binary opposition that generated conflict in the first place by demonizing the Beloved Disciple (2001, 98). Not only does the resistant reader reject the gift; she invalidates the gift for the compliant reader.

The sympathetic reader, in contrast, acknowledges value in the text. Devising a strategy for a Jewish reading sympathetic to the Fourth Gospel, Reinhartz demonstrates how Jewish texts and the Gospels share similar ideas. Of course, parallels between ancient Jewish literature and the Gospels have long been noted by historical critics, but Reinhartz uses this approach not to demonstrate a formal, historical relationship between these texts but rather as a basis for forming a relationship with the text of the Fourth Gospel. Thus, the Passover haggadah, like the Gospel of John, invites the reader to actually experience the historical tale and view it as a paradigm for the reader's own experiences. Likewise, both Jewish tradition and the Fourth Gospel utilize scriptural texts such as Song as Songs to construct meaning out of their historical experience (2001, 102–12). Readers of midrash and readers of the Gospel of John can talk about the Song of Songs as a parabolic intertext employed to articulate human and/or divine love (provided they do not discuss their irreconcilable disagreement regarding the historical expression of that love). Although Reinhartz cannot completely accept the metaphorical world in the cosmological tale of the Beloved Disciple, she does derive some value from this imaginative construct. Thus, Reinhartz can relate to the Beloved Disciple's anxiety about death and sees a similar response in classical Jewish texts, namely, the idea of overcoming death with eternal life (2001, 113–15). Likewise, both Jews and the Beloved Disciple imagine living simultaneously in this world and the world to come. For example, phrases such as "the hour is coming and is now here, when the dead will hear the voice of the Son of God, and those who hear will live" blur the distinction between present and future time (John 5:24–25; Reinhartz 2001, 117). Similarly, for Jews, the Sabbath as a "foretaste of the world to come" inserts the future holy world into the mundane secular world of the rest of the week.[10] Because of the practical nature and historical contingency of the ecclesiological narrative, this story is most conducive to a sympathetic reader. Reinhartz identifies with the women in the church, since contemporary Jews struggle with their ancient texts to define the role of women (2001, 119–26). Moreover, conflicts within the leadership typify religious organizations (not to mention most social groups). Tensions between Peter and the Beloved Disciple evoke images of Hillel and Shammai, while the problem of succession after the death of a leader parallels the story of Shabbetai Zevi and Rabbi Menahem Mendel Schneerson (2001, 126–30). As a person who belongs to a community of faith, the sympathetic Jewish reader and the Beloved Disciple have much to discuss, and this realization may form the basis of a friendship. Nonetheless, there are limits: in order to avoid conflict, the sympathetic reader ignores the most inflammatory topics. For example, even the sympathetic reading of the ecclesiological tale founders on the rocks of the specific historical circumstances (2001, 130). While a Jewish reader may sympathize with what Jesus' continued absence means for the Johannine community, she certainly does not believe or even want Jesus to return. Similarly, for the Beloved Disciple, Shabbetai Zevi must be a false Messiah.

It is in the engaged reading of the Fourth Gospel that Reinhartz addresses the tough, irreconcilable questions. For Reinhartz, the task is not to reach resolution but rather to label explicitly and precisely the areas of deep difference. In the case of the historical tale, Reinhartz cannot accept the image of Jesus in the Fourth Gospel—as a Jew, Reinhartz considers Jesus' humanity (not divinity) and Jewishness as axiomatic. Nevertheless, in one of the few opaque passages in her book, Reinhartz adopts a somewhat different perspective when discussing two fictional portrayals of Jesus by Norman Mailer and Philip Roth as particularly provocative Jewish responses to the Jesus question (2001, 137–40). Reinhartz describes how Mailer portrays a Jesus with the full range of human emotions and how Roth legitimates all discussion of God's omnipotence. I think that Reinhartz is suggesting two ideas here: she can relate to the Fourth Gospel in so far as it explores Jesus' inner consciousness, although she still assumes Jesus to be human; while Jews reject Jesus' divinity, they cannot deny the possibility of the virgin birth without denying God's omnipotence. Thus, the engaged reader can agree with the Beloved Disciple

---

10. Although the Beloved Disciple does not advocate Sabbath observance, Reinhartz reads Jesus' defense of Mary's anointing (John 12:7) as a transformation of present time into future time (2001, 117–18).

about God's power even if she disagrees about the particular exercise of that power in the case of Jesus. When Reinhartz cites Roth's character Ozzie, "You should never hit anybody about God" (2001, 140), I think she is simultaneously advocating the engaged reading and cautioning against the potentially violent responses that may come from the acknowledgment of irreconcilable differences.

Reinhartz has serious concerns about John's cosmological tale because its dichotomous, binary valence conflicts with her own deep commitment to pluralism (2001, 140). Although one could respond by finding scraps in the Fourth Gospel that valorize dissenting views, the sheer rareness of this appreciation of the Other reinforces the text's binary opposition between those who believe and those who do not. Similarly, Reinhartz rejects the possibility of a different metaphor of exclusivism, such as the "truth" of Judaism, because it reinscribes the binary opposition that she seeks to counter. Based on some contemporary examples within the Catholic Church and Judaism, Reinhartz ingeniously suggests that the binary view of the Fourth Gospel may not be a response to another exclusivist system but rather a response to a nonexclusivist pluralism (2001, 145–52). Thus, the argument is not whether or not Jesus is the Messiah but whether the fundamental core of Judaism was the monotheistic, covenantal relationship between God and Israel or a salvific messianism. In other words, the dispute in the cosmological tale is not over who are the good and who are the wicked but rather whether the world can be divided so neatly. Thus, Reinhartz does not disagree with FG's cosmological tale simply because it is incarnated in Jesus (a point at which Jews and Christians can never agree), but rather because it rejects a pluralistic view. Such a dispute may not be easier to resolve. This rejection of binary thinking makes Reinhartz seem more like a resistant rather than an engaged reader.

Enter, then, the ecclesiological tale. Here Reinhartz suggests that the Beloved Disciple is somewhat at odds with his own community (2001, 152–57). The Beloved Disciple reflects an internal Jewish conflict, but the issue is not over faith in Jesus as the Messiah but rather the significance of messianism within Judaism. His overemphasis on Christology underdetermines the portrayal of Mary and Martha at Bethany: both believe in Jesus but are also comfortably involved within the Jewish community (2001, 155). In short, the engaged reading of FG's ecclesiological tale leads Reinhartz to the conclusion that the Beloved Disciple imposed a binary history of exclusivism on a community that initially coexisted with the Jewish community. He did this because his worldview, so incompatible with a pluralistic system, made him feel as Other in relationship to the Jewish community. An engaged Jewish reader can certainly understand the experience of Otherness.

Ultimately, however, Reinhartz cannot befriend the Beloved Disciple (2001, 162–63). Friendship is impossible through a compliant or resistant reading: the former requires the Jew to reject her Judaism; the latter requires her to reject the Fourth Gospel's message. A sympathetic reading could produce an unhealthy friendship undermined by denial of the irreconcilable differences. The greatest potential lies in the engaged reading, but Reinhartz cannot relate to the Beloved Disciple as an equal who accepts difference (nor can the Beloved Disciple accept her). Even though she may understand the source of the Beloved Disciple's binary discourse, she simply cannot accept it. Nor can the Beloved Disciple surrender that discourse without, for all intents and purposes, ceasing to be the Beloved Disciple.

On the surface then, Reinhartz does indeed reflect the typical response of the Jewish reader of the Fourth Gospel. She reiterates the essential Jewish axiomatic rejection of salvation through Jesus. She exemplifies why it is important for there to be Jewish scholars of the New Testament: as a necessary reminder of the implications of these texts and as an existential stimulus to the question of scholarly objectivity (considerations that should apply to all scholars, regardless of their backgrounds). She does go beyond Sandmel, however, in two important ways: she has a much more positive view of the Fourth Gospel's literary qualities; and she offers an additional reason for Jewish rejection of the Beloved Disciple's gift. In addition to rejecting Johannine Christology, Jewish people should reject the binary thinking that characterizes the text.[11] Moreover, she offers a new way for Jewish people to engage in the text: Jews can relate to the story of an emerging community of faith. And even on the more specific historical level, Jews can identify with the struggle between an exclusivist and pluralistic ideology.

When Robinson wrote his article on the "new look" in 1957, he hardly could have imagined a Jewish feminist literary reading of the Fourth Gospel. Having said that, however, the result of Reinhartz's analysis very much correlates with Robinson's fifth trend: increasing interest in the Johannine tradition and issues facing the Johannine community. Reinhartz argues that the Gospel of John embodies a binary worldview because it opposed the more pluralistic Jewish community and emerged from an internal Jewish conflict over the role of messianism in Judaism. Reinhartz's reading rests on the assumption that the Gospel of John has a degree of independence. Also in line with the new look, Reinhartz argues that FG reflects a Jewish background, that its theology reflects an independent theological tradition (not simply the culmination of a

---

11. Reinhartz's claim to be *a* Jewish reader is crucial here, because one could find other Jewish readers who have a binary view of the world.

historical theological progression), and that its authorship must be discussed in terms of the Johannine community. The one dimension of the "new look" that does not affect Reinhartz is the question of the historicity of the information about Jesus in the Fourth Gospel. This stems, I believe, from her literary approach to the text. Following the new historicism, she attempts to situate the general ideology of the text, rather than specific details of the narrative, within a historical context. Her interest in history centers on the Johannine community rather than on Jesus.

Such a summary of Reinhartz's position effaces the self-acknowledged fact of her Jewishness because it represents a legitimate scholarly reading of the Gospel of John that any contemporary researcher could make. Rather, Reinhartz utilizes her Jewishness as a vehicle for presenting her thoughts about the text. In essence, Reinhartz is performing what I have argued from the beginning, a distinction between the scholar as discoverer of new knowledge and transmitter of new knowledge. Her interpretations, analyses, and research adhere to the canons of objective scholarship. In order to transmit this scholarship, she embraces the persona of a Jewish woman. As a result, she situates the reading of the Gospel of John into a late twentieth-century context. Rather than assume that academic analysis of the Fourth Gospel has no relevance or impact on society as a whole, Reinhartz explores what it means for a modern Jew to encounter this book through an academic exegetical tradition. In addition to answering the question, What do we know about the Gospel of John? Reinhartz also asks, How do we talk about the Gospel of John?

Summary of Jewish Readings

This brief survey of four Jewish academics enables us to develop a taxonomy of Jewish scholarship on the Fourth Gospel. (1) Jewish scholarship will always have an internal and external apologetic character. Even Reinhartz herself admits this. The Jewish scholar must always confront anti-Jewish implications of New Testament texts, whether by acknowledging their existence or demonstrating their unhistoricalness.

(2) Jewish scholarship has an additional apologetic role: to explain Christianity to Jews. In explaining why a Jewish scholar reads the Gospels, the Jewish scholar also explains why Jews should read the Gospels. Jewish scholars must also explain to Jews why they should reject the gift of the Beloved Disciple.

(3) Jewish scholarship begs the question of scholarly objectivity. I do not mean that Jewish scholars are not objective but that acknowledging their Jewishness requires them to address this issue. This is simply a small subset of the

broader reality that scholarship is contingent upon historical and sociological circumstances.

(4) What makes a reading Jewish is the Jewishness of the reader, not the use of Jewish sources to interpret the New Testament. Past notions that only Jews could interpret the New Testament in relationship to its Jewish background were fallaciously based on historically determined demographic realities. For most of the twentieth century, the scholars of Jewish literature were primarily Jewish, for a variety of sociological and historical reasons. There is no reason, however, to assume that Jewish people somehow understand the rabbinic literature better than non-Jews. To be sure, there will always be more incentives for Jewish scholars to become familiar with Jewish sources and consequently to bring these to bear on their studies. But this is a far cry from characterizing a reading based on Jewish sources as Jewish.

(5) Jewish scholarship on the New Testament is critical simply because the New Testament continues to play a prominent role in social discourse in society as a whole. Specifically here, since the Fourth Gospel continues to play a formative role in contemporary society and because it clearly impacts attitudes towards Jews, Jewish scholars must continue to bear witness to the broader social implications of Johannine scholarship. I do not mean to exclude other constituencies as well—the same arguments would apply *mutatis mutandis*. Having said that, however, the fact that Jews play such a prominent role in the Fourth Gospel does make a Jewish presence in the guild of scholars essential.

(6) What can we say about the future of Jewish readings of the Gospel of John? In identifying her work as *a* Jewish person's reading of the Gospel of John, Reinhartz invites other Jewish scholars to do the same. If Jewish scholars follow her model, we will be able to explore further what a "Jewish reading" might entail.

The taxonomy outlined above indicates that Jewishness plays a central role in one's teaching about the Gospel of John rather than in one's research on the Gospel of John. Both Sandmel and Reinhartz have employed their Jewish personae in popular works that primarily transmit contemporary scholarship about the Fourth Gospel rather than contribute to academic discussion.[12] Fredriksen's Jewishness hardly emerges in her academic writing but rather in her participation in public debate outside of academia. Boyarin's Jewishness is more tricky because he follows the canons appropriate to the academic venue in which he writes about the Fourth Gospel. Nevertheless, he is acutely

---

12. Of course, Sandmel and Reinhartz have also published serious academic books and articles in scholarly journals without emphasizing their Jewishness.

aware of the ideological implications of scholarship; see, for example, his review of Lawrence Hoffman's *Covenant of Blood*, which criticizes Hoffman's attempt to invoke scholarly objectivity in a work deeply imbricated with the valorization of Reform Judaism (Boyarin 1997b). Since Boyarin is Jewish, his argument for a Jewish binitarianism should not be read as a reinscription of Christian supersessionism ("if Jews followed their own theology, they would recognize Christ"). Rather, I think his argument should be read more as a critique of contemporary Jewish binary thinking, particularly as manifested in a common discursive distinction between Judaism and Christianity. In other words, speaking to scholars as a scholar, Boyarin lays out an argument that may or may not convince his colleagues. Speaking as a Jew to Jews, Boyarin presents a challenge that would be understood much differently coming from a Christian.

Befriending Nicodemus

As a rabbi and a scholar, I will test my theory that Jewishness matters more in the presentation of the Fourth Gospel than in the research concerning it by imagining how I would explain the Nicodemus episode to two distinct audiences, one Jewish and the other Christian. I would begin both explanations in the same way with a description of the episode and the common issues discussed by scholars. Then I would move the presentation in different directions, depending on the audience. The following discussion should not be seen as an exact script for a teaching session but rather as an outline of the salient points.

The Issues

Nicodemus appears only in the Gospel of John, where we encounter him three times (3:1–21; 7:49–52; 19:38–42). Since the primary episode occurs in chapter 3, it deserves quoting several verses at length:

> Now there was a man of the Pharisees, named Nicodemus, a ruler of the Jews. This man came to Jesus by night and said to him, "Rabbi, we know that you are a teacher come from God; for no one can do these signs that you do, unless God is with him." Jesus answered him, "Truly, truly, I say to you, unless one is born anew, he cannot see the kingdom of God." Nicodemus said to him, "How can a man be born when he is old? Can he enter a second time into his mother's womb and be born?" Jesus answered, "Truly, truly, I say to you, unless one is born of water and the Spirit, he cannot enter the kingdom of God. That which is born of the flesh is flesh, and that which is born of the Spirit is spirit. Do not marvel that I said to you, 'You must be born anew.' The wind blows where it wills, and you hear the sound of it, but you do not know whence it comes or whither it goes;

so it is with every one who is born of the Spirit." Nicodemus said to him, "How can this be?" Jesus answered him, "Are you a teacher of Israel, and yet you do not understand this? Truly, truly, I say to you, we speak of what we know, and bear witness to what we have seen; but you do not receive our testimony. If I have told you earthly things and you do not believe, how can you believe if I tell you heavenly things? No one has ascended into heaven but he who descended from heaven, the Son of Man. And as Moses lifted up the serpent in the wilderness, so must the Son of Man be lifted up, that whoever believes in him may have eternal life." (John 3:1–15; unless otherwise noted, all biblical quotations are taken from the NRSV)

Late one evening, the Pharisee and Jewish leader Nicodemus visits Jesus and engages in a dialogue about being "born again/from above" (*anōthen*; John 3:3). In a Gospel that divides the world between believers in Christ and "Jews," Nicodemus plays an ambiguous, liminal role. On the one hand, addressing Jesus as a rabbi and teacher who has performed miracles, he acknowledges that God is with Jesus. On the other hand, Jesus criticizes Nicodemus for not understanding what it means to be born again or born from above. Such ignorance implies that Nicodemus will not be able to enter the kingdom of God. The context of the story particularly highlights Nicodemus's liminality (see Brown 1966–70, 1:129, 137–38; Paulien 1992). In the verses immediately preceding chapter 3, we learn that Jesus does not entrust himself to those who believe in his name as a result of the signs he has performed, because he knows what is in a person (*anthrōpos*, 2:24–25). The Fourth Gospel utilizes the term *anthrōpos* ("human being") to describe the believer or potential believer in Jesus. It is the *anthrōpos* who could be "born again" (3:4), and Jesus is the son of *anthrōpos* (3:14). As we see throughout the narrative, the term "Jews" refers to the opponents of Jesus. Therefore, the description of Nicodemus as both *anthrōpos* ("*man* of the Pharisees") and Jewish (leader of the Jews; 3:1) situates him in both the anti-Jesus Jewish camp and the potentially believing human camp at once. Similarly, in the discourse following the episode, Jesus concludes with a distinction between light and darkness: the good and truthful love the light, while the evil embrace darkness (Brown 1966–70, 1:130; Reinhartz 2001, 68). Thus, the timing of Nicodemus's visit has symbolic significance. Although a legitimate reading of the text indicates that Nicodemus came "at night," the text could also be translated "from night" (3:1). Nicodemus represents a person coming *from* the night of unbelief into the light of Christ (3:19). Jesus' gentle rebuke of Nicodemus indicates that he still remains somewhere between the darkness and light (Tanzer 1991, 293).

Even when Nicodemus appears again in the story, he occupies an in-between space in the Fourth Gospel's binary scheme (Sevrin 2001, 367). When the high priests and Pharisees castigate their servants for not arresting

Jesus, Nicodemus defends him. "Nicodemus, who had gone to him before, and who was one of them, said to them, 'Does our law judge a man without first giving him a hearing and learning what he does?' " (John 7:50–51). Nicodemus does not, however, publicly profess his faith in Jesus but rather argues only that Jesus should be given a chance to defend himself. Finally, when Nicodemus appears in the story a third time to bury Jesus, John associates him with a secret believer, Joseph of Arimathea, and attributes his motivations not to full-fledged belief but rather to the desire to provide Jesus a decent Jewish burial.

> After this Joseph of Arimathea, who was a disciple of Jesus, but secretly, for fear of the Jews, asked Pilate that he might take away the body of Jesus, and Pilate gave him leave. So he came and took away his body. Nicodemus also, who had at first come to him by night, came bringing a mixture of myrrh and aloes, about a hundred pounds' weight. They took the body of Jesus, and bound it in linen cloths with the spices, as is the burial custom of the Jews. (John 19:38–40)

The questions raised by scholars concerning Nicodemus typify developing trends in Johannine scholarship (see Paulien 1992; Sevrin 2001, 357 n. 1, 358 n. 2; Tanzer 1991). Scholars once wondered whether Nicodemus represents an actual historical figure who can be equated to certain Jews of the same name who appear in rabbinic literature. With the rise of literary studies, however, the focus has shifted from Nicodemus's historicity to his characterization and function. How does Nicodemus relate to the narrative? Does the text view him positively or negatively? Does he develop throughout the story or remain the same? How does he appeal to the Fourth Gospel's potential audience? A variety of answers have been given to these questions. Nicodemus ranges from the positive Jewish sympathizer to the rejected partial believer to the consistently ambiguous figure.

FOR A JEWISH AUDIENCE

What are we to make of this Jewish leader who shows interest in and sympathy for Jesus? As a Jew, I would certainly view Nicodemus differently than the author of the Fourth Gospel did. Rather than wondering to what extent Nicodemus accepts the gift of the Beloved Disciple, I, to paraphrase Reinhartz, see Nicodemus as a good person teetering on the brink of faith in Jesus, one who, I hope, will not succumb but remain committed to Judaism (Reinhartz 2001, 97). Another Jewish scholar also shares Reinhartz's perspective. After arguing that the Nicodemus episode should be understood as an appeal to Jewish-Christians (Christians who both believed in Jesus and adhered to Jewish practices) to choose Christianity instead of Judaism, Sarah Tanzer concludes,

"John makes a powerful hortatory appeal to these closet Christian Jews. One only wishes that history had preserved the appeal made by the other [Jewish] side" (1991, 300). Instead of wondering whether and how Nicodemus commits to faith in Jesus, Jewish readers positively imagine him remaining within the Jewish fold.

In alluding to the possibility of a Jewish counterargument to Johannine teaching, Tanzer also points to the historical interest Jews might have in Nicodemus. He is like an archaeological artifact of antiquity that provides information about Jews of the first century C.E. Our interpretation of Nicodemus, however, depends heavily on its context. We cannot ignore that his portrayal is highly colored by the ideology of the Fourth Gospel. Despite this representation, Nicodemus can also tell us something about ancient Jews who showed interest in Jesus without surrendering their Judaism. Here our own context becomes relevant. Western Jews, deeply embedded in a Christianized society, can identify with a Jew who shows interest in Christianity. We, however, represent a minority that is subject to a dominant majority culture, whereas Nicodemus represents the majority culture approaching the minority ideology. Moreover, the Judaism and Christianity of our times reflect the developments of two millennia. Therefore, when we say that the Jew Nicodemus was interested in Jesus, we have to understand that "Jew" and "Jesus" meant something different then than they do now. Finally, we have the legacy or burden of a history of Jewish-Christian encounters, whereas Nicodemus did not really have a well-developed model.

For me, then, the story of Nicodemus indicates that the Judaism of his time could be in sympathetic dialogue with Johannine teaching. Nicodemus symbolizes the Jew who chooses to engage Jesus open-mindedly and—contrary to the desire of the Beloved Disciple but to my own delight—does not fully believe in the Fourth Gospel's teachings. Put in the terms of Reinhartz, Nicodemus tries to befriend Jesus, but Jesus rejects him. Even so, Nicodemus publicly defends Jesus' right to be heard and provides him with a decent burial. Like Nicodemus, we might not fully understand or agree with Christian theology, but we can still treat Christians with respect. Such a Jew may seem ambiguous from a Christian point of view, but I would argue (from my own liberal Jewish perspective) that Nicodemus unambiguously models how Jews should relate to Christians.

For a Christian Audience

Despite the clearly anti-Jewish sentiments of the Gospel of John, Nicodemus seems to be one of the few positive Jewish characters. I would like to suggest, however, that in fact Nicodemus reinscribes the binary, anti-Jewish model. For Christian readers, or rather, in accordance with the ideology of the Fourth Gospel, Nicodemus represents someone on the path to Christianity (Tanzer 1991, 287). Thus, as one scholar puts it, "one could think that the Fourth Gospel develops the character of Nicodemus as a way to leave an opening to the Jews in their relation to Jesus" (Sevrin 2001, 369). Yet from a Jewish point of view this positive portrayal of a Jew is intimately related to a severe critique of Judaism. What makes Nicodemus positive is the extent of his attraction to Jesus. Since the story demonstrates the sheer power of the Gospel's message (the identity of Jesus as Christ and the possibility of eternal life through faith), it simultaneously diminishes the power of Jewish teaching. Framed in a different way, the attraction of Nicodemus to Jesus indicates that his own community did not offer him something (Reinhartz 2001, 65).

It is certainly nothing new to suggest that categorizing Jews at different stages on the path to Christianity deeply offends Jewish sensibilities. Having said that, however, I think that Jews and Christians must acknowledge that the Fourth Gospel does view Jews in this manner. According to the Gospel of John, a Jew who adheres to Judaism and refuses to identify Jesus as the Christ has left the road that leads to the teaching offered by the Beloved Disciple. Therefore, in order to accept Jews as Jews, Christian readers must reject the gift of the Beloved Disciple. By contrast, in order to accept the gift, Christian readers must reject the legitimacy of Judaism. I can live with Christian acceptance of the Beloved Disciple's gift, however, out of respect for a Christian ideology that has numerous other assumptions that I cannot accept. In a sense, like Nicodemus, I will listen to Christians and defend their right to be heard. I will even risk providing Jesus with a decent Jewish burial. Christians must realize that Jews cannot go as far as the Fourth Gospel requires, but Jews should realize that they can go further than the Pharisees. Like Reinhartz, I cannot befriend the Beloved Disciple. I can, however, befriend Nicodemus.

The Johannine Community: Caught in "Two Worlds"

Yak-hwee Tan

In the early 1990s the term "globalization" was used primarily by people in the world of economics. The word was used to teach students in business administration with respect to how to market and often to establish production beyond the boundaries of their own nation-state. However, by the turn of the millennium, globalization had become a central topic of debate across the social-science disciplines. Anthony Giddens, a renowned British social political scientist, sees globalization beyond the dimension of economics. He defines "globalization" as follows:

> Globalisation can ... be defined as the intensification of world-wide social relations which link distant localities in such a way that local happenings are shaped by events occurring many miles away and vice versa. This is a dialectical process because such local happenings may move in an obverse direction from the very distanciated relations that shape them. Local transformation is as much a part of globalisation as the lateral extension of social connections across time and space. (Giddens 1990, 64)

In other words, besides the global marketplace, every fabric of our lives is influenced by globalization, "restructuring the ways in which we live, and in a very profound manner" (Giddens 2000, 22), but Giddens also acknowledges that globalization is a complex and paradoxical process. Some think that the result of globalization is a "pulling away" of power or influence from local communities and nations into the global arenas, but the effect can also be seen in the revival of local cultural identities and rise of nationalism (Giddens 2000, 30–31).

With respect to the revival of local cultural identities, some traditional societies resist the impact of globalization. For example, global influences may lead women to stake their claim to greater equality; to counter such threats to the established social order, some traditional societies maintain even more fervently the belief of the "traditional family," whereby the equality of sexes and the sexual freedom of women are suppressed. An example is seen when respectable girls are praised for their virginity and wives are applauded for their fidelity and virtues (Giddens 2000, 73). Giddens sees the opposition of sexual equality and freedom as "one of the defining features of religious fundamentalism across the world" (2000, 83). That is to say, religious traditions are required to justify, for example, the subordination of women and children. Samuel Huntington foresaw that such inharmonious relationships, in light of the conditions of modernization brought about by globalization, are likely to happen. Huntington portrays such discordant relationships as "the clash between civilizations" (1993, 22–50). The term "civilizations" is defined as idea systems, which take two main forms: (1) universal religions, whereby the social and religious fabric of the society are "culturalized" successfully; (2) political ideologies "that sought to unify diverse collectivities of people in the pursuit of common goals" (Waters 2001, 161).

Cultural identities not only also seek to legitimize the general idea of a "traditional family" or a social group ("a people") but also, for some societies, lead to the construction of the idea of a nation-state or nationalism (Ashcroft, Griffiths, and Tiffin 1998, 150–51). The idea of the nation-state arises when the once-colonized people begin to engage in a complex process of contesting, as well as appropriating, colonialist versions of the past with respect to their history and culture. The once-colonized people seek to reconstruct their histories, cultures, and identities from their own viewpoints.

The process of globalization has also impacted biblical criticism and biblical hermeneutics. That is to say, readers from the once-colonized societies have now begun to read ancient texts, including the Bible, from their own cultural perspectives. These readers employ a variety of methods and theories from other disciplines, including literary criticism, sociology, and cultural anthropology. Moreover, some readers use these methodologies with a specific strategy in mind, such as the promotion of a feminist or liberationist stance. Such approaches depart dramatically from John A. T. Robinson's "new look" on John. In his article "The New Look on the Fourth Gospel," Robinson revisited five presuppositions that raised questions regarding the authorship of the Fourth Gospel and the historical factors that might have influenced the writing of that book (1962b, 94–106). However, many contemporary readers of the Fourth Gospel would propose other ways of reading the text, raising questions beyond authorship and sources. In this essay I will offer a reading of John's "vine discourse" (John 15:1–11) that is conditioned by the impact of globalization, that is, a reading that is postcolonial in nature.

The effects of globalization give rise to the revival of cultural identities and nationalism, as well as what postcolonial theorists call "postcoloniality."

In the words of Leela Gandhi, postcoloniality "is just another name for the globalisation of cultures and histories." That is to say, in light of the globalized nature of the world, exemplified in prevailing and extensive cybertechnologies such as the Internet, national borders can no longer be maintained. With the movement of people and information from one location to another made more accessible, "identitarian" politics are called into question (Gandhi 1998, 126). In other words, the preservation and perpetuation of essentialized racial/ethnic identities by the metropolitan center, which seeks to confirm and stabilize the hegemonic notion of their superiority over an ethnicity that is always seen as marginal or peripheral, must be interrogated (Hall 1990, 227).[1]

In his work *Orientalism,* Edward Said demonstrates the close relationship between the production of Western knowledge and the non-Western world. He asserts that "Orientalism" is a discourse whereby European culture manages and produces the Orient (Said 1979, 1–9). That is to say, the representation of the civilization and culture of the Orient is ideologically constructed through writings, doctrines, vocabulary, and scholarships in various disciplines of academic institutions as well as colonial bureaucracies. As such, the basic distinction between "the West" (Occident) and "the East" (Orient) becomes the starting point for the study of the Orient (and the Occident). Consequently, the idea "of European identity as a superior one in comparison with all the non-European peoples and cultures" and the notion that there is such a thing as "a pure, or unconditional Orient" are brought to the fore (Said 1979, 7, 23). However, paradoxically, the encounter between the West and the Orient brought about a "dangerously unOtherable," and, in the words of Rey Chow, "the native is no longer available as the pure, unadulterated object of Orientalist inquiry—she is contaminated by the West" (Chow 1993, 12). Moreover, in the face of globalization and postcolonialism, the notion of the "pure Other of the West" is jeopardized as such phenomena bring about the "mutual contagion and subtle intimacies" of the colonizers and the colonized, or of the "Self" and "Other" or "center" and "margins" (first quotation Spivak 1990, 8; second quotation Gandhi 1998, 129). In short, globalization brought about the meeting of two identities, resulting in the construction of a new identity, one that is *"neither the one nor the other"* (Bhabha 1994b, 25). Through globalization, a hybridized identity is created for both the Self and the Other.

---

1. In his observations on Thatcherite Britain, Hall contends that essentialism is a convenient way of constructing the identity of the Other as "exotic" or "ethnic." In the process, the hegemonic notion of "Englishness" is confirmed and stabilized. "Englishness" or "Americanness" is never represented as "ethnicity."

Poetics and Politics of the Text

According to Michel Foucault, a "discourse" may be defined as "some material medium" whereby all ideas are ordered, organized, and patterned by certain unspoken rules. The "order of discourse" includes what could be said and what not, what is included as acceptable and what is rejected as unacceptable, and so forth (Foucault 1970, 100). Thus, Foucault raises questions regarding the nature of the unspoken rules that determine the nature of a discourse and also the identity of the authors who ordered such a discourse. At the end of his analysis, he advances the notion that knowledge and power are interdependent. That is to say, knowledge and power are connected and also serve and reinforce each other; "there is no power relation without the correlative constitution of a field of knowledge, nor any knowledge that does not presuppose and constitute at the same time power relations" (Foucault 1977, 27). In other words, the powerful have the power to construct and regulate knowledge and, more precisely, to construct the *kind* of knowledge concerning the "powerless." To put it another way, one sees both the *poetics* and *politics* of the discourse/text at work (Tolbert 1995, 305–17).[2] The *poetics* of the text lie in the discursive nature of the text, such as the imperial-colonial ideology embedded in the Fourth Gospel, while the *politics* of the text lie in the imperial-colonial framework of its real flesh-and-blood readers.

The real flesh-and-blood readers of a text, who are influenced by their political, social, economic, and cultural conditions, will use what Fernando Segovia has called a "postcolonial optic" to uncover and question the embedded colonial ideologies that have been inscribed in the text by those in power (Segovia 1998a, 49–65).[3] The disclosure of such colonial ideology in ancient texts by the Other challenges people, namely, the Self who "regulates conduct, makes up or constructs identities and subjectivities" (Hall 1997a, 6). In current postcolonial theory, the Other is the colonized subject whose identity is established by the colonizing culture and worldview. The Other is characterized as dependent, and his or her identity is understood in relation to the Self, namely, the colonizers (Ashcroft, Griffiths, and Tiffin 1998, 170–71). As Hall

---

2. Tolbert argues that the *politics* of location emphasizes the "multiplicity, complexity, and contextuality of human experience" and raises questions concerning the writing of the text, its ideology, and so forth. On the other hand, the *poetics* of location analyzes the text understood as "constitutive of reality," raising the question of the language of power and the construction of positive or negative representations of others.

3. In this essay Segovia shows the relationship between postcolonial biblical hermeneutics and postcolonial theory and discourse. The purpose of such hermeneutical strategy, he argues, should be not only descriptive but also prescriptive; that is, it should effect transformation.

argues, the meaning of representation could not exist without *difference*. *Difference* is critical for the construction of the binary opposites Self and Other or center and margins; that is, the Self defines "the way certain things are represented, thought about, practised and studied" (Hall 1997a, 6; see also 1997b, 229). The colonizers, and/or the subjugated people themselves, select and design information concerning the subjugated group and re-present them from their perspective; in the process, the subjugated are encouraged to appropriate the idiom of the colonizers (Pratt 1992, 7). Such a stance is the result of the colonial encounter, whereby the boundaries of colonizer and colonized or Self and Other or center and margins are no longer fixed or exclusive. The real flesh-and-blood reader of the Fourth Gospel, such as I, is thus hybrid in nature.

Furthermore, since power functions in a capillary fashion, no discourse is privileged to be exercised by any binary opposites (Gandhi 1998, 14).[4] Any individual can be a vehicle of power. Therefore, with respect to the *poetics* of a text, texts are not neutral or static but rather can be contested as "contact zones." According to Pratt, a "contact zone" is a temporal space where both the colonizers and the colonized come in contact with each other, interacting and coercing one another's understanding and practices (Pratt 1992, 6–7). In so doing, the fixed binary opposites of Self and Other or center and margins become fluid, paving the way for the outworking(s) of hybridity.

Hybridization takes many forms: linguistic, cultural, political, and so forth. Bakhtin's model of linguistic hybridity broaches on what he calls "intentional hybridity," the notion that every text is "inevitably internally dialogic. Two points of view are not mixed, but set against each other dialogically" (Bakhtin 1981, 360). That is to say, within the boundaries of a syntactical linguistic whole, or even within a single sentence, different meanings or viewpoints contest one another, each with the potential to expose the other. Hybridity is thus a dialectic process. In a similar fashion, Bhabha discusses hybridity on the basis of his analysis of colonizer-colonized relations and asserts that relationships between the colonizer and the colonized give rise to the "splitting" of different facets within different cultures. As such, one's identity is never stable: one is never fully a colonizer nor fully colonized but "something else besides" (Bhabha 1994b, 107, 97). Both Bakhtin and Bhabha concur that hybridity implies the notion that "the fixity or essentiality of identity is continually contested" (Sanga 2001, 75). In other words, the "multivocal language situations" of the text and the "something else besides" identity of

---

4. With reference to Foucault's notion of "power," Gandhi comments that "if power is available as a form of 'subjection,' it is also a procedure which is 'subjectivised' through, and within, particular individuals."

the colonizer/colonized offer an opportune strategy for postcolonial critics to dismantle the fixed boundaries of colonizer and colonized, Self and Other, center and margins

The present study will explore the question, What does globalization and postcoloniality have to do with the question of the identity of the Johannine community? On the one hand, the Johannine community was subjected to the rule of the Roman Empire; on the other hand, they were followers of Jesus Christ. Such a situation poses the question of the community's allegiance: Are they for Rome or against Rome? The issue of allegiance, in turn, raises the question of the identity of the Johannine community. The vine discourse, I will argue, delineates the Johannine community as a group caught between the world of the Roman Empire and the world of Jesus Christ.

The Vine Discourse and the Johannine Community

In the recent history of research, scholars have undertaken the characterization of the Johannine community, applying different theoretical approaches and reading strategies to the Fourth Gospel. From the point of view of historical criticism, many have seen the community as a group expelled from the synagogue because of their belief in and understanding of Jesus' identity as the Christ. Such (re)constructions focus on the environment—Jewish, Christian, and Gentile—surrounding the Johannine community/communities (see Martyn 1979; Brown 1979). Other scholars use reading strategies that explicitly bring their own personal ideologies to the text; that is, they openly identify "specific sets of interests and commitments" in their readings (Pregeant 1997, 19; Pippin 1996, 51–78). For example, writing from a feminist perspective, Gail O'Day highlights the significant role that women play in the Fourth Gospel and thus argues for an egalitarian community (1998, 381–93).[5] Another ideological approach is propounded by Glass, who uses the vine discourse to demonstrate that discursive practices are at work in the text, "in the act of building a new nation-ness—that is, the vine." Glass associates the themes of membership and assimilation into the vine with modern concepts of citizenship. In so doing, she argues that "membership into a new political order" is constructed through a dialectic of binary opposites, such as "inclusion" and "exclusion" (Glass 2002, 162–64).

While Glass focuses on the question of citizenship and nation, my reading of the vine discourse from a postcolonial perspective will attempt to delin-

---

5. O'Day cites seven passages from the Fourth Gospel in support of her thesis: 2:1–11; 4:4–42; 7:53–8:11; 11:1–44; 12:1–8; 19:25–27; 20:1–18. For another example of an ideological approach, see Rensberger 1988.

eate the identity of the Johannine community as one caught in "two worlds." Such an approach is pertinent, since the vine discourse describes the relationship between vine and the branches, representing the relationship between Jesus and the disciples as well as the disciples' relationship with the "world." As such, the disciples are caught in the contentious relationship between Jesus and the world, in "two worlds." The "two worlds" model as used here is adapted from Fernando Segovia's notion of "two worlds," which he describes as "this-world" and "other-world." For him, "this-world" refers to the world where the disciples will be left behind after Jesus' departure to the world of the Father, the "other-world." The term "this-world" refers to the encompassing imperial reality of the Roman Empire, which includes the political, social, cultural, and religious conditions (Segovia 1998b, 183–209). My discussion will follow Segovia's model of "two worlds"; here I will refer to his "this-world" as "world-below" and to his "other-world" as "world-above."

In applying Segovia's model, my reading of John 15 will reflect the intersection of methodological concerns and personal experience. In terms of method, my reading will utilize insights from postcolonial studies, applied to a literary-rhetorical analysis of the vine discourse. From the field of postcolonial studies, the question of binary opposites, identity, and hybridity will be used to construct the identity of the Johannine community. Literary and rhetorical devices such as ambiguity and irony will assist me in characterizing the Johannine community as "hybridized." In terms of experience, I will approach the text as a real flesh-and-blood reader informed by my own colonial and postcolonial experiences. As one whose heritage is Chinese and Confucian but who became a Christian during her youth at a Christian mission school and whose education has been primarily Western, Christian, and Eurocentric in character, I cannot deny that my encounters with the West and Christianity have produced a "mixed" Yak-hwee, an "in-between" person. My identity is no longer an essentialized one but one that embodies a clashing of classes, nationalities, religions, and ethnicities. Therefore, my analysis of the Johannine community as "hybridized" is a personally engaging and challenging project.

THE VINE DISCOURSE AT THE INTERSECTION OF "TWO WORLDS"

At different periods of biblical history, the dominance of empires with respect to the land and people of their colonies was overarching. The biblical writers were not unaffected by the colonial environment to which they belonged. Therefore, the "full artistic production and hence the full literary production of the imperial framework in question, whether of the center or of the margins" in both the "world of antiquity" and the "world of contemporary

Christianity" must be taken into consideration in one's reading strategy of the biblical texts (Segovia 1998a, 56–63). In other words, the Bible is a discourse where both *poetics* and *politics* are at work. The vine discourse of John 15 is no exception.

The structure of the vine discourse falls naturally into two major divisions, 15:1–17 and 15:18–27 (see Segovia 1991).[6] The first division focuses on Jesus and the disciples, whereas the second is about the world's hostility toward the disciples because of their collusion with Jesus. Unlike the discourses in John 13 and 14, which focus on Jesus' departure and its ramifications for the disciples, the vine discourse of John 15 focuses on the role of the Johannine community, represented by the disciples, with respect to their relationships with Jesus, with one another, and with the world-below. Such relationships are underscored by the underlying themes of "love," "hate," and "remaining/abiding." Using the vine discourse as an illustration, I will characterize the Johannine community as one that is in a "flux"—"caught in two worlds."

In his previous statements Jesus has declared that there was no other "way," "truth," and "life" (John 14:6); similarly, at the beginning of the vine discourse, Jesus affirms that he is not only the vine but the "true" vine (15:1a). He thus claims exclusivity vis-à-vis all other allegations. In so doing, Jesus sets up the *difference* between Self and Other. Metaphorically, the Self is the vine, while the Other is the branches. By delineating the *difference*, which is a convenient way of defining the Other, Jesus fortifies the hegemonic identity of the Self (Hall 1989, 227). Therefore, within the introductory section of the discourse, the boundaries and identity of the community are delineated. The self-definition of the members of the Johannine community is tied with Jesus, the Self of the community, and they are bound by certain conditions, such as fruit-bearing, lest they be thrown out.

The hegemonic identity of the Self is further strengthened in the way Jesus exercises "a politics of internal positioning" (Glass 2002, 166). Jesus sets himself as "a politically conscious, unified revolutionary Self, standing in unmitigated opposition" to all others who challenge his position (Parry 1987, 30). This challenge is illustrated by way of the "unfruitful" branches. Jesus is "the source of life and fruitfulness," and the disciples will not bear fruit if they do not abide in him (John 15:4; Moloney 1998, 417). The disciples, who have already received and accepted Jesus' word while in the process of being pruned, are warned that they must not take the mutual union between Jesus

---

6. In his analysis of the Johannine Farewell Discourse proper, Segovia proposes four units of discourse: 13:31–14:31; 15:1–17; 15:18–16:4a; 16:4b–33. Segovia thus sees 15:1–17 as the second unit of the Farewell, and 15:18 is the point of departure for the third unit.

and them for granted. In other words, to be a member of the community means that they must continuously "remain" in the vine. Any "unfruitful" branches will be thrown out, gathered, and burned (15:6). As such, the "fruitful" branches must be wary of the "unfruitful" branches, lest they also be cast out. Moreover, these "unfruitful" branches are threats to Jesus and to the maintenance of a steady and strong community (Hall 1997b, 230). Unless they are restored to their proper place, that is, in a "structured relationship" as deemed by Jesus, they are to be thrown out (Glass 2002, 167).[7] *Difference* defines the boundaries of the community, indicating who is included or excluded.

In the face of the imperial reality of the Roman Empire, the presentation of Jesus as the "unmitigated opposition" is significant. Despite the confines of imperial-colonial rule, Jesus emerges as the new Self, alleging that he is the "something that occupies a space within the frontiers that it divides" (Glass 2002, 163). By drawing the disciples to himself as the new Self, Jesus is creating an alternative community in resistance to the imperial rule, defined as the world-below. And by portraying the world-below as the premier enemy, Jesus "elicits and integrates the randomly distributed energies" of the members of the community. In other words, for the community to resist the world-below, they must "acquire a cohesive revolutionary shape and form" demonstrated in the rhetoric of "love" (Gandhi 1998, 111).[8] The rhetoric of love also discloses the binary opposites of Jesus as the Self and the disciples as the Other.

Jesus exhorts his disciples to observe his commandments unconditionally as well as to remain in his love, premised upon the Father's love for him (John 15:9–10; Moloney 1998, 422). Moreover, Jesus calls the disciples his "friends" and alleges that "to be called friends" means that they are obligated to carry out the commandments he has given to them. The nature of one's love is demonstrated in the laying down of "one's life for one's friends" (cf. 15:10–11, 13b), an expression of "commitment that flows directly from the relationship among friends" (Howard-Brook 1994, 336). Furthermore, to name his disciples as "friends" is to mark *difference* between them and "slaves"—"a slave does not know what the master is doing; but I have called you friends, because I have made known to you everything" (15:15; cf. 14:26). Therefore, in naming the disciples "friends" as opposed to "slaves," Jesus endows the disciples not only with a privileged status but also, ironically, with a responsibility. The status of

---

7. Glass suggests that certain norms entail membership in a group, of which structuring relationships is one. This notion of "structured relationship" is reflected in the practice of the discourse.

8. See, e.g., Guha, who argues that Indian nationalism could only be achieved through the mobilization, regulation, and harnessing of the "subaltern" energy (1992, 64–120).

the disciples as "friends" is double-edged. On the one hand, being designated as "friends" puts them in a privileged position, though they have to do all the things that have been disclosed to them by Jesus. However, on the other hand, they might have to sacrifice their lives for him. In other words, Jesus shapes the psyche of the disciples so that his own interests can be served (Loomba 1998, 58).[9]

Jesus also calls the disciples to love each other, premised upon Jesus' love for them (John 15:9, 12, 17). In their love for each other, the community comes to an understanding "about themselves, their relationship to each other and their place in the world" (see 13:35; 15:18–27). In short, Jesus' discourse on reciprocal love "organises social existence and social reproduction" of the community (both quotations Ashcroft, Griffiths, and Tiffin 1998, 71). As such, the identity of the community is complex: on the one hand, the disciples know that they are subjected to Jesus, the vine; on the other hand, the reciprocal love relationship among the disciples enables them to resist the world-below.

In summary, for the disciples to "remain" in Jesus means that they are to step out from the world to which they belong, the world-below, and into the world of Jesus, the world-above. The world of Jesus, the world-above offers (1) truth, because he is the "true" vine; (2) fruit-bearing, because the disciples remain in him; and (3) love, because Jesus loves them just as the Father loves him. Therefore, the mutual relationship between the disciples and Jesus proves to be challenging for the disciples in the face of the hostile world-below. This challenge is further delineated in the second section of the vine discourse, John 15:18–27.

At the outset of this second section, Jesus does not mince words concerning the harsh realities the disciples would encounter from the world-below. Thus, he marks the *difference* between the world-below and the disciples. The world-below's hatred toward the disciples is grounded on the disciples' non-alliance with the world-below. Indeed, Jesus has already claimed the disciples for his own and taken them out of the domain of the world-below (John 15:19b; cf. 15:16). This in seen in two respects: (1) with respect to the way in which the disciples are treated: while Jesus loves the disciples, the world-below will hate them because it has previously hated Jesus (15:18; cf. 15:9a–b, 12); (2) with respect to knowledge: the disciples know Jesus' sender but the world-below does not, even though they have witnessed Jesus' works in their midst. Had Jesus not made known his sayings and works to the world-below,

---

9. The encounter between the European and non-European as a result of colonialism established the notion of the inferiority of non-Europeans, a notion that was reshaped in order to serve specific colonial practices.

the world-below would be justified for their hostile behavior toward Jesus and the disciples; however, they have known and seen them (15:22, 24). Moreover, the failure and falsehood of the world-below is reinforced by Jesus' use of a rhetorical contrary-to-fact condition statement ("If you belonged to the world, the world would love you as its own"; 15:19a).[10]

Again, *difference* is used to highlight the incisive division between the world-below and the world-above, the world that was introduced by Jesus to the disciples. By way of the analogy of the "master/slave" relationship, Jesus warns his disciples of future dire consequences: if Jesus, their Master, is persecuted by the world-below, the disciples, who are under his rule, will also be persecuted, perhaps even more intensely (John 15:20). Moreover, the conflict between the disciples and the world-below is already a present reality that will grow in intensity, from mere hatred to persecution and finally to sin (15:22b, 24a).[11] Such is the severe hostility of the world-below, against which the disciples must be cautioned.

Thus, the ambivalent nature of the community emerges. On the one hand, the disciples have been chosen by Jesus and therefore belong to him, yet they are in a subordinate position because they are designated "slaves," with Jesus as their master. At the same time, from the perspective of the world-below, their subordinate status is inverted, because the world-below is not in control of the disciples. Ultimately, the world-below's antagonism is a fulfillment of scriptural prophecy ("they hated me without a cause"; John 15:25; cf. Ps 69:4?), a fact that implies that their hostility toward the community is under the directive of God. As Talbert notes, "this hatred is not evidence that things are out of God's control" (1992, 216).[12] God is still in charge of the situation, and thus the world-below's hatred can still be contained and resisted. The role

---

10. See Brooks and Winbery 1970, 182–83. This type of conditional clause (second class) suggests that the condition stated in the protasis (the "if" clause) is untrue, as indicated by the use of *ei* with a past tense in the indicative mood. The apodosis (the "then" clause) states what would have been true in the event that the protasis had been true, usually indicated by the use of *an* with a past tense of the indicative mood.

11. Brooks and Winbery 1970, 182. The conditional clauses in this unit of the discourse can be classified as first-class conditions, meaning that the condition stated in the protasis (the "if" clause) is believed by the speaker to be a reality, as indicated in the use of *ei* plus the indicative mood (John 15:18a, 19a, 20c, 20d). The apodosis (the "then" clause) may use other moods, and the verb can be in any tense. The conditional clause may be framed in the form of a direct statement, a question, an exhortation, or a request.

12. John 15:25 contains the only scriptural citation in the whole of the Farewell Discourse, usually identified as Ps 35:19 or 69:4. The Johannine version is not identical to the Masoretic Text or the LXX. See Segovia 1991 for a concise discussion of the textual difficulties of the reference (194 n. 40).

and status of the world-below is thus given an ironic twist. The binary opposites Self and Other or center and margins are inverted: the world-below is placed at the margins, with the disciples at the center. This inversion of binary opposites is further elucidated in the sending of the Paraclete, who will equip the disciples to confront the hatred of the world-below (15:26–27; cf. John 17). In sum, the community is caught "in between"; that is, they must negotiate their role with reference to Jesus and the world-below.

In summary, the first division of the vine discourse (John 15:1–17) delineates the *difference* between the vine and the branches (representing Jesus and the disciples, respectively), and its delineation is one that establishes Jesus as the Self and the disciples as the Other. The disciples, representing the Johannine community, are described as dependent upon Jesus for sustenance and maintenance. But this portrayal of the disciples is inverted in the second division of the vine discourse (15:18–27), where they are established as the Self with respect to the world-below. In light of the whole vine discourse, the identity of the disciples, representing the Johannine community, is seen to be in flux. The community straddles between the world that they were called into by Jesus, the world-above, and the world of the imperial Roman empire, the world-below. How should they respond in light of their hybridity? Should they be exclusive? Or should they compromise with the world-below? Or could they live in these two worlds at once, with an identity that they define for themselves—one that is "something else besides"?

According to Bhabha, both language and the construction of nation or community are connected; that is, they are full of contradictions and ambiguities. Hence, they are not stable. They scatter and dissolve any *difference* and ambiguity because the boundaries of nation or community disintegrate and their interiors cease to remain distinct. Bhabha suggests that one should pay attention to the "margins of the nation-space and … the boundaries *in-between* nations and peoples" (1994a, 1–7). Reading the vine discourse from this perspective, the hybridized stance of the Johannine community proves to be advantageous. On the one hand, they belong to Jesus and the world-above; on the other hand, they are still in the world-below, yet not defenseless in the face of its hostility. As such, the community could "slide" into either world and, hence, be a challenge to either world. But more important, the fluid nature of the community means that they are defined neither by the world-below nor by the world-above. That is to say, the self-definition of the Johannine community is grounded upon their own understanding of their relationship to these two worlds.

The above analysis of the vine discourse with respect to the characterization of the disciples raises several questions. What are some of the implications of such an analysis, in light of globalization and postcolonialism, for a real flesh-and-blood reader (like me), and for biblical criticism and hermeneutics in general?

Conclusion

In light of globalization and postcolonialism, every aspect of life is affected on an international and local scale: what happens in the local affects the international and vice versa. Our lives are intertwined, so to set ourselves as exclusive is bound to meet with challenge and resistance. As Giddens states, the current world order "is emerging in an anarchic, haphazard, fashion carried along by a mixture of influences. It is not settled or secure, but fraught with anxieties as well as scarred by deep divisions. Many of us feel in the grip of forces over which we have no power." Giddens proceeds to ask, Can we reimpose our will upon them [these forces]?" His answer is affirmative: "We need to reconstruct those we have, or create new ones. For globalization is not incidental to our lives today. It is a shift in our very life circumstances. It is the way we now live" (2000, 37). I see his answer as a challenge for those of us engaged in biblical criticism and biblical hermeneutics, because the field of biblical criticism and hermeneutics is not unaffected by globalization. This paper has sought to give a "new look" on John, if I may use Robinson's term, but a "new look" that recognizes the important role of the real flesh-and-blood reader in the reading of the ancient text, using a myriad of methodologies and approaches.

This "new look," with an emphasis on real readers, is seen within the academy in the growth of emerging voices from different parts of the world. These voices primarily represent the perspectives of biblical scholars who are influenced by their social location and who use various interpretive methodologies and strategies from the fields of liberation theology, feminist criticism, minority studies, diasporic studies, and postcolonial studies in their reading and interpreting of the Bible. They are " 'speaking in other tongues,' in one's own tongue," lest they be usurped and be spoken by other tongues (Segovia 1995, 31). My project speaks of one such interpretive methodology and offers one approach to reading the vine discourse, grounded upon my social location as one whose identity is hybridized and diasporic. Hence, my representation the Johannine community is, like myself, "caught in two worlds."

Part 3
Reflection and Forecast

Social Location and Johannine Scholarship: Looking Ahead

Francisco Lozada Jr.

When John A. T. Robinson set out to delineate several new perspectives on Johannine scholarship in his article "The New Look on the Fourth Gospel" in 1957, I am sure he would have never imagined that the question of the role of social location of the reader (i.e., the flesh-and-blood-reader) vis-à-vis readings of the Fourth Gospel would have been an issue or a topic among today's studies. Among the "new looks" that he discussed, not one of them focused on the world "in front" of the text. This is not surprising, since the question of the role of the reader did not figure in either the "old look" or the "new look" phases of Johannine scholarship. The reader was an invisible and universal reader whose primary role was to extract the meaning of the text, or to excavate the many layers of tradition supporting the text, by way of either identifying its sources, editing its history, or unearthing the various general historical realities behind the Fourth Gospel. In short, the focus was on the world "behind" the text rather than the world "in front" of the text.

This "behind the text" approach, performed by historical critics, has been clearly documented in New Testament scholarship in general and in Johannine scholarship in particular. It is reflected by those Johannine studies that developed in the 1990s out of literary criticism (e.g., reader-response criticism) and postmodern approaches to biblical studies (Segovia 1996; 1998c). The question of the role of social location vis-à-vis biblical interpretation, I believe, has been recognized by many New Testament scholars as relevant to understanding the process of interpretation, but I am sure many still long for the days when the question of the social location of the reader was disregarded and the principles of positivism, objectivity, and universality were heralded by everyone. In other words, I characterize Robinson's era as a time when conformity was aimed for and difference was marginalized. Nonetheless, the question of the social location of the reader is very important to New Testament scholarship generally and Johannine studies in particular. It is essential because it offers another avenue for those frustrated by the narrow parameters of historical criticism or, for that matter, by any methodological approach that consumes the social location of the reader. More important, the question of the social location of the reader is important because it allows readers to begin to acknowledge difference. It is my ideological position that to know where readers and their readings are coming from leads to a better understanding, or at least an appreciation, of the Other and how we are more alike rather than different across the globe. For me, biblical interpretation is not only about understanding the world "behind" the text; it is also about understanding this world "in front" of the text and its power dynamics and ramifications for the Other.

With this brief discussion of social-location hermeneutics, I would also argue that those who embark on the question of social location begin to move away from making themselves (as scholars) the heroes of the process of interpretation and toward exploring the complex concept of identity that makes up social location. It is not that I think the question of the social location of the reader is finished; rather, I believe that to understand better how we read (social location) could lead to a better understanding of what we read with (identities), which will, in turn, eventually lead us back to a clearer understanding on the question of how (social location). In other words, the identity factors that make up social location must be explored in order to understand biblical interpretation, including the interpretation of the Fourth Gospel. Factors such as racial and ethnic identity (including "whiteness"), religious identity, class identity, motherhood, fatherhood, sexual orientation, gender, and diasporic identity and their complexities underscore the importance of social location and ought to be explored as well (Woodward 1997).

In this paper I will not examine the question of identity per se but will rather explore the question of the reader's social location. I aim to review critically three works on the Gospel of John that employ social location in various ways. This review will not only illustrate how social location has been used in recent scholarship but will also highlight aspects of each study that support my argument that the question of social location opens doors for further exploration of the identity of the reader. In the process, I will show that the question of social location deserves greater critical scrutiny than it received in the 1990s. The three studies are: *Reading with a Passion: Rhetoric, Autobiography, and the American West in the Gospel of John*, by Jeffrey L. Staley (1995); *The Shining Garment of the Text: Gendered Readings of John's Prologue*, by Alison Jasper (1998); and *Befriending the Beloved Disciple: A Jewish Reading of the Gospel of John*, by Adele Reinhartz (2001). All three of these studies examine the Fourth Gospel from the theoretical perspective of cultural studies and also engage the social location of the authors themselves. Most important, as I shall try to demonstrate, all three studies contribute to a clearer understanding of the reader's social location and/or the nature of his or her critical moves in the reading experience when social location aspects are disclosed. It is also my contention that engaging the real reader's social location leads one to begin to confront one's own social location, namely, my own social location. However, I shall postpone this encounter for another time. This critical review serves as a point of departure for my own thinking on how best to use social location to interpret the Fourth Gospel.

In what follows I will focus on how each Johannine scholar noted above uses social location in his or her reading experience of the Fourth Gospel. I will first briefly summarize the main thrust and orientation of these three works, following their order of publication date. I will then provide some concluding comments vis-à-vis the question of social location and the Fourth Gospel.

Jeffrey L. Staley's *Reading with a Passion*

Jeffrey L. Staley's *Reading with a Passion* (1995) focuses on two major methodological issues. The first, which occupies part 1 of the book, focuses on engaging the text of the Fourth Gospel from a literary perspective, involving reader-response criticism from three perspectives: the implied reader, the resistant reader, and the agonistic reader. The second issue, encompassed in part 2 of the book, centers on engaging the real reader (Staley himself) of the Fourth Gospel from a literary perspective, involving primarily autobiographical criticism and informed by aspects of postcolonialism, feminism, and postmodernism. Staley specifically argues that both the text and the reader must undergo a rigorous and engaged study. His overarching emphasis in this book, however, is with the latter component, the reader. Staley stresses the reader in reaction to criticisms that his previous work was too formalistic, with the real reader (himself) hiding behind the implied or encoded reader (1995, 18).

Staley aims to show in this work how the real reader (himself) began the professional reading of the Fourth Gospel hidden behind the implied reader and how he now openly thinks and writes on those ideological and social constraints that informed him as a real reader of the Fourth Gospel (see Staley 2000). This discussion of how the real reader (himself) slowly comes out of the tomb is organized in a succeeding chapter-to-chapter arrangement in part 1 of the book, with the real reader beginning in-the-text disguised as the implied reader reading John 5 and 9 (ch. 1). His next move is a focus on the real reader, influenced by intertextuality and feminist theory, taking on the role of the resistant reader in reading John 11 (ch. 2). Finally, Staley focuses again on the real reader, influenced by reception theory, taking on the role of the agonistic reader in reading John 18:1–24 (ch. 3). In part 2 of the book Staley unapologetically and shamelessly writes about certain events stemming from his childhood to young adulthood and puts his autobiography into practice with a postmodern reading of John 18:24–19:42. The three most important chapters of the book, I believe, are found in part 2: chapter 4 focuses on autobiographical criticism; chapter 5 entails the autobiography of Staley; and chapter 6 provides a postmodern reading of the passion narrative informed by autobiographical criticism.

Chapter 4, "The Father of Lies: Autobiographical Acts in Recent Biblical Criticism and Contemporary Literary Theory," is the methodological foundation of the book. This chapter follows a sevenfold division centered on the genre of autobiography and its implications. In the first division of the chapter, entitled "Making Whoppers," Staley points out that using autobiography is not simply about demarcating identity factors at the beginning of our readings but rather about seriously analyzing those social and ideological constraints that form real readers of the Bible (see Staley 2000). The next three divisions of chapter 4—"A Cyborg Meets Jesus"; "Nothing in the Text about Merlin"; and "A Reader's Alchemy"—focus on atypical autobiographical studies by three white European-American biblical scholars who write about their lives but then keep the personal voice out of their interpretations. These three scholars are Marcus Borg, *Meeting Jesus Again for the First Time* (1994); Sandra Schneiders, *The Revelatory Text: Interpreting the New Testament as Sacred Scripture* (1991); and Mikeal Parsons, "What's 'Literary' about Literary Aspects of the Gospels and Acts?" (1992). Staley points out, using images to illustrate his argument, that Borg reads like a cyborg, separating his spiritual and academic experience and assuming that both lives are objective and independent (Staley 1995, 127). Schneiders reads like Merlin (a wizard) in that she mutters some very interesting personal reflections in the beginning of her work but succeeds in keeping them out of her reading (Staley 1995, 127). Parsons reads like an alchemist, mixing up the autobiographical with the intellectual, yet he refrains from becoming an active reader of any biblical text (Staley 1995, 135). All three decide not to integrate the autobiographical aspects of their lives with their interpretations. This is the problem, for Staley, with most social-location works: they fail to integrate social location with interpretation. In the final three divisions of the chapter—"A Myth of Origins"; "Losing the Formula"; and "Where the Future Lies"—Staley defines "autobiography" as a literary genre that goes beyond the traditional representation of the self toward a critical reflection of the self, knowing full well that this reflection is always a construction.

Staley's fifth chapter, the longest in *Reading with a Passion*, entails his autobiography, which is delineated around five textual markers: (1) metaphor, (2) difference, (3) distance, (4) tools, and (5) place.

First, with regard to metaphor, Staley employs the metaphor of "dog" to start his autobiography (1995, 155). It is the dog that comes to mind when he begins to write about his childhood, which he spent on a Navajo reservation in northeastern Arizona with his family, who were members of the Emmanuel Mission. Why the dog? In the Navajo tradition, dogs are despised and treated quite abusively by their owners, yet they are everywhere on the reservation. For instance, in the recollection of one particular event, Staley recounts a time when he and his brothers befriended a dog but reluctantly had to return the dog to its rightful owners. The Navajo owners, according to Staley, angrily "took the dog and tied an old piece of briar-like barbed wire around his neck. With the husband pulling the [dog], the wife kicked [it] the entire mile to their house" (1995, 157). Staley goes on to write that "two days later the dog returned to [his home]"; however, he and his brothers had to chase the dog away because it would not leave and they did not want the owners to assume that they had stolen it (1995, 157). As such, the metaphor "dog" repetitively emerges in Staley's memory when he recounts his childhood. The metaphor also reminds Staley that the Navajo saw him and his family in a negative way, like dogs. They even thought Staley was a direct descendant of Kit Carson, "the white man who had burned their family orchards and cornfields, starved their old women and young children, and forced those who survived into exile in a foreign land" (1995, 197–98). Interestingly, Staley, after reviewing his ancestry, learned that he was indeed related to Kit Carson, who also participated in Buffalo Bill's Wild West Show in the U.S. and abroad. In short, for Staley, to recount his past is simply to point out "how we read our own interests into canonical texts" (1995, 231). In other words, the dog represents the intermingling between the text and the reader.

Second, Staley writes part of his autobiography through the textual lens of "difference," with a focus on the different values and perceptions between the Navajo and himself. Without going into further detail here, Staley writes how difference has impacted his family and professional life. For Staley, difference is still seen as a threat by many people and a risk to many academic disciplines, especially when these disciplines try to contain difference as a way to control it (1995, 179).

Staley's third autobiographical marker is "distance." Staley writes about how far he had to travel from place to place growing up, about the distance between his home and college (Wheaton College in Illinois), about how his brothers (Rob and Greg) moved away both geographically and ideologically from the family, and also about how he also influenced several Navajo peers to attend Wheaton College. Distance forces Staley to reflect upon how "good" scholars must put distance between one's personal life and interpretation—unlike what he is doing in his own book.

Staley's fourth autobiographical marker is entitled "tools." With regard to tools, Staley devotes time to his religious identity. No longer connected to his religious roots of the Plymouth Brethren tradition, Staley's encounter with difference on the Navajo reservation leads him "to challenge the authoritarian, anti-intellectualism of [his] Plymouth Brethren upbringing, replacing it with a mindful curiosity and a natural pluralism" (1995, 186). In other words, it leads him to "see things differently," which he believes is "part of [his] psychological makeup from the age of seven." Thus, difference, distance, and defamiliarization are the tools that characterize his way of reading the Fourth Gospel.

Staley's fifth and final autobiographical marker is "place." With regard to place, Staley engages his geographical location. He centers attention on his exploration of the landscape of northern Arizona, particularly the lower reaches of the San Juan Basin. Like an explorer of the land, Staley, a Johannine explorer, sees himself moving temporally and spatially through a specific narrative region (the Fourth Gospel) in order to learn the feel of the land and to "negotiate its texture with all its detours" (1995, 193). His passion to explore the geography and topography of the Navajo reservation in northeastern Arizona thus correlates with his reading passion for the Fourth Gospel. The overarching point of this autobiography, therefore, is to point out that the Gospel of John can easily be found in Staley's life and that he can also find his life in the Gospel of John.

In chapter 6 Staley provides a postmodern reading of the passion narrative (John 18:28–19:42), informed by autobiographical criticism. Briefly, Staley aims to "move toward the formation of a reader-critic ... who is increasingly aware of how autobiographical matters ... formalist reader criticism, and cultural studies all affect his readings of the Fourth Gospel" (1995, 199). In other words, his postcolonial, autobiographical reading of himself leads Staley to a postmodern, dramatic reading of the Johannine passion narrative. How so? Staley constructs a dialogue between the three corpses on their crosses (see John 19:18). One of the corpses is a social-world-of-Jesus critic, another is a literary critic, and another is an autobiographer. The intent of the dialogue between these three interlocutors is to show how all interpreters fight for interpretive control of meaning at the site of Jesus' crucifixion (1995, 21). To demonstrate Staley's point, the metaphor of "dog" reappears on the scene. The social-world-of-Jesus critic wants to include dogs in the crucifixion scene because they likely would have been there. The literary critic keeps pointing out that dogs were not on the scene because they are not mentioned in the text. The autobiographer realizes that dogs are not mentioned in the Fourth Gospel but emphasizes that the dogs are present anyway. However, the dogs are not present objectively, as the social-world critic wants to contend, but rather intertextually, as a text from another story—this other story being Staley's own autobiography. As such, this postmodern reading aims to point out that all readers and readings are a function of social location(s), as is the case with Staley's reading of the passion narrative in John.

Staley's attitude toward social location allows him to approach the Fourth Gospel in a creative and open way. Staley is quite aware of his social location and is forthcoming in his discussions. For instance, Staley discusses his sociocultural (Navajo context), socioeducational (Wheaton College), and socioreligious (Plymouth Brethren missionary tradition) experiences in quite an expansive fashion, particularly in the latter half of his study. In fact, as was mentioned above, part 2 of *Reading with a Passion* sets out to illustrate how Staley moved away from the notion of a universal reader toward a particular, non-first-time reader. Using one's social location is quite uncommon in most biblical interpretation studies; however, Staley is using autobiographical criticism, which will allow for a more explicit use of one's social location. He reads in a resistant manner: not resistant toward the text per se, but rather resistant to the way he and others have read the text in the past by not disclosing one's social location during the reading process. The use of social location by Staley can be characterized, therefore, as autobiographical. *Reading with a Passion* challenges and confronts Johannine scholars to be more explicit about their autobiographies (Kitzberger 1999). Unfortunately, this is a call not heard, or at least not well received, by the following study of the Fourth Gospel by Alison Jasper.

ALISON JASPER'S *THE SHINING GARMENT OF THE TEXT*

Alison Jasper's *The Shining Garment of the Text* (1998) focuses on the Prologue of the Gospel of John (John 1:1–18), with an emphasis on how this text has been read throughout history by other readers and how she reads it from a women-centered or feminist perspective. As such, the book unfolds in two main parts. The first part is a study of the Prologue by way of a close, deconstructive reading of five interpretations by Augustine, Hildegard von Bingen, Martin Luther, Adrienne von Speyr, and Rudolf Bultmann. Jasper argues that all these interpreters clothe the Prologue with the same patriarchal or phallogocentric garment, namely, a garment that reduces any trace of the feminine or women to descriptions of imperfection (Augustine), seduction (von Bingen), spiritual fault (Martin Luther), valuelessness (Bultmann), or nonobedience (von Speyr). Part 2 of the book consists of four main chapters, although I will focus on the first three. These three chapters aim to deconstruct and reconstruct the Prologue of the Fourth Gospel. The main thrust of the argument in part 2 is that the Prologue could be read in multiple ways that are advantageous to women. In other words, Jasper aims to show the "feminine face" reflected within the Prologue. Jasper, therefore, aims not to avoid the patriarchal tendencies of the Prologue but rather to engage and confront her oppressor. Such is the overarching aim of the book. In the following analysis, I will focus on part 2 of *Shining Garment*, with attention given to how Jasper uses her gendered identity in reading the Prologue of the Gospel of John.

Jasper begins her quest to engage the Prologue with a twofold aim in chapter 7, "Which Came First: Word or the Words? Towards a Feminist Transformation." The first aim is to deconstruct what Jasper calls "rhetorical mythology." Rhetorical mythology is an interpretation of a narrative that aims to persuade readers to comply with the worldview of the text, such as the patriarchal underpinnings of the Prologue (Jasper 1998, 165). In other words, Jasper does not agree with institutional interpretations of the Prologue—a mythological narrative—that reinscribe patriarchy and authoritative texts. She begins by challenging Ernst Käsemann's interpretation of the Prologue in *The Testament of Jesus* (1968), who argues that the Fourth Gospel is not primarily about the incarnation of the flesh but rather about the divine glory revealed in the world (Jasper 1998, 167). Jasper understands this interpretation as a mythic construction in that the divine descends to humanity without becoming involved or conditioned by humankind, that is, a humankind that is "symbolized by woman or the feminine" (1998, 167). She sees this mythic interpretation as nothing other than the exaltation of the male gender through masculine representation vis-à-vis divinity. In other words, the feminine is excluded or marginalized, since women represent the Other—the human world. Käsemann rejects this "Otherness."

Jasper's next methodological move is to deconstruct this phallogocentric tendency in the Prologue by proposing another interpretation from the point of view of "focalization." However, the Prologue will not be interpreted from the point of view of the divine or the narrator but rather from the perspective of John the Baptist, who reminds readers, according to Jasper, of the significance of human work to bear witness to the Word. It is the Baptist who first speaks to authorize Jesus (John 1:29–34), thus pointing to the importance of human participation in divine revelation (Jasper 1998, 176). Jasper, therefore, is aiming to restore the importance of humanity and, consequently, the importance of women, who symbolize humanity. Jasper states, "I am reading the text of the Prologue in order to reveal a God who is necessarily dependent upon the materiality (John 1.14) of both word (witness) and flesh (glorified presence), in order to enter into relationship with humankind" (1998, 178). In other words, working with the traditional gender binary construct of "masculine/feminine" correlated with the binary construct "divine/human," Jasper is arguing that the feminine/human component is actually first, since "only the one who was sent can reveal the one who has sent him" (1998, 24). Jasper thus provides an interpretation that restores the feminine face.

In the second reading of the Prologue in chapter 8 of her study, "Flesh Insights on the Prologue of John's Gospel," Jasper focuses on the term "flesh" at John 1:13 to interpret the incarnational statement of John 1:14, "And the Word became flesh" (1998, 183). The major thrust of her interpretation begins with the argument that the word "flesh" in the Fourth Gospel typically functions as the lower term within a hierarchy that prioritizes spiritual values (e.g., John 3:4–7; 6), with the feminine or women identified with the lower term, flesh. If this is the case, the divine word becoming flesh in John 1:14 suggests that the divine makes a humiliating descent into a feminine humanity, and, for humanity to receive salvation, humanity must remove themselves from this fleshly realm to be received into the divine realm (1998, 209). However, the divine does take on "human flesh," thus indicating the importance of the world of the flesh. Jasper even provides a brief interpretation of John 6 to illustrate that the term "flesh" there also represents, on the one hand, something flawed and dangerous but, on the other hand, something essential to life. Her argument here in this second reading of the Prologue is to point out the apparent contradiction in the Fourth Gospel's presentation of "flesh," with the hope that this contradiction emphasizes that the term "flesh," which typically correlates with women or the feminine, does not have to be read negatively.

In her third reading of the Prologue (in my opinion the most challenging) in chapter 9, "In the Beginning Was Love," Jasper reads the Prologue as a description of the human subject *en procès*, a concept emanating from Julia Kristeva's work on intertextuality. This concept is also part of the second objective of part 2, which aims to construct a new mythological narrative of the Prologue in order to contest the one supported by orthodox Christianity. For instance, Jasper's aim with this third examination of the Prologue is to analyze the text as a "drama of developing human subjectivity" (1998, 24). It is Jasper's position that the incarnation is a "description of the divine which integrates the symbolism of gender but manages not to copy into that symbolism the hierarchical framework that ... devalues the feminine term" (1998, 215). In other words, for Jasper, the Word takes on a necessary heterogeneity of subjectivity, which encompasses both the joy of living as well as the dark suffering of living. Women must construct an imaginative narrative, therefore, out of the Prologue that deals with this "textual confusion ... that accounts for ... the painful dissociations to (by) which they are subject(s)" (1998, 233). Women, for Jasper, are represented as fundamentally maternal but also represent resistance to any form of exclusion in the Prologue. These latter deconstructive and constructive readings surely demonstrate that Jasper's women-centered identity and her feminist readings are a function of her social location as a women-centered reader.

Unlike Staley's reading of other readers of the Fourth Gospel and his own reading of the Fourth Gospel per se, the study by Jasper can be characterized as liberationist. Her project, from my perspective and with respect to the question of social location, is one that turns to the question of women and uses this social location to provide a feminist or gendered reading of the Prologue of the Fourth Gospel. However, her reading is much more reserved in orientation than Staley's. In other words, we are not learning about how she became a feminist (sociocultural world), where she studied that perhaps informed her feminist educational background (socioeducational world), or her experience within Christianity as a feminist (socioreligious world)—although, with regard to the latter, she does engage ecclesiastical readings and the history of scholarship on the Prologue, with its patriarchal proclivities, in an open and creative fashion. She is resistant toward other readings of the Prologue, as well as to what the Fourth Gospel has to say with regard to incarnation. However, she does provide a constructive and creative reading of the Prologue, one that is liberating in orientation for humanity. Jasper's use of social location is surely reserved compared to Staley's, yet it is apropos in the sense that she uses social location in a way that is specific to her goal of deconstructing and reconstructing a reading or readings of the Prologue. Jasper's reading is in keeping with other feminist studies, but social location along these lines tends to be much more distant in disclosing the particularities of one's social location.

Adele Reinhartz's *Befriending the Beloved Disciple*

The final work that I wish to examine is Adele Reinhartz's *Befriending the Beloved Disciple* (2001). In this book Reinhartz turns her attention to both the reader and the text and provides a fourfold reading of the Fourth Gospel. With regard to the reader, Reinhartz reveals to her readers how her own personal and intellectual life is involved in her involvement with the Fourth Gospel. With regard to the text, Reinhartz introduces four reading strategies in relationship to her encounter with the implied author, namely, the Beloved Disciple. The overarching question of her work is, Can a Jewish, professional reader of the Fourth Gospel befriend this Beloved Disciple? For Reinhartz, the response to her question is, It depends! It depends upon what reading strategy she adopts, but she will eventually favor one of the four reading strategies at the end.

I shall focus here on two major sections of Reinhartz's book. The first section (chs. 1 and 2) covers Reinhartz's identity and social location as a Jewish New Testament scholar, followed by a discussion of how she will approach the Fourth Gospel as a Jewish New Testament scholar. The second major section (chs. 4–7) focuses on Reinhartz's four reading positions, which she calls "the compliant reader," "the resistant reader," "the sympathetic reader," and "the engaged reader."

First, with regard to the reader, Reinhartz begins with a disclaimer that she does not claim to read for all Jews. Rather, what she offers as *a* Jewish reader is not "the Jewish reading" but one of several possible Jewish readings, thus suggesting that no one of these Jewish readings is by any means normative, objective, or positivistic. She then moves to provide some autobiographical notes on her identity. Her first confession is that she is Jewish and a child of Holocaust survivors, thus indicating to her readers why she has spent so many years studying texts that have contributed to hatred and anti-Semitism (2001, 11). She recounts a story from her childhood in which she suffered discrimination by Christians and wonders if this is perhaps also part of the reason why she works with the New Testament, namely, to work out her Jewish identity. Her second confession is that she only recently began to acknowledge her Jewish identity in the university and professional arena. She acknowledges that it has been difficult to express her social location, primarily in the profession with its notions of objectivity and scientific method, but she came to realize that this meant desensitizing herself toward the hostile anti-Jewish texts in the New Testament. In other words, it was time to "come out" as a Jew, if she really wanted to change how Jews are represented in the world. This coming out took place both in the classroom and in the academy, and she realized that this disclosure "deepened her understanding of the New Testament, and of the field of Johannine scholarship as well" (Reinhartz 2001, 14). Her third confession concerns her identity as a feminist. Having been persuaded by the principles undergirding feminism and its ethical focus toward the liberation of women and the marginalized, Reinhartz's vocation as a New Testament scholar is further defined. She concludes her brief autobiographical remarks on her Jewish identity with a further question: How does a Jewish woman read the Fourth Gospel? This is the question she will begin to answer in chapter 2, where she focuses on how she will begin to read the Fourth Gospel.

Reinhartz begins to explain her reading strategy with another autobiographical confession. Reinhartz introduces her love and passion for fiction. In fact, she calls it a healthy addiction. She uses this passion for fiction as a point of departure in explaining her reading strategy. For Reinhartz, reading fiction is akin to the experience of human friendship, and she will use this experience as a metaphor to relate to the Fourth Gospel as a friend (2001, 18). This metaphor of a book as a friend actually comes from Wayne Booth's *The Company We Keep: An Ethics of Fiction* (1988) and is the foundation of a critical approach he calls "ethical criticism," which argues that our interactions with books as friends parallels our relations with friends in the real world, "not only in the pleasures they bring but also in the ethical stances they foster" (Reinhartz 2001, 18). As such, ethical criticism refers not only to the way we judge stories but also to the responsibilities readers must bear when they read stories. In other words, Who do we become when we enter into a relationship with a book?

Reinhartz's reading of the Fourth Gospel is an exercise in ethical criticism. But how does one negotiate this relationship, especially when a book such as the Fourth Gospel is hostile to her as a Jew and when the Fourth Gospel cannot speak back? Acknowledging this latter limitation, Reinhartz believes the "friendship as a metaphor" approach is a good model or framework to use to befriend the Fourth Gospel. As such, she extends an invitation for conversation to the implied author of the Fourth Gospel. For Reinhartz, this implied author is the Beloved Disciple (see John 13:23; 19:26; 20:2). She opens the conversation by opening the Fourth Gospel and is greeted by the Beloved Disciple with a gift. This gift is the promise of eternal life through faith in Jesus as the Christ and Son of God (John 20:30–31). However, as a practicing Jew, Reinhartz finds it difficult to accept this gift. She realizes that if she rejects the gift she will be judged as evil and cast to eternal damnation. Realizing these dire consequences, Reinhartz begins to work on how to befriend the Beloved Disciple, given the nature of his gift. Her strategy is to take up various reading positions, and in so doing, the Beloved Disciple becomes a particular sort of friend. This friendship is explored in the second part of her reading of the Fourth Gospel by way of four reading strategies.

The first of Reinhartz's four reading strategies is to adopt the posture of "the compliant reader." In this reading, the Beloved Disciple is portrayed as mentor. The compliant reader is one who accepts faith in Jesus as the Christ and Son of God without resistance and who accepts the Beloved Disciple as a mentor or guide who leads one to salvation. A compliant reader is a good position to embrace, since the path of faith has been chosen. However, Reinhartz admits that reading the Fourth Gospel as compliant reader can only be done temporarily, for she cannot accept the Beloved Disciple's gift, since it is uncongenial to her as a Jew. What does feel more natural for Reinhartz is the second reading position, namely, "the resistant reader." The resistant reader views the Beloved Disciple not as a mentor but rather as an opponent. As such, under this model of reading, Reinhartz rejects the gift of salvation and reads from the point of view of the Johannine Jews. From this point of view, Reinhartz is portrayed as "good" because she has rejected the gift of the Beloved Disciple, and those (believers) who accept the gift consider her "bad." However, as with the compliant reader, Reinhartz chooses not to adopt this reading position because both of these reading positions hide behind the characters of the story. The compliant reader hides behind those who accept the gift, and the resistant reader behind those characters who do not accept the gift of salvation.

The final two reading positions emanate from Reinhartz's lived experience as Jewish, as an Other who must "constantly negotiate relationships with those who are other to her" (2001, 28). The third reading position is one of "sympathetic reader," and the Beloved Disciple is portrayed as a colleague. This reading position tends to focus on those gifts from the Beloved Disciple that unite Reinhartz with others, while ignoring those elements that divide her with others. However, this position does not allow Reinhartz to confront those issues that separate her from the Beloved Disciple, and it fails to take seriously the Otherness of the Beloved Disciple. Therefore, Reinhartz chooses a fourth option to read the Fourth Gospel. This fourth position is called "the engaged reader," and here the Beloved Disciple is portrayed as an Other. The engaged reader confronts what separates the reader from the Other, not in order to persuade the Other, but rather to recognize and accept the Other's difference.

In short, these four reading strategies demonstrate that Reinhartz's readings of the Fourth Gospel, like Staley's and Jasper's, emanate from her social location as a Jewish New Testament scholar who ascribes to certain feminist principles. Unlike Staley, Reinhartz does not draw in depth upon these social, autobiographical factors that make up her social location, only to the point that these factors pertain to her reading relationship with the Fourth Gospel. However, similar to Staley's reading, Reinhartz proposes various readings of the Fourth Gospel and, similar to Jasper's approach, argues for a plurality of readings rather than one positivistic reading. Unlike Jasper, Reinhartz does not use her feminist social location in an explicit way. She is not arguing for a feminist reading of the Fourth Gospel, although she does draw upon some principles of feminism, such as liberation, to read the Fourth Gospel. Reinhartz is concerned with the ethical implications of the text, with respect to the question of anti-Jewish readings of the Fourth Gospel. As such, I would surely characterize Reinhartz's reading as one that uses social location as ethical criticism, that is, social location with the intent of examining critically the effects and implications of one's readings.

Social Location and Its Contributions

The three studies discussed above represent a major and invaluable contribution to the field of Johannine scholarship, as well as a significant contribution in the area of social-location hermeneutics, especially given their very different theoretical perspectives, methodological approaches, and use of social location in reading the Fourth Gospel. I do believe these major studies point to a number of rather distinctive and recurrent issues and developments; I confine myself to three I consider to be the important for Johannine studies in general. The first is the question of social location. Each of these authors uses an understanding of social location that emerges out of postmodernism: social location and autobiography (Staley); social location and liberation (Jasper); and social location and ethical criticism (Reinhartz). Each application of social location shares a nonessentialist understanding of identity and highlights how the construction of social location is complex and not something fixed across time and place. The use of social location needs to continue to be explored, critiqued, and scrutinized in order for it to continue to benefit Johannine scholarship and readers of the Fourth Gospel. These three approaches, as I have defined them, do so in a very challenging way.

The second contribution, which was not the focus of this paper, is the question of identity. It is identity or identities that give shape to one's social location. All three scholars use identity in a nonessentialist way and as something not fixed across time and place. Staley defines his identity primarily along the lines of sociocultural, socioreligious, and socioeducational terms, using autobiographical criticism to do so. Jasper defines her social location along the lines of gender identity, using feminist liberation criticism to do so. Reinhartz defines her social location primarily along the lines of her religious and ethnic identity but also makes reference to other identities such as feminism and her professional identity as a New Testament scholar, using cultural studies with its ethical impetus of examining the implications and ramifications of one's reading. All the authors understand identity as relational. In other words, identity is constructed in relationship to other identities. Staley constructs his identity in relationship to Navajo culture, Jasper in relationship to male interpretation of the Prologue of the Gospel of John, and Reinhartz in relationship to Christian readings of the Fourth Gospel. They also understand identity as fluid. Their identities are changed by events in their lives, but also their changed identities provoke changes in how they read the Fourth Gospel. Finally, their identities are multiple and multidimensional and always in process. As I mentioned in the introduction, the next move social-location advocates must make is this exploration of identity in order better to understand the use of social location in the field of biblical interpretation.

The third contribution to Johannine scholarship, and the area that intrigues me the most, is how the question of understanding the construction of readings and readers paves the way for biblical scholars to begin to read the Fourth Gospel alongside the sacred texts of cultures other than their own. All three of the studies that I examined above contributed to understanding the Other. Whether it was learning a bit more about the Navajo culture, the sociocultural world of women, or the socioreligious/cultural world of Judaism, the use of social location in reading the Fourth Gospel was very valuable in understanding the particularities of the Other. This is the direction I would like to see the use of social location move toward in the future of Johannine scholarship. We must be "born again, anew," not in the traditional sense of an individualistic spirituality, but rather in a pluralistic and global way that moves toward not only trying to the understand the worlds "behind" or "in" but also that "in front" of the text for a more just and liberating world. Social location does matter, and it must continue to matter for the sake of understanding difference and understanding one another.

The question of social location is not an "old look" but surely a "new look" in today's study of the Fourth Gospel. It is a "new look" that will need to be continually examined and explored with the focus toward the study of identity. The studies above lay the groundwork for the study of social location and identity, and, in particular, for defining oneself, one's community, one's nation, one's world, and one's religion.

Looking Downstream:
Where Will the New Currents Take Us?

R. Alan Culpepper

This volume was conceived as a collection of essays by a group of emerging Johannine scholars, written in light of John A. T. Robinson's analysis of the "new look" in the Johannine scholarship of fifty years ago. Most of the contributors had not yet been born when Robinson published "The New Look on the Fourth Gospel." These men and women represent different nationalities, ethnicities, schools, and religious traditions, and they have written on a variety of different topics. They were all given the same assignment, however, and they share in common that their approach(es) to the study of John were shaped in the latter years of the twentieth century, well after the publication of Robinson's essay. The contributors have each engaged an issue that has some currency in contemporary research, so their choice of topics and the ways in which they have developed their topics provide a panoramic view of the state of Johannine scholarship today.

Robinson's essay is a milestone because it signaled pervasive changes in the study of John in the 1950s and anticipated some of the developments that would emerge in the coming decades, especially the importance of first-century Judaism for the study of the Fourth Gospel (FG) and the attention that would be given to John's social context (the Johannine community). The extent to which Robinson's own conservatism is reflected in the five points of his "new look," and the failure of scholarship in succeeding decades to follow his lead on this matter, should remind us of how difficult it is to predict the future on the basis of the present. Each of us has a limited perspective, and the contours of the land mean that we always see more looking upstream than downstream. Before assessing the promise of the "new currents" reflected in the essays in the present volume, some attention must be given to the half century of scholarship between Robinson and the publication of this volume. Johannine scholarship in this period has been so vigorous that any general observations can be challenged with exceptions. Recognizing this limitation, the literature on John nevertheless gives evidence of a series of developments along two axes, the first generally historical and the second generally literary.

Robinson's concerns in his "New Look" essay fall almost exclusively along the historical axis. The first of his five points justifies the qualifier "almost," since it relates to the Fourth Evangelist's use of sources and FG's relationship to the Synoptics, issues that might be deemed "literary" in the broad sense. The other four points of Robinson's "new look," however, all relate to the identity of the Fourth Evangelist and his setting: the similarity of his background to those of the events and teaching he records, his role as an eyewitness to the Jesus of history, the context of his theology, and his possible identity as the apostle John. Even this cursory listing of the five elements of Robinson's "new look" suggests that the primary concerns of mid-twentieth century Johannine scholarship revolved around the composition and historical setting of FG: its author, sources, relationship to the Synoptics, and the context of its theology—both the broader context of Judaism and Hellenism and the narrower context of the development of Christian thought in the first century.

Robinson's own penchant for challenging "assured results" and critical orthodoxy would emerge clearly in his *Redating the New Testament* (1976), in which he argued that the evidence scholars use to assign dates to New Testament documents is much weaker than is generally supposed and that a reasonable case can be made for dating the composition of all the books of the New Testament before the fall of Jerusalem in 70 C.E. In retrospect, we can see this line of thought already becoming apparent in "The New Look on the Fourth Gospel." The full development of the five points of the "new look" can be seen in one of Robinson's last books, *The Priority of John* (1985). The question of John's sources and alleged dependence on the Synoptics is important not merely for understanding the composition of the Fourth Gospel and its place among the Gospels but also because the date of the text and the role (and therefore possible identity) of the Fourth Evangelist are bound up with this question. An eyewitness would not have had to depend on sources or Gospels written by others. Therefore, if the Gospel of John reflects dependence on lost sources, such as Bultmann proposed (a signs source, revelatory discourses, and a passion narrative), or on the Synoptics (at least Mark), as C. K. Barrett maintained, then the Fourth Evangelist was probably not an eyewitness to Jesus and therefore not the apostle John. In the first chapter of *The Priority of John*, Robinson challenges "the long shadow of dependence," argues for a move "from sources to source," and proposes that rather than being the "Fourth" Gospel, John is "a first gospel."

In spite of the perceptiveness of Robinson's characterization of the "new look" in the study of John in the mid-1950s and his observations that anticipated future directions of research, we should not view Robinson's "New

Look" essay as a synopsis of the concerns or conclusions of Johannine studies over the next half century. Robinson's argument drew primarily on the work of other British scholars (J. B. Lightfoot, B. F. Westcott, P. Gardner-Smith, C. H. Dodd, and, with more disagreement, C. K. Barrett). Where he found support from Continental scholars, it was in the work of J. Jeremias, B. Reicke, Bultmann's critics (E. Schweizer, E. Ruckstuhl, and P.-H. Menoud), and the Scandinavian scholar Bent Noack. The "new look," therefore, did not reflect the general status of Johannine scholarship in Germany even at the time Robinson wrote his essay. American Johannine scholarship hardly enters the picture, although Robinson cites the work of W. F. Albright, W. H. Brownlee, and E. R. Goodenough on Palestinian geography, the Dead Sea Scrolls, and John the Baptist. In a recent essay on Raymond Brown's contribution to Johannine studies, I compare his views to the five points of Robinson's "new look" and conclude that "while there is certainly an affinity between Brown and the 'new look,' Brown generally nuanced the points and resisted simplification rather than championing Robinson's cause" (Culpepper 2005, 45).

When Robinson's "new look" was fully developed in *The Priority of John* (1985), Johannine scholarship had generally moved beyond him, with the result that the book appeared to many to be a rather idiosyncratic reminting of the concerns and scholarship of an earlier era. Robinson's concern in "The New Look" for the identity of the Fourth Evangelist, the early date of FG, and its potential value as eyewitness testimony was almost immediately muted by the reference commentaries that were published shortly thereafter. Brown proposed a five-stage process for the composition of FG, subordinating the identity of the author to the coherence of the Johannine tradition. In his Anchor Bible commentary on John (1966–70), Brown affirmed that the Beloved Disciple was the apostle John, but he later abandoned this view, concluding that "he [the BD] was a minor disciple whose name we cannot know" (2003, 191; 1966–70, 1:xcviii; 1979, 31–34). Rudolf Schnackenburg also proposed stages in the composition of the Fourth Gospel, and he too affirmed and then later abandoned the view that the Beloved Disciple was the apostle John (see 1982, 381). Like Brown and Schnackenburg, G. R. Beasley-Murray distinguished the Fourth Evangelist from the Beloved Disciple and proposed an extended composition process (1987, lxx–lxxv).

Rather than the identity of the Evangelist, scholars turned their attention to reconstructing the history of the community that preserved and developed the Johannine tradition. A continuous tradition and the composition of a Gospel in stages implied a distinct community, the history of which might be reconstructed from the concerns and interpretations of the Johannine tradition at various stages in the text's development. Robinson observed that "there are now signs of a corresponding interest in the Johannine *tradition* as such and in the community behind it," citing Bent Noack's *Zur johanneischen Tradition* (1962b, 105; Noack 1954). Research on the Johannine community resulted in a series of publications by J. Louis Martyn (1968, 1978), Wayne Meeks (1972), R. Alan Culpepper (1975), Oscar Cullmann (1976), and Raymond Brown (1979). Work on John's sources continued primarily in the publications of Robert Fortna (1988) and Urban von Wahlde (1989) and in the critical assessment of the signs-source hypothesis by Gilbert van Belle (1994). But historical research soon shifted away from the Evangelist (for a notable exception, see Charlesworth 1995) and from the history of the Johannine community to social-scientific study of the context of the Fourth Gospel. M. C. de Boer (1996) traces the christological terms and themes in John's interpretation of Jesus' death to three crises that marked off four periods in the development of the Johannine tradition. Moving further afield, Tom Thatcher (2006) has discovered new perspectives on the composition of FG by employing social-memory theory in an effort to answer the very basic question, why did John *write* a Gospel?

A similar mutation of interest is evident along the second axis of Johannine research, literary studies. Motivated by David Rhoads's work on the Gospel of Mark and the research of Norman Petersen and other colleagues in the Literary Aspects of the Gospels Group in the Society of Biblical Literature, I spent a sabbatical leave in Cambridge writing *Anatomy of the Fourth Gospel* (1983) under Frank Kermode's guidance. *Anatomy* began as a kind of experiment to see what the Gospel of John looks like from the perspective of current literary theory, informed especially by Wayne Booth, Seymour Chatman, and Gérard Genette. It was an "anatomy" in the sense that it studied the various components, structures, or organs of the vital literary organism we call the Gospel of John to see how they function. The theoretical underpinnings of the book were eclectic: formalism, new criticism, communication theory, reader-response theory, and, to a lesser extent, structuralism. My focus was more on the text itself as narrative and the ways the text manipulates readers in the reading process than on real readers and readings of the Gospel of John.

Anatomy of the Fourth Gospel was just a cursory mapping of the territory, but it opened the way for others to explore individual areas of John's narrative more fully. Gilbert van Belle (1985) analyzed the role of the parentheses or narrative asides in John. Paul Duke (1985) and Gail O'Day (1986) produced groundbreaking studies on Johannine irony. Jeffrey Staley (1988) amplified the role of the implied reader. Jan du Rand (1990; 1991) introduced Johannine narrative criticism to South African scholarship. A 1991 issue of the journal *Semeia* explored *The Fourth Gospel from a Literary Perspective*. Adele Reinhartz (1992) read the opening verses of John 10 as a "cosmological tale." Mark W. G. Stibbe (1992) examined especially the passion narrative in *John as Storyteller* and then produced a narrative-critical commentary on John (1993). In the same year the first volume of Francis J. Moloney's narrative-critical commentary on John appeared (1993). Dorothy Lee analyzed the interplay of form and meaning in *The Symbolic Narratives of the Fourth Gospel* (1994). Craig Koester (2003) wrote on the symbolism, representative figures, and symbolic actions in John. D. F. Tolmie (1995) extended narrative criticism to the interpretation of the Farewell Discourse. David Ball (1996) examined the "I Am" sayings in the light of their literary function. David Beck (1997) studied the function of FG's anonymous characters, and Larry Jones (1997) analyzed the symbolism of water in John. Derek Tovey engaged both narrative criticism and speech-act theory in his work *Narrative Art and Act in the Fourth Gospel* (1997). While Andrew Lincoln's work is broader than narrative criticism, the role of the lawsuit motif in FG is the focus of his *Truth on Trial* (2000). Francisco Lozada (2000) moved narrative criticism in the direction of ideological criticism in his reading of John 5. Jan van der Watt (2000) explored John's metaphorical system and the role of familial language in particular. James Resseguie (2001) treated various aspects of point of view in John. Mary Coloe (2001) showed how temple symbolism in the Fourth Gospel develops thematically and ties together FG's Christology and the self-understanding of the Johannine community. William Bonney (2002) analyzed the role of Thomas in John 20 as an "enabler of faith" at the climax of the Gospel. Building on the work of narrative criticism, rhetoric, and sociolinguistics, Peter M. Phillips (2006) offers a sequential reading of the Prologue. And the work goes on: Kasper Larsen (2006) recently completed a fine dissertation on the role of the recognition scenes in John. Other titles could be included, of course, but these are sufficient to convey the richness of the new issues that narrative criticism has opened up to Johannine studies. At least when judged by the sheer number of published dissertations and monographs, one can legitimately conclude that narrative-critical studies have been the most productive current in Johannine scholarship over the last two decades.

Once narrative-critical perspectives were introduced, methodological innovations appeared quickly (see Moore 1989). Jeffrey Staley (1995) introduced autobiographical criticism. Margaret Davies drew from rhetorical theory, structuralism, reader-response criticism, and feminist interpretation in her *Rhetoric and Reference in the Fourth Gospel* (1992). Responding to the history of patriarchal interpretations of John's Prologue, Alison Jasper (1998) drew on structuralist criticism and deconstruction for her feminist readings of the text. Sandra Schneiders (1999) wove together narrative-critical interpretation of John's symbolic narratives with concerns for feminism and spirituality. In the course of developing her own Jewish reading, Adele

Reinhartz (2001) showed how the Fourth Gospel might look from the perspective of compliant, resistant, sympathetic, and engaged readers. Jo-Ann Brant (2004) profitably combined structuralism with a study of John's use of conventions from ancient Greek drama. Jean Kim's *Woman and Nation* (2004) interprets the women in the Gospel of John from a postcolonial feminist perspective. And tellingly, Robert Kysar (2005) recently organized his volume of collected essays into four groups that reflect the methodological shifts we have surveyed: historical criticism, theological criticism, literary criticism, and postmodern criticism.

The literature on John is endless, but this selection of books in English is sufficient to document the methodological advances and the variety of topics that have guided the interpretation of John over the past several decades. Along both axes, the historical and the literary, one finds methodological innovation and increasingly eclectic approaches to the task of interpretation. The almost exclusive dominance of historical criticism in Robinson's day has given way to two lines of inquiry, both of which have become increasingly diverse and eclectic.

This book, representing "new currents" in Johannine scholarship, is divided into two parts, the first related to "history and theology" and the second to "readers and readings." These rubrics are apt and reflect not only the two major groupings of the essays included here but also the two lines of study, historical and literary, that were traced above through the past quarter century of Johannine scholarship. Reflecting the proliferation of new methodologies, and the allegiances they have created, the Society of Biblical Literature polled its members not long ago, asking them to identify both their areas of expertise and their chosen methodology. The methodological uniformity of the "new look" has collapsed, but rival camps have developed, each advocating certain concerns and certain methods or approaches to the text. At times one can still hear judgmental comments, such as "historical criticism is bankrupt" or "Oh, you're one of those 'lit-crit' people." Scholarship is well on its way to accepting that readers from various ethnic, cultural, and global perspectives read FG differently, but prejudices regarding what constitutes "real scholarship" or cutting edge issues still remain.

One can cite exceptions, but some of the dialogue with Robinson in this collection of essays reminds us of the extent to which historical issues regarding the authorship, historical value, and composition history of the Fourth Gospel have been eclipsed by other concerns. Studies of the theology of FG generally have not benefited from methodological innovations, though observations regarding theological issues often appear scattered in articles and books devoted to historical or literary issues. Regardless of how productive work in other areas may be, Johannine scholarship cannot overlook the realities that the Gospel of John was written in particular historical circumstances about a historical figure and that it is one of the early church's most important theological documents. History and theology will therefore always be vital areas for Johannine scholarship.

One of the encouraging signs of the work of the new generation of scholars represented in this volume is their eclectic methodology, as Tom Thatcher observes at the end of his introductory essay. Jamie Clark-Soles explores Johannine eschatology in light of FG's anthropology. Indeed, she provides a useful lexicon of Johannine anthropology. Rejecting Robinson's diachronic approach, she also reads the Fourth Gospel as a literary whole, drawing on the nuances of terms and observations regarding its literary patterns. Carsten Claussen develops a synchronic reading of John 21, showing how it reinterprets John 1–20, but he still refers to John 20:30–31 as "the original ending of the Fourth Gospel" (p. 66). His conclusion that "John 21 may serve the same purpose as the Johannine Epistles" (p. 67)—that is, to provide hermeneutical guidance to the readers of John 1–20—is both suggestive and a creative blending of diachronic and synchronic approaches to interpretation. Mary Coloe's essay is particularly interesting as a reflection of the breakdown of methodological exclusivism, in that she works with the social conventions surrounding footwashing in antiquity, John's narrative texture, and "the living experience of the Johannine community" in an effort to understand the text's spirituality more fully (p. 80). Extending Robinson's observation that the "new look" in Johannine studies would find a closer similarity between John and its Jewish thought world, Brian Johnson offers readers "a more positive appropriation of the themes and symbols of Judaism" (p. 83), while Beth Sheppard introduces observations regarding Roman family structure, inheritance, and the property rights of the *paterfamilias* that cast John's sayings about the relationship between the Father and the Son in John in a new light. Both Johnson and Sheppard may be making valid observations; one perspective does not necessarily render the other invalid.

The ongoing tension between diachronic and synchronic approaches to the text is still visible, however. Jamie Clark-Soles writes, "Today it seems odd to operate with models of trajectories and growth, primitive and mature—heavily judgmental language that forces biblical texts to compete with one another on the basis of age and development" (p. 52). Coloe notes, "Scholars of the past five decades have fought against the 'critical orthodoxy' expressed in the five presuppositions Robinson described, successfully opening the way for a new generation of scholars to address new issues and to employ new methodologies" (p. 82). As apt as both observations are, we will do well to remember that the study of Jesus, the Johannine tradition, and the Johannine community—for which one needs to employ historical or diachronic methods—continue as valid and important tasks for Johannine scholarship. One approach to the task of interpretation is not necessarily better than another. Each has its place. Different questions require different methods, and scholarship needs to be concerned with both the newer and the traditional questions.

The three essays in part 2 of this volume treat "Readers and Readings" of the Fourth Gospel from different perspectives. Armand Barus engages in a narrative-critical reading of John 2:12–25 in which he analyzes seven aspects of John's account of Jesus' action in the temple. His major conclusion is that this scene leads readers to a postresurrection understanding of "the universality of Jesus' body as the new temple in which the Jews and the Gentiles are united" (p. 139). He also suggests that the Gospel of John was read in settings where nonbelievers were present, so that the text served both to initiate faith among nonbelievers and to deepen faith among believers. The readers and readings that Barus constructs are therefore the historical or original readers of FG. After reviewing the contributions of four Jewish Johannine scholars, Matthew Kraus briefly explains how he, as a Jew, would interpret the figure of Nicodemus for Jewish audiences and for Christian audiences. For Jews, Nicodemus represents a figure teetering on the brink of renouncing Judaism and accepting Jesus (something Kraus hopes he will not do), yet he also models how Jews should relate to Christians. For Christians, Nicodemus poses the dilemma that in order to accept Jews as Jews, Christian readers must reject the gift of the Beloved Disciple (i.e., the gospel of eternal life through faith in Jesus as the Christ, the Son of God). But in order to accept the gift of the Beloved Disciple, Christian readers must reject the legitimacy of Judaism. For Kraus, therefore, the readers and readings in question are modern Jewish scholars and Jewish and Christian readers of the Fourth Gospel. Yak-hwee Tan enters the text through the vine discourse in John 15 and establishes a dialogue between the Johannine community and modern readers, who are encountering the rapid process of globalization. Johannine Christians straddled the divide between the world above, to which Jesus called them, and the world below, the world of the Roman Empire in which they lived. For modern readers, Tan sketches a postcolonial reading of the text that focuses on real readers reading from the perspectives of their social locations. The concluding essay by Francisco Lozada extends the significance of social location for Johannine scholarship, as he reviews the construction of the reader in recent monographs by Jeffrey L. Staley (1995), Alison Jasper (1998), and Adele Reinhartz (2001). Lozada underscores the different ways in which these three scholars reference social location and the dynamic shaping of identity in the work of all three. He also proposes the value of reading the Gospel of John alongside sacred texts of other cultures. Clearly, these four essays illustrate the fruitfulness, one might even say the seemingly limitless diversity, of interpretations or readings to which the text of the FG opens itself once the constructs of implied, intended, historical, and real readers are introduced into the interpretive process.

At the end of his introductory article, Tom Thatcher notes the methodological diversity and the diversity of global perspectives represented in this volume. In the years since Robinson wrote "The New Look on the Fourth Gospel," the community of scholars has become much more diverse and inclusive. As a result, scholars today can make fewer assumptions about perspectives their readers will share with them and with one another, so they must be much more forthcoming about why they are engaging a particular topic and how they will go about it. Our work is done on a much larger stage, engaging a wider range of conversations and conversation partners. Although the requirements that come with the larger stage can at times be demanding and may seem tedious, the result is generally a healthy transparency of method and argument.

Where will these "new currents" take us? Put another way, what do we see when we look ahead and try to read the water downstream? Moody Smith's doctoral students have all been cautioned more than once about "giving hostages to fortune," and nothing invites contradiction so much as an attempt to predict the future of Johannine scholarship. John A. T. Robinson was not troubled about giving hostages to fortune, with the result that he appears brilliant and prophetic where the work of later scholars confirmed directions he foresaw. Where future scholarship took altogether new and unpredictable directions, it simply confirms the limitations of any effort to predict the future.

Recognizing these limitations, and pleading that part of my assignment for this essay was to venture some observations about what the "new currents" in Johannine scholarship portend for the future, I offer the following rather general observations and plead caution as the better part of valor in not venturing more specific predictions.

We may begin with the observation—confirmed by the diversity reflected in the contributors to this volume and the diversity of authors in the list of works cited—that the work of Johannine scholarship is now no longer being done primarily by white, Eurocentric males. Articles, dissertations, monographs, and commentaries on John are now being written by men and women from all parts of the globe, and social location has become—for many—a conscious aspect of their scholarship. The interpretation of FG has therefore become linked with various ethnic, gender, economic, racial, religious, and geopolitical agendas. It is natural that those who have been marginalized should call out for a place at the table and remind those already at the table that their work is laden with implications regarding power and privilege, ethics and political processes. This conscious attention to the social location and identity of the interpreter is salutary, both because it recognizes real factors in the interpretation of the text that have otherwise have been ignored or denied and because it repeatedly confronts interpreters with the otherness of the readings of scholars who start from different vantage points. Nevertheless, one may still wish to confess an uneasiness when it becomes apparent that the real agenda is not the interpretation of the Gospel of John but the concerns that arise from an interpreter's social location. It is inevitable and right that the table of Johannine scholarship should be open to all who wish to participate in the ongoing dialogue about FG. This new openness has not come easily, and battles for full inclusion and recognition remain to be fought.

The diversity of readings of the Gospel of John, some of which are based on the interpreter's social location, raises the specter of sheer subjectivity in interpretation. The tension between objectivity and subjectivity still calls for methodological resolution. While the mask of objectivity has been pulled from the face of those interpreters who do not address the effects of their social locations or predispositions, scholars have not agreed on just how the rules of scholarship have changed. Part of the challenge in this new era continues to be defining norms for the conversation that allow for full inclusion while recognizing that some readings of the text are more perceptive, have greater explanatory power, or are more fully validated by the text and the community of readers than are other readings. In a word, not all readings are equally valid, but what makes one reading more probative or convincing than another?

Second, the movement from the methodological uniformity of the historical criticism of Robinson's day to the methodological plurality of recent decades, and the first tentative efforts to bridge methodologies, suggests a direction that should engage Johannine scholarship in the future. It is almost inevitable that exaggerated claims are made when new approaches to interpretation are introduced, but the exaggerated claims, the sometimes defensive responses of traditionalists, and the privileging of certain issues and methods over others all confirm that Johannine scholarship is still in its infancy. Particular issues or questions are not necessarily better or more important than others just because they are well established or new, currently in vogue or deeply rooted in the history of the discipline, accepted or experimental in their methodologies. One cannot say, therefore, that one methodology is better than another, whether it be historical, literary, social-scientific, theological, or postcolonial. Different issues require different methods or approaches to the text, and there is no more virtue in working in one field than in another. The enterprise of scholarship needs to continue to be informed by all of these areas, to explore new areas, and to test both "assured results" and new theories.

We may applaud the ways in which some "new currents" are drawing from multiple methods of study and beginning to establish dialogues between them. New advances will still be made in each area of study, but some of the most interesting developments downstream may well be the ways in which data, theories, and models from one interpretive method suggest new insights for other approaches to the text. We may therefore look ahead with anticipation to see how the research of social-science scholars sheds light on some of the presumed conventions in the Fourth Gospel and how narrative criticism reshapes our understanding of the ideology and theology of the text. No theory regarding the composition history of FG or the history of the Johannine community has significantly altered the state of these issues in the past couple of decades (see, however, Waetjen 2005), so it will be interesting to see how the work of these decades will change our understandings when these questions are revisited. The reception of the Gospel of John and its role in the second century also appears to be a contested but promising area for further study (see Hill 2004).

Physicists continue to seek the unified theory that will allow them to understand the reasons for some of the paradoxes in contemporary physics. Johannine scholarship and Gospel studies more generally still have not developed a methodology that unifies the various current approaches to the text and harnesses the contributions of the plurality of methods of interpretation. As long as all are welcomed at the table, all questions are received, all original contributions are critically appraised, and dialogue is fostered without prejudice toward certain scholars, methods, or theories, the future of Johannine scholarship will be both vigorous and fruitful.

Works Cited

Adam, A. K. M. 1995. *Making Sense of New Testament Theology: "Modern" Problems and Prospects*. StABH. Macon, Ga.: Mercer University Press.

Anderson, Paul N. 1996. *The Christology of the Fourth Gospel: Its Unity and Disunity in the Light of John 6*. Valley Forge, Pa.: Trinity Press International.

———. 1999. The Having-Sent-Me Father: Aspects of Agency, Encounter, and Irony in the Johannine Father-Son Relationship. Pages 33–57 in *Semeia 85: God the Father in the Gospel of John*. Edited by Adele Reinhartz. Atlanta: Society of Biblical Literature.

Ando, Clifford. 2000. *Imperial Ideology and Provincial Loyalty in the Roman Empire*. Berkeley and Los Angeles: University of California Press.

Appleby, Joyce, Lynn Hunt, and Margaret Jacob. 1995. *Telling the Truth About History*. New York: Norton.

Ashcroft, Bill, Gareth Griffiths, and Helen Tiffin. 1998. *Key Concepts in Post-colonial Studies*. London: Routledge.

Ashton, John. 1994. *Studying John: Approaches to the Fourth Gospel*. Oxford: Clarendon.

Bacon, Benjamin Wisner. 1910. *The Fourth Gospel in Research and Debate*. New York: Moffatt & Yard.

Bakhtin, Mikhail M. 1981. *The Dialogic Imagination: Four Essays*. Edited by Michael Holquist. Translated by Caryl Emerson and Michael Holquist. Austin: University of Texas Press.

Balch, David L., and Carolyn Osiek, eds. 2003. *Early Christian Families in Context: An Interdisciplinary Dialogue*. Grand Rapids: Eerdmans.

Ball, David Mark. 1996. *'I Am' in John's Gospel: Literary Function, Background and Theological Implications*. JSNTSup 124. Sheffield: Sheffield Academic Press.

Barber, Benjamin R. 1996. *Jihad vs. McWorld: How Globalism and Tribalism are Reshaping the World*. New York: Ballantine.

Bar-Efrat, Shimon. 2000. *Narrative Art in the Bible*. Bible and Literature 17. Sheffield: Sheffield Academic Press.

Barrett, C. K. 1973–74. John and the Synoptic Gospels. *ExpTim* 85:228–33.

———. 1978. *The Gospel according to St. John*. 2nd edition. Philadelphia: Westminster.

Barthes, Roland. 1967. *Writing Degree Zero*. Translated by Annette Lavers and Colin Smith. London: Jonathan Cape.

———. 1974. *S/Z*. Translated by Richard Miller. New York: Hill & Wang.

———. 1977. The Death of the Author. Pages 142–48 in *Image—Music—Text*. Edited and translated by Stephen Heath. New York: Hill & Wang.

Bauckham, Richard. 1988. Jesus' Demonstration in the Temple. Pages 72–89, 171–76 in *Law and Religion: Essays on the Place of the Law in Israel and Early Christianity*. Edited by Barnabas Lindars. Cambridge: Clarke.

———, ed. 1998. *The Gospels for All Christians: Rethinking the Gospel Audiences*. Grand Rapids: Eerdmans.

Beasley-Murray, G. R. 1999. *John*. 2nd ed. Nashville: Nelson.

Beck, David R. 1997. *The Discipleship Paradigm: Readers and Anonymous Characters in the Fourth Gospel*. BibInt 27. Leiden: Brill.

Belle, Gilbert van. 1985. *Les parenthèses dan l'Evangile de Jean*. Leuven: Leuven University Press.

———. 1994. *The Signs Source in the Fourth Gospel*. BETL 116. Leuven: Leuven University Press.

Berger, Peter. 1969. *The Sacred Canopy: Elements of a Sociological Theory of Religion*. Garden City, N.Y.: Anchor Books.

Berger, Peter, and Thomas Luckman. 1980. *The Social Construction of Reality: A Treatise in the Sociology of Knowledge*. New York: Irvington.

Bhabha, Homi. 1994a. "Introduction: Narrating the Nation." Pages 1–7 in *Nation and Narration*. Edited by Homi Bhabha. New York: Routledge.

———. 1994b. *The Location of Culture*. London: Routledge.

Biville, Frédérique. 2002. The Graeco-Romans and Graeco-Latin: A Terminological Framework for Cases of Bilingualism. Pages 77–102 in *Bilingualism in Ancient Society*. Edited by J. N. Adams, Mark Janse, and Simon Swain. Oxford: Oxford University Press.

Blomberg, Craig. 2001. *The Historical Reliability of John's Gospel: Issues and Commentary*. Downers Grove, Ill.: InterVarsity Press.

Boer, M. C. de. 1996. *Johannine Perspectives on the Death of Jesus*. Kampen, The Netherlands: Kok Pharos.

Boismard, M.-E., and A. Lamouille, with G. Rochais. 1977. *L'Evangile de Jean: Commentaire*. Vol. 3 of *Synopses des quarte Evangiles en français*. Paris: Cerf.

Bonney, William. 2002. *Caused to Believe: The Doubting Thomas Story as the Climax of John's Christological Narrative*. BibInt 62. Leiden: Brill.

Booth, Wayne C. 1988. *The Company We Keep: An Ethics of Fiction*. Berkeley and Los Angeles: University of California Press.

Borg, Marcus J. 1994. *Meeting Jesus Again for the First Time: The Historical Jesus and the Heart of Contemporary Faith*. San Francisco: HarperSanFrancisco.

Böttrich, Christfried. 2001. "Suchen und Finden": Aspekte des johanneischen Menschenbildes nach Joh 1,35–51. Pages 379–96 in *Menschenbild und*

Menschenwürde. Edited by Eilert Herms. Veröffentlichungen der Wissenschaftlichen Gesellschaft für Theologie 17. Gütersloh: Christian Kaiser, Gütersloher Verlagshaus.

Boyarin, Daniel. 1997a. Jewish Studies as Teratology: The Rabbis as Monsters. *JQR* 88:57–66.

———. 1997b. Review of *Covenant of Blood* by Lawrence Huffman. *JQR* 88:57–66.

———. 1997c. *Unheroic Conduct: The Rise of Heterosexuality and the Invention of the Jewish Man*. Berkeley and Los Angeles: University of California Press.

———. 1999. *Dying for God: Martyrdom and the Making of Judaism and Christianity*. Stanford, Calif.: Stanford University Press.

———. 2001. The Gospel of the Memra: Jewish Binitarianism and the Prologue to John. *HTR* 94:243–84.

———. 2002. The Ioudaioi in John and the Prehistory of "Judaism." Pages 216–39 in *Pauline Conversations in Context: Essays in Honor of Calvin J. Roetzel*. Edited by Janice Capel Anderson, Philip Sellew, and Claudia Setzer. JSNTSup 221. London: Sheffield Academic Press.

———. 2004. *Border Lines: The Partition of Judaeo-Christianity*. Philadelphia: University of Pennsylvania Press.

Boyer, Peter. 2003. The Jesus War: Mel Gibson's Obsession. *The New Yorker*. September 15:58–83.

Boys, Mary. 2003. "I Didn't See Any Anti-Semitism": Why Many Christians Don't Have a Problem with The Passion of the Christ. *Cross Currents* 52. Online: http://www.crosscurrents.org/BoysSpring2004.htm

Bradley, Keith. 1991. *Discovering the Roman Family: Studies in Roman Social History*. Oxford: Oxford University Press.

Brant, Jo-Ann A. 2004. *Dialogue and Drama: Elements of Greek Tragedy in the Fourth Gospel*. Peabody, Mass.: Hendrickson.

Bremmer, Jan. 2002. *The Rise and Fall of the Afterlife*. London: Routledge.

Brodie, Thomas. 1993. *The Quest for the Origin of John's Gospel: A Source-Oriented Approach*. New York: Oxford University Press.

Brooks, James A., and Carlton L. Winbery. 1970. *Syntax of New Testament Greek*. Lanham, Md.: University Press of America.

Brown, Raymond. 1966–70. *The Gospel according to John*. AB 29–29A. Garden City, N.Y.: Doubleday.

———. 1978. Other Sheep Not of This Fold: The Johannine Perspective on Christian Diversity in the Late First Century. *JBL* 97:5–22.

———. 1979. *The Community of the Beloved Disciple: The Life, Loves, and Hates of an Individual Church in New Testament Times*. New York: Paulist.

———. 2003. *An Introduction to the Gospel of John*. Edited by Francis J. Moloney. New York: Doubleday.

Brumberg-Kraus, Jonathan D. 1997. A Jewish Ideological Perspective on the Study of Christian Scripture. *Jewish Social Studies* 4:121–52.

———. 2000. Jesus as Other People's Scripture. Pages 155–66 in *The Historical Jesus through Catholic and Jewish Eyes*. Edited by Leonard J. Greenspoon, Dennis Hamm, and Brian F. Le Beau. Harrisburg, Pa.: Trinity Press International.

Bultmann, Rudolf. 1971. *The Gospel of John: A Commentary*. Translated by G. R. Beasley-Murray, Rupert W. N. Hoare, and John K. Riches. Oxford: Basil Blackwell.

Cassem, N. H. 1972–73. A Grammatical and Contextual Inventory of the Use of *Kosmos* in the Johannine Corpus with Some Implications for a Johannine Cosmic Theology. *NTS* 19:81–91.

Cassidy, Richard J. 1992. *John's Gospel in New Perspective*. Maryknoll, N.Y.: Orbis.

Chancey, Mark. 2004. "Hellenization," "Romanization" and Galilean Judaism. Paper presented at the Society of Biblical Literature Annual Meeting. San Antonio, Tex., 21 November.

Charlesworth, James H., ed. 1985. *The Old Testament Pseudepigrapha*. London: Darton, Longman & Todd.

———, ed. 1990. *John and the Dead Sea Scrolls*. New York: Crossroads.

———. 1995. *The Beloved Disciple: Whose Witness Validates the Gospel of John?* Valley Forge, Pa.: Trinity Press International.

Chow, Rey. 1993. *Writing Diaspora: Tactics of Intervention in Contemporary Cultural Studies*. Bloomington: Indiana University Press.

Claussen, Carsten. 2005. The Eucharist in the Gospel of John and in the *Didache*. Pages 135–63 in *Trajectories through the New Testament and the Apostolic Fathers*. Edited by Andrew F. Gregory and Christopher M. Tuckett. Oxford: Oxford University Press.

Cohn-Sherbok, Dan. 1996. The Resurrection of Jesus: A Jewish View. Pages 184–200 in *Resurrection Reconsidered*. Edited by Gavin D'Costa. Oxford: Oneworld.

Coloe, Mary L. 2000. Households of Faith (Jn 4:46–54; 11:1–44). *Pacifica* 12:326–33.

———. 2001. *God Dwells with Us: Temple Symbolism in the Fourth Gospel*. Collegeville, Minn.: Liturgical Press.

———. 2004. Welcome to the Household of God: The Footwashing in John 13. *CBQ* 66:400–15.

Cook, Michael J. 1974. Jesus on Trial. *Religious Education* 69:278–80.

———. 1978. *Mark's Treatment of the Jewish Leaders*. NovTSup 51. Leiden: Brill.

———. 1983. Anti-Judaism in the New Testament. *USQR* 38:125–37.

———. 1987a. The Gospel of John and the Jews. *RevExp* 84:259–71.

———. 1987b. The New Testament and Judaism: An Historical Perspective on the Theme. *RevExp* 84:183–99.

———. 1988. Confronting New Testament Attitudes on Jews and Judaism: Four Jewish Perspectives. *Chicago Theological Seminary Register* 78:3–30.

———. 1996. The Jewish Scholar and New Testament Images of Judaism. *Lutheran Theological Seminary Bulletin* 77:21–41.
———. 1999. Christian Appropriation of the Passover: Jewish Responses Then and Now. *LTQ* 34:13–39.
———. 2000. Jewish Reflections on Jesus: Some Abiding Trends. Pages 95–111 in *The Historical Jesus through Catholic and Jewish Eyes*. Edited by Leonard J. Greenspoon, Dennis Hamm, and Bryan F. Le Beau. Harrisburg, Pa.: Trinity Press International.
Crook, J. A. 1967. Patria Potestas. *CQ* 17 (NS):113–22.
Cullmann, Oscar. 1976. *The Johannine Circle*. Translated by John Bowden. Philadelphia: Westminster.
Culpepper, R. Alan. 1975. *The Johannine School*. SBLDS 26. Missoula, Mont.: Scholars Press.
———. 1983. *Anatomy of the Fourth Gospel: A Study in Literary Design*. Philadelphia: Fortress.
———. 1991. The Johannine *Hypodeigma*: A Reading of John 13. Pages 133–52 in *Semeia 53: The Fourth Gospel from a Literary Perspective*. Edited by R. Alan Culpepper and Fernando F. Segovia. Atlanta: Society of Biblical Literature.
———. 1998. *The Gospel and Letters of John*. Interpreting Biblical Texts. Nashville: Abingdon.
———. 2002. Inclusivism and Exclusivism in the Fourth Gospel. Pages 85–108 in *Word, Theology, and Community in John*. Edited by John Painter, R. Alan Culpepper, and Fernando F. Segovia. St. Louis: Chalice.
———. 2005. "The Legacy of Raymond E. Brown and Beyond: A Response to Francis J. Moloney." Pages 40–51 in *Life in Abundance: Studies of John's Gospel in Tribute to Raymond E. Brown*. Edited by John R. Donahue. Collegeville, Minn.: Liturgical Press.
Culpepper, R. Alan, and Fernando F. Segovia, eds. 1991. *Semeia 53: The Fourth Gospel from a Literary Perspective*. Atlanta: Society of Biblical Literature.
D'Angelo, Mary Rose. 1999. Imitating Deity in the Gospel of John: Theological Language and "Father" in "Prayers of Jesus." Pages 59–82 in *Semeia 85: God the Father in the Gospel of John*. Edited by Adele Reinhartz. Atlanta: Society of Biblical Literature.
Daube, David. 1984. *The New Testament and Rabbinic Judaism*. Salem, N.H.: Ayer.
———. 1987. *Appeasement or Resistance and Other Essays on New Testament Judaism*. Berkeley and Los Angeles: University of California Press.
Davies, Margaret. 1992. *Rhetoric and Reference in the Fourth Gospel*. JSNTSS 69. Sheffield: Sheffield Academic Press.
Destro, Adriana, and Mauro Pesce. 1995. Kinship, Discipleship, and Movement: An Anthropological Study of John's Gospel. *BibInt* 3:266–84.

Dixon, Suzanne. 1992. *The Roman Family*. Baltimore: Johns Hopkins University Press.

Dodd, Charles Harold. 1963. *Historical Tradition in the Fourth Gospel*. Cambridge: Cambridge University Press.

Duke, Paul D. 1985. *Irony in the Fourth Gospel*. Atlanta: John Knox.

Dunn, James D. G. 2006. *Unity and Diversity in the New Testament: An Inquiry into the Character of Earliest Christianity*. 3rd ed. London: SCM.

Eisenbaum, Pamela Michelle. 1997. *The Jewish Heroes of Christian History: Hebrews 11 in Literary Context*. SBLDS 156. Atlanta: Scholars Press.

———. 2004. Jews and the Study of the New Testament. Paper presented at the Society of Biblical Literature Annual Meeting. San Antonio, Texas.

Encyclopedia Judaica Decennial Book, 1973–1982. 1982. Jerusalem: Keter.

Eyben, Emiel. 1991. Fathers and Sons. Pages 114–43 in *Marriage, Divorce and Children in Ancient Rome*. Edited by Beryl Rawson. Oxford: Clarendon.

Fitzgerald, John T. 2000. Hospitality. *DNTB*, 522–25.

Flusser, David. 1983. The Jewish-Christian Schism, Part 1. *Imm* 16:32–49.

———. 1992. Jesus and Judaism: Jewish Perspectives. Pages 80–109 in *Eusebius, Christianity, and Judaism*. StPB 42. Edited by Harold W. Attridge and Gohei Hata. Leiden: Brill.

Fortna, Robert T. 1970. *The Gospel of Signs: A Reconstruction of the Narrative Source Underlying the Fourth Gospel*. SNTSMS 11. Cambridge: Cambridge University Press.

———. 1988. *The Fourth Gospel and Its Predecessor: From Narrative Source to Present Gospel*. Philadelphia: Fortress.

Foucault, Michel. 1970. *The Order of Things: An Archeology of the Human Sciences*. Translated by Alan Sheridan-Smith. New York: Pantheon.

———. 1977. *Discipline and Punishment: The Birth of the Prison*. Translated by Alan Sheridan. New York: Random House.

Frankfurter, David. 2001. Jews or Not? Reconstructing the "Other" in Rev. 2:9 and 3:9. *HTR* 94:403–425.

Fredriksen, Paula. 1988. *From Jesus to Christ: The Origins of the New Testament Images of Jesus*. New Haven: Yale University Press.

———. 2000. *Jesus of Nazareth, King of the Jews: A Jewish Life and the Emergence of Christianity*. New York: Knopf.

———. 2003. Mad Mel: The Gospel according to Gibson. *New Republic* July 28.

———. 2004. The Pain Principle. *The New Republic Online*. February 27. Online: https://ssl.tnr.com/p/docsub.mhtml?i=express&s=fredriksen022704.

Frymer-Kensky, Tikva, ed. 2000. *Christianity in Jewish Terms*. Radical Traditions. Boulder, Colo.: Westview.

Funk, Robert W., Roy W. Hoover, and the Jesus Seminar. 1993. *The Five Gospels: The Search for the Authentic Words of Jesus*. New York: Macmillan.

Gandhi, Leela. 1998. *Postcolonial Theory: A Critical Introduction*. New York: Columbia University Press.

Gardner-Smith, Percival. 1938. *St. John and the Synoptic Gospels*. Cambridge: Cambridge University Press.

Gärtner, Bertil. 1965. *The Temple and the Community in Qumran and the New Testament: A Comparative Study in the Temple Symbolism of the Qumran Texts and the New Testament*. SNTSMS 1. London: Cambridge University Press.

Gaventa, Beverly Roberts. 1996. The Archive of Excess: John 21 and the Problem of Narrative Closure. Pages 240–54 in *Exploring the Gospel of John: Essays in Honor of D. Moody Smith*. Edited by R. Alan Culpepper and C. Clifton Black. Louisville: Westminster John Knox.

Geertz, Clifford. 1973. *Interpretations of Cultures*. New York: Basic.

Giddens, Anthony. 1990. *The Consequences of Modernity*. Cambridge: Polity.

———. 2000. *Runaway World: How Globalization Is Reshaping Our Lives*. New York: Routledge.

Glass, Zipporah G. 2002. Building Toward "Nation-ness" in the Vine: A Postcolonial Critique of John 15:1–8. Pages 153–69 in *John and Postcolonialism. Travel, Space and Power*. Edited by Musa W. Dube Shomanah and Jeffrey L. Staley. Bible and Postcolonialism 7. New York: Sheffield Academic Press.

Goldhill, Simon, ed. 2001. *Being Greek under Rome: Cultural Identity, the Second Sophistic and the Development of Empire*. Cambridge: Cambridge University Press.

Greenspoon, Leonard J., Dennis Hamm, and Bryan F. LeBeau, eds. 2000. *The Historical Jesus through Catholic and Jewish Eyes*. Harrisburg, Pa.: Trinity Press International.

Guha, Ranajit. 1992. Discipline and Mobilise. Pages 64–120 in *Subaltern Studies 7: Writings on South Asian History and Society*. Edited by Partha Chatterjee and Gyanendra Pandey. Delhi: Oxford University Press.

Hall, Stuart. 1989. New Ethnicities. In *Black Film, British Cinema*. ICA Document 7. London: Institute of Contemporary Arts.

———. 1990. Cultural Identity and Diaspora. Pages 222–37 in *Identity, Community, Culture, Difference*. Edited by J. Rutherford. London: Lawrence & Wishart.

———. 1997a. Introduction. Pages 1–11 in *Representation: Cultural Representations and Signifying Practices*. Edited by Stuart Hall. London: Sage.

———. 1997b. The Spectacle of the "Other." Pages 225–92 in *Representation: Cultural Representations and Signifying Practices*. Edited by Stuart Hall. London: Sage.

Hamid-Khani, Saeed. 2000. *Revelation and Concealment of Christ: A Theological Inquiry into the Elusive Language of the Fourth Gospel*. WUNT 2/120. Tübingen: Mohr Siebeck.

Haran, Menahem. 1969. The Divine Presence in the Israelite Cult and the Cultic Institutions. *Bib* 50:251–67.

Hauser, Alan J., and Duane F. Watson, eds. 2003. *The Ancient Period*. Vol. 1 of *A History of Biblical Interpretation*. Grand Rapids: Eerdmans.

Hays, Richard B. 1989. *Echoes of Scripture in the Letters of Paul*. New Haven: Yale University Press.
Hellerman, Joseph H. 2001. *The Ancient Church as Family*. Minneapolis: Fortress.
Hengel, Martin. 1977. *Crucifixion in the Ancient World and the Folly of the Message of the Cross*. Translated by John Bowden. Philadelphia: Fortress.
———. 1989. *The Johannine Question*. Translated by John Bowden. London: SCM.
Heschel, Susannah. 2003. Quest for the Aryan Jesus: The Archaeology of Nazi Orientalist Theology. Pages 65–84 in *Jews, Antiquity, and the Nineteenth-Century Imagination*. Edited by Hayim Lapin and Dale B. Martin. Bethesda, Md.: University Press of Maryland.
Hill, Charles E. 2004. *The Johannine Corpus in the Early Church*. Oxford: Oxford University Press.
Horst, Pieter W. van der. 1995. The *Birkath ha-Minim* in Recent Research. *ExpTim* 105:363–68.
Hoskyns, Edwyn Clement. 1947. *The Fourth Gospel*. 2nd ed. Edited by F. N. Davey. London: Faber & Faber.
Howard-Brook, Wes. 1994. *Becoming Children of God. John's Gospel and Radical Discipleship*. Maryknoll, N.Y.: Orbis.
Hultgren, Arland J. 1982. The Johannine Footwashing (13:1–11) as Symbol of Eschatological Hospitality. *NTS* 28:539–46.
Huntington, Samuel P. 1993. The Clash of Civilizations? *Foreign Affairs* 72/3:22–49.
Hurtado, Larry W. 2003. *Lord Jesus Christ: Devotion to Jesus in Earliest Christianity*. Grand Rapids: Eerdmans.
Ilan, Tal. 1995. *Jewish Women in Greco-Roman Palestine*. Peabody, Mass.: Hendrickson.
Jasper, Alison. 1998. *The Shining Garment of the Text: Gendered Readings of John's Prologue*. JSNTSup 165. Sheffield: Sheffield Academic Press.
Jeffers, James S. 1999. *The Greco-Roman World of the New Testament Era: Exploring the Background of Early Christianity*. Downers Grove, Ill.: InterVarsity Press.
Jewett, Robert. 1971. *Paul's Anthropological Terms : A Study of Their Use in Conflict Settings*. AGJU 10. Leiden: Brill.
Johnson, Brian D. 1998. Review of *The Gospels for All Christians*. *Stone-Campbell Journal* 1:269–70.
Jones, Larry Paul. 1997. *The Symbol of Water in the Gospel of John*. JSNTSup 145. Sheffield: Sheffield Academic Press.
Jonge, Marinus de. 1988. *Christology in Context: The Earliest Christian Response to Jesus*. Philadelphia: Westminster.
Käsemann, Ernst. 1968. *The Testament of Jesus: A Study of the Gospel of John in the Light of Chapter 17*. Translated by Gerhard Krodel. Philadelphia: Fortress.
Keck, Leander E. 1992. Death and Afterlife in the New Testament. Pages 83–96 in *Death and Afterlife: Perspectives of World Religions*. Edited by Hiroshi Obayashi. Westport, Conn.: Greenwood.

Keener, Craig S. 2003. *The Gospel of John: A Commentary*. Peabody, Mass.: Hendrickson.
Kerr, Alan. 2002. *The Temple of Jesus' Body: The Temple Theme in the Gospel of John*. JSNTSup 220. London: Sheffield Academic Press.
Kilgour, Frederick G. 1998. *The Evolution of the Book*. Oxford: Oxford University Press.
Kim, Jean K. 2004. *Woman and Nation: An Intercontextual Reading of the Gospel of John from a Postcolonial Feminist Perspective*. BibInt 69. Leiden: Brill.
Kitzberger, Ingrid Rosa, ed. 1999. *The Personal Voice in Biblical Interpretation*. London: Routledge.
Klenicki, Leon, ed. 1991. *Toward a Theological Encounter: Jewish Understanding of Christianity*. New York: Paulist.
Koester, Craig. 2003. *Symbolism in the Fourth Gospel: Meaning, Mystery, Community*. 2nd ed. Minneapolis: Fortress.
Köstenberger, Andreas J. 1999. *Encountering John: The Gospel in Historical, Literary, and Theological Perspective*. Grand Rapids: Baker.
Kümmel, Werner George. 1975. *Introduction to the New Testament*. Rev. ed. Translated by Howard Clark Kee. Nashville: Abingdon.
Kysar, Robert. 1993. *John, the Maverick Gospel*. Louisville: Westminster John Knox.
———. 2005. *Voyages with John: Charting the Fourth Gospel*. Waco, Tex.: Baylor University Press.
LaBahn, Michael. 1999. *Jesus als Lebensspender: Untersuchungen zu einer Geschichte der johanneischen Tradition anhand ihrer Wundergeschichten*. BZNW 98. Berlin: de Gruyter.
Larsen, Kasper Bro. 2006. "Recognizing the Stranger: *Anagnōrisis* in the Gospel of John." Ph.D. diss. University of Aarhus, Denmark.
Lee, Dorothy A. 1994. *The Symbolic Narratives of the Fourth Gospel: The Interplay of Form and Meaning*. JSNTSup 95. Sheffield: Sheffield Academic Press.
———. 2002. *Flesh and Glory: Symbolism, Gender and Theology in the Gospel of John*. New York: Crossroad.
Levine, Amy-Jill. 1988. *The Social and Ethnic Dimensions of Matthean Salvation History*. Lewiston, N.Y.: Mellen.
Levine, Amy-Jill, with Marianne Blickenstaff, eds. 2003. *A Feminist Companion to John*. 2 vols. FCNTECW 4–5. New York: Sheffield Academic Press.
Lieu, Judith M. 1998. The Mother of the Son in the Fourth Gospel. *JBL* 117:61–77.
———. 2001. Anti-Judaism and the Fourth Gospel: Explanation and Hermeneutics. Pages 101–17 in *Anti-Judaism and the Fourth Gospel*. Edited by Reimund Bieringer, Didier Pollefeyt, and Frederique Vandecasteele-Vanneuville. Louisville: Westminster John Knox.
Lincoln, Andrew T. 2000. *Truth on Trial: The Lawsuit Motif in the Fourth Gospel*. Peabody, Mass.: Hendrickson.

Lindbeck, Kristen H. 2000. A Jewish Jesus (Review of Paula Fredriksen, *Jesus of Nazareth, King of the Jews*). *First Things* 108:46–48.

Long, A. A. 1986. *Hellenistic Philosophy: Stoics, Epicureans, Sceptics*. 2nd ed. Berkeley and Los Angeles: University of California Press.

Loomba, Ania. 1998. *Colonialism/Postcolonialism*. New York: Routledge.

Lozada, Francisco, Jr. 2000. *A Literary Reading of John 5: Text as Construction*. Studies in Biblical Literature 20. New York: Lang.

MacMullen, Ramsay. 2000. *Romanization in the Time of Augustus*. New Haven: Yale University Press.

Malina, Bruce J. 1985. *The Gospel of John in Sociolinguistic Perspective*. Berkeley, Calif.: Center for Hermeneutical Studies.

Malina, Bruce J., and Richard Rohrbaugh. 1998. *Social-Science Commentary on the Gospel of John*. Minneapolis: Fortress.

Manns, Frédéric. 1981. Le lavement des pieds: Essai sur la structure et la signification de Jean 13. *RSR* 55:149–69.

———. 1991. *L'Évangile de Jean à la lumière du Judaïsme*. Jerusalem: Franciscan Printing Press.

Marcus, Joel. 1992. *The Way of the Lord: Christological Exegesis of the Old Testament in the Gospel of Mark*. Louisville: Westminster John Knox.

———. 2000. *Mark: A New Translation with Introduction and Commentary*. 2 vols. AB27–27A. New York: Doubleday.

Martyn, J. Louis. 1968. *History and Theology in the Fourth Gospel*. New York: Harper & Row.

———. 1977. "Glimpses into the History of the Johannine Community." Pages 149–76 in *L'Évangile de Jean: Sources, Rédaction, Théologie*. Edited by Marinus de Jonge. BETL 44. Leuven: Leuven University Press.

———. 1978. *The Gospel of John in Christian History: Essays for Intepreters*. New York: Paulist.

———. 1979. *History and Theology in the Fourth Gospel*. 2nd ed. Nashville: Abingdon.

———. 2003. *History and Theology in the Fourth Gospel*. NTL. Louisville: Westminster John Knox.

McGowan, Andrew. 1999. *Ascetic Eucharists: Food and Drink in Early Christian Ritual*. Oxford Early Christian Studies. Oxford: Clarendon.

McNamara, Martin. 1992. *Targum Neofiti 1: Genesis*. Edinburgh: T&T Clark.

Medved, Michael. 2004. Crucifying Mel Gibson. No pages. Online: http://www.taemag.com/issues/articleid.17815/article_detail.asp.

Meeks, Wayne A. 1972. The Man From Heaven in Johannine Sectarianism. *JBL* 91:44–72.

Meyer, Ben F. 1994. *Reality and Illusion in New Testament Scholarship: A Primer in Critical Realist Hermeneutics*. Collegeville, Minn.: Liturgical Press.

Meyers, Carol L., Toni Craven, and Ross S. Kraemer, eds. 2000. *Women in Scripture: A Dictionary of Named and Unnamed Women in the Hebrew Bible, the Apocryphal/Deuterocanonical Books and the New Testament*. New York: Houghton Mifflin.

Moloney, Francis J. 1993. *Belief in the Word: Reading John 1–4*. Minneapolis: Fortress.

———. 1998. *The Gospel of John*. Sacra Pagina. Collegeville, Minn.: Liturgical Press.

Moore, Stephen D. 1989. *Literary Criticism and the Gospels: The Theoretical Challenge*. New Haven: Yale University Press.

Morris, Leon. 1969. *Studies in the Fourth Gospel*. Grand Rapids: Eerdmans.

Motyer, Stephen. 1997. *"Your Father the Devil?": A New Approach to John and "the Jews."* Carlisle: Paternoster.

Nanos, Mark D. 1996. *The Mystery of Romans: The Jewish Context of Paul's Letter*. Minneapolis: Fortress.

———. 2000. Challenging the Limits That Continue to Define Paul's Perspective on Jews and Judaism. Pages 212–24 in *Reading Israel in Romans: Legitimacy and Plausibility of Divergent Interpretations*. Edited by Cristina Grenholm and Daniel Patte. Romans through History and Cultures. Harrisburg, Pa.: Trinity Press International.

———. 2002. *The Irony of Galatians: Paul's Letter in First Century Context*. Minneapolis: Fortress.

Neill, Stephen, and Tom Wright. 1988. *The Interpretation of the New Testament 1861–1986*. Oxford: Oxford University Press.

Neirynck, Franz. 1977. John and the Synoptics. Pages 73–106 in *L'Évangile de Jean: Sources, Rédaction, Théologie*. Edited by Marinus de Jonge. BETL 44. Leuven: Leuven University Press.

Neusner, Jacob. 1989. Money Changers in the Temple: The Mishnah's Explanation. *NTS* 35:287–90.

Nielsen, Helge Kjaer. 1999. Johannine Research. Pages 11–33 in *New Readings in John: Literary and Theological Perspectives*. Edited by Johannes Nissen and Sigfred Pedersen. JSNTSup 182. Sheffield: Sheffield Academic Press.

Niemand, Christopher. 1993. *Die Fusswaschungserzählung des Johannesevangeliums: Untersuchungen zu ihrer Entstehung und Überlieferung im Urchristentum*. Rome: Pontificio Anteneo S. Anselmo.

Nisbet, Robert A. 1964. Kinship and Political Power in First Century Rome. Pages 257–71 in *Sociology and History: Theory and Research*. Edited by Werner J. Cahnman and Alvin Boskoff. London: The Free Press of Glencoe.

Noack, Bent. 1954. *Zur johanneischen Tradition*. Copenhagen: Rosenkilde og Bagger.

O'Day, Gail R. 1986. *Revelation in the Fourth Gospel: Narrative Mode and Theological Claim*. Philadelphia: Fortress.

———. 1998. John. Pages 381–93 in *Women's Bible Commentary: Expanded Edition with Apocrypha*. Edited by Carol A. Newsom and Sharon H. Ringe. Louisville: Westminster John Knox.

Parry, Benita. 1987. Problems in Current Theories of Colonial Discourse. *Oxford Literary Review* 9:27–58.
Parsons, Mikeal. 1992. What's "Literary" about Literary Aspects of the Gospels and Acts? Pages 14–39 in *Society of Biblical Literature 1992 Seminar Papers.* SBLSP 31. Atlanta: Scholars Press.
Patterson, Stephen J. 2001. The Prologue to the Fourth Gospel and the World of Speculative Jewish Theology. Pages 323–32 in *Jesus in Johannine Tradition*. Edited by Robert T. Fortna and Tom Thatcher. Louisville: Westminster John Knox.
Paulien, Jon. 1992. Nicodemus. *ABD* 4:1105–6.
Perry, Menakhem. 1979. Literary Dynamics: How the Order of a Text Creates Its Meaning. *Poetics Today* 1:35–64, 311–61.
Philips, Peter Michael. 2004. The Prologue of the Fourth Gospel: An Exploration into the Meaning of at Text. Ph.D. thesis, University of Sheffield.
———. 2006. *The Prologue of the Fourth Gospel: A Sequential Reading*. Library of New Testament Studies 294. London: T&T Clark.
Pippin, Tina. 1996. Ideology, Ideological Criticism and the Bible. *CurBS* 4:51–78.
Pratt, Mary Louise. 1992. *Imperial Eyes: Traveling, Writing and Transculturation.* London: Routledge.
Pregeant, Russell. 1997. *Engaging the New Testament: An Interdisciplinary Introduction*. Minneapolis: Augsburg Fortress.
Rad, Gerhard von. 1972. *Genesis: A Commentary*. London: SCM.
Rand, Jan A. du. 1990. *Johannese Perspektiewe*. Pretoria: Orion.
———. 1991. *Johannine Perspectives: Introduction to the Johannine Writings—Part I*. Pretoria: Orion.
Rawson, Beryl. 1986. *The Family in Ancient Rome: New Perspectives*. Ithaca, N.Y.: Cornell University Press.
Reinhartz, Adele. 1992. *The Word in the World: The Cosmological Tale in the Fourth Gospel*. SBLMS 45. Atlanta: Scholars Press.
———. 1999. "And the Word Was Begotten": Divine Epigenesis in the Gospel of John. Pages 83–103 in *Semeia 85: God the Father in the Gospel of John*. Edited by Adele Reinhartz. Atlanta: Society of Biblical Literature.
———. 2001. *Befriending the Beloved Disciple: A Jewish Reading of the Gospel of John*. New York: Continuum.
Rensberger, David. 1988. *Johannine Faith and Liberating Community*. Philadelphia: Westminster.
Resseguie, James L. 2001. *The Strange Gospel: Narrative Design and Point of View in John*. Bib Int 56. Leiden: Brill.
Riesner, Rainer. 1992. Teacher. *DJG,* 807–11.
Riley, George. 2001. *The River of God*. San Francisco: HarperCollins.
Rissi, Mathias. 1979. Voll grosser Fische, hundertdreiundfünfzig, Joh. 21,1–14. *TZ* 35:73–89.

Robinson, John A. T. 1962a. The Destination and Purpose of St. John's Gospel. Pages 107–25 in idem, *Twelve New Testament Studies*. SBT 34. London: SCM.
———. 1962b. The New Look on the Fourth Gospel. Pages 94–106 in idem, *Twelve New Testament Studies*. SBT 34. London: SCM.
———. 1962c. The Parable of the Shepherd (John 10:1–5). Pages 67–75 in idem, *Twelve New Testament Studies*. SBT 34. London: SCM.
———. 1965. The Destination and Purpose of the Johannine Epistles. Pages 126–38 in idem, *Twelve New Testament Studies*. 2nd ed. London: SCM.
———. 1976. *Redating the New Testament*. Philadelphia: Westminster.
———. 1985. *The Priority of John*. Edited by J. F. Coakley. Oak Park, Ill.: Meyer-Stone.
Sabbe, Maurits. 1977. The Arrest of Jesus in Jn 18, 1–11 and Its Relation to the Synoptic Gospels: A Critical Examination of A. Dauer's Hypothesis. Pages 203–34 in *L'Évangile de Jean: Sources, Rédaction, Théologie*. Edited by Marinus de Jonge. BETL 44. Leuven: Leuven University Press.
Said, Edward W. 1979. *Orientalism*. New York: Vintage.
Saldarini, Anthony J. 1998. Passover in the Gospel of John. *TBT* 36:86–91.
Saller, Richard P. 1994. *Patriarchy, Property and Death in the Roman Family*. Cambridge: Cambridge University Press.
Sanders, E. P. 1985. *Jesus and Judaism*. London: SCM.
Sandmel, Samuel. 1956. *A Jewish Understanding of the New Testament*. New York: Ktav.
———. 1965. *We Jews and Jesus*. New York: Oxford University Press.
———. 1978. *Judaism and Christian Beginnings*. New York: Oxford University Press.
Sanga, Jaina C. 2001. *Salman Rushdie's Postcolonial Metaphors: Migration, Translation, Hybridity, Blasphemy, and Globalization*. Westport, Conn.: Greenwood.
Saunders, Ernest W. 1982. *Searching the Scriptures: A History of the Society of Biblical Literature, 1880–1980*. SBLBSNA 8. Chico, Calif.: Scholars Press.
Schlier, H. 1964–76. Deiknymi. *TDNT* 2:25–33.
Schnackenburg, Rudolf. 1968. *The Gospel according to St. John*. Translated by Kevin Smith. HTKNT. New York: Herder & Herder.
———. 1982. *The Gospel according to St. John*. Volume 3. Translated by David Smith and G. A. Kon. New York: Crossroad.
Schneiders, Sandra M. 1999. *The Revelatory Text: Interpreting the New Testament as Sacred Scripture*. San Francisco: HarperSanFrancisco.
———. 1999. *Written That You May Believe: Encountering Jesus in the Fourth Gospel*. New York: Crossroad.
———. 2005. The Resurrection (of the Body) in the Fourth Gospel: A Key to Johannine Spirituality. Pages 168–98 in *Life in Abundance: Studies in Tribute to Raymond E. Brown, S.S.* Edited by John R. Donahue. Collegeville, Minn.: Liturgical Press.

Schüssler Fiorenza, Elisabeth. 1992. *But She Said: Feminist Practices of Biblical Interpretation.* Boston: Beacon.

Schwartz, Seth. 2001. The Rabbi in Aphrodite's Bath: Palestinian Society and Jewish Identity in the High Roman Empire. Pages 335–61 in *Being Greek under Rome: Cultural Identity, the Second Sophistic and the Development of Empire.* Edited by Simon Goldhill. Cambridge: Cambridge University Press.

Scott, J. Julius, Jr. 1995. *Jewish Backgrounds of the New Testament.* Grand Rapids: Baker.

Segal, Alan F. 1990. *Paul the Convert: The Apostolate and Apostasy of Saul the Pharisee.* New Haven: Yale University Press.

Segovia, Fernando F. 1991. *The Farewell of the Word: The Johannine Call to Abide.* Minneapolis: Fortress.

———. 1995. "And They Began to Speak in Other Tongues": Competing Modes of Discourse in Contemporary Biblical Criticism. Pages 1–31 in vol. 1 of *Reading from This Place: Social Location and Biblical Interpretation in the United States.* Edited by Fernando F. Segovia and Mary Ann Tolbert. Minneapolis: Augsburg Fortress.

———. 1998a. Biblical Criticism and Postcolonial Studies: Toward a Postcolonial Optic. Pages 49–65 in *The Postcolonial Bible.* Edited by R. S. Sugirtharajah. The Bible and Postcolonialism 1. Sheffield: Sheffield Academic Press.

———. 1998b. Inclusion and Exclusion in John 17: An Intercultural Reading. Pages 183–209 in *Literary and Social Readings of the Fourth Gospel.* Vol. 2 of *What Is John?* Edited by Fernando F. Segovia. SBLSymS 7. Atlanta: Scholars Press.

———, ed. 1996. *Readers and Readings of the Fourth Gospel.* Vol. 1 of *What is John?* SBLSymS 3. Atlanta: Scholar's Press.

———, ed. 1998c. *Literary and Social Readings of the Fourth Gospel.* Vol. 2 of *What is John?* SBLSymS 7. Atlanta: Scholars Press.

Setzer, Claudia. 2004. *Resurrection of the Body in Early Judaism and Early Christianity: Doctrine, Community, and Self-Definition.* Boston: Brill.

Sevrin, Jean-Marie. 2001. The Nicodemus Enigma: The Characterization and Function of an Ambiguous Actor of the Fourth Gospel. Pages 357–69 in *Anti-Judaism and the Fourth Gospel: Papers of the Leuven Colloquium, 2000.* Edited by R. Bieringer, D. Pollefeyt, and F. Vandecasteele-Vanneuville. Assen: Van Gorcum.

Skinner, Christopher W. 2004. Another Look at "the Lamb of God." *BSac* 161:89–104.

Smith, D. Moody. 1984. *Johannine Christianity: Essays on Its Setting, Sources, and Theology.* Columbia: University of South Carolina Press.

———. 1999. *John.* Nashville: Abingdon.

———. 2001. *John among the Gospels.* 2nd ed. Columbia: University of South Carolina Press.

Sperling, S. David. 1992. *Students of the Covenant: A History of Jewish Biblical Scholarship in North America*. Confessional Perspectives Series. Atlanta: Scholars Press.

———. 2001. Jewish Perspectives on Jesus. Pages 251–59 in *Jesus Then and Now*. Edited by Marvin Meyer and Charles Hughes. Harrisburg, Pa.: Trinity Press International.

Spivak, Gayatri Chakravorty. 1990. *The Postcolonial Critic: Interviews, Strategies, Dialogues*. Edited by Sarah Harasym. New York: Routledge.

Staley, Jeffrey Loyd. 1988. *The Print's First Kiss: A Rhetorical Investigation of the Implied Reader in the Fourth Gospel*. SBLDS 82. Atlanta: Scholars Press.

———. 1995. *Reading with a Passion: Rhetoric, Autobiography, and the American West in the Gospel of John*. New York: Continuum.

———. 2000. Autobiography. Pages 14–19 in *Handbook of Postmodern Biblical Interpretation*. Edited by A. K. M. Adam. St. Louis: Chalice.

Stauffer, Ethelbert. 1955. *Christ and the Caesars*. Translated by K. and R. Gregor Smith. Philadelphia: Westminster.

Stibbe, Mark W. G. 1992. *John as Storyteller: Narrative Criticism and the Fourth Gospel*. SNTSMS 73. Cambridge: Cambridge University Press.

———. 1993. *John*. Readings: A New Biblical Commentary. Sheffield: JSOT Press.

———. 1994. *John's Gospel*. New Testament Readings. London: Routledge.

Strauss, David Friedrich. 1860. *The Life of Jesus Critically Examined*. Translated by M. Evans from the 4th German ed. New York: Blanchard.

Streeter, B. H. 1964. *The Four Gospels: A Study of Origins*. Rev. ed. London: MacMillan.

Talbert, Charles H. 1992. *Reading John: A Literary and Theological Commentary on the Fourth Gospel and the Johannine Epistles*. New York: Crossroad.

Tanzer, Sarah. 1991. Salvation Is for the Jews: Secret Christian Jews in the Gospel of John. Pages 285–300 in *The Future of Early Christianity: Essays in Honor of Helmut Koester*. Edited by Birger A. Pearson, A. Thomas Kraabel, George W. E. Nickelsburg, and Norman R. Petersen. Minneapolis: Fortress.

Thatcher, Tom. 2006. *Why John Wrote a Gospel: Jesus—Memory—History*. Louisville: Westminster John Knox.

Thomas, John Christopher. 1991. *Footwashing in John 13 and the Johannine Community*. JSNTSup 61. Sheffield: JSOT Press.

Thompson, Marianne Meye. 1999. The Living Father. Pages 19–31 in *Semeia 85: God the Father in the Gospel of John*. Edited by Adele Reinhartz. Atlanta: Society of Biblical Literature.

Thyen, Hartwig. 1977. Entwicklungen innerhalb der johanneischen Theologie im Spiegel von Joh 21 und der Lieblingsjüngertexte des Evangeliums. Pages 259–99 in *L'Évangile de Jean: Sources, Rédaction, Théologie*. Edited by Marinus de Jonge. BETL 44. Leuven: Leuven University Press.

———. 2005. *Das Johannesevangelium*. HNT 6. Tübingen: Mohr Siebeck.

Tolbert, Mary Ann. 1995. The Politics and Poetics of Location. Pages 305–17 in vol. 1 of *Reading from This Place: Social Location and Biblical Interpretation in the United States*. Edited by Fernando F. Segovia and Mary Ann Tolbert. Minneapolis: Augsburg Fortress.

Tolmie, D. F. 1995. *Jesus' Farewell to the Disciples: John 13:1–17:26 in Narratological Perspective*. BibInt 12. Leiden: Brill.

Tovey, Derek. 1997. *Narrative Art and Act in the Fourth Gospel*. JSNTSup 151. Sheffield: Sheffield Academic Press.

Trumbower, Jeffrey A. 1992. *Born from Above: The Anthropology of the Gospel of John*. Tübingen: Mohr Siebeck.

VanderKam, James. 1990. John 10 and the Feast of Dedication. Pages 203–14 in *Of Scribes and Scrolls: Studies on the Hebrew Bible, Intertestamental Judaism, and Christian Origins*. Edited by Harold W. Attridge, John J. Collins, and Thomas H. Tobin. Lanham, Md.: University Press of America.

Vermes, Geza. 1981. *Jesus the Jew: A Historian's Reading of the Gospels*. Philadelphia: Fortress.

Veyne, Paul. 1987. *From Pagan Rome to Byzantium*. Vol. 1 of *A History of Private Life*. Translated by Arthur Goldhammer. Cambridge: Harvard University Press.

Visotsky, Burton L. Methodological Considerations in the Study of John's Interaction with First-Century Judaism. Pages 91–107 in *Life in Abundance: Studies of John's Gospel in Tribute to Raymond Brown, S.S.* Edited by John R. Donahue. Collegeville, Minn.: Liturgical Press.

Waetjen, Herman C. 2005. *The Gospel of the Beloved Disciple: A Work in Two Editions*. New York: T&T Clark.

Wahlde, Urban von. 1989. *The Earliest Version of John's Gospel: Recovering the Gospel of Signs*. Wilmington, Del.: Glazier.

Waters, Malcolm. 2001. *Globalization*. 2nd ed. London: Routledge.

Watson, Francis J. 1998. Toward a Literal Reading of the Gospels. Pages 195–217 in *The Gospels for All Christians: Rethinking the Gospel Audiences*. Edited by Richard Bauckham. Grand Rapids: Eerdmans.

Watt, Jan G. van der, ed. 2000. *Family of the King: Dynamics of Metaphor in the Gospel according to John*. Biblical Interpretation Series 47. Leiden: Brill.

Weiss, Herold. 1979. Foot Washing in the Johannine Community. *NovT* 21:298–325.

Westermann, Claus. 1985. *Genesis 12–36: A Commentary*. Minneapolis: Augsburg.

Wevers, John William. 1993. *Notes on the Greek Text of Genesis*. SBLSCS 35. Atlanta: Scholars Press.

White, L. Michael. 2003. Paul and *Pater Familias*. Pages 457–74 in *Paul and the Greco-Roman World: A Handbook*. Edited by J. Paul Sampley. Harrisburg, Pa.: Trinity Press International.

Wills, Lawrence M. 1997. *The Quest of the Historical Gospel: Mark, John, and the Origins of the Gospel Genre*. New York: Routledge.
Wolff, Hans. 1974. *Anthropology of the Old Testament*. Translated by Margaret Kohl. Philadelphia: Fortress.
Woodward, Kathryn, ed. 1997. *Identity and Difference*. London: Sage.
Wright, N. T. 1992. *The New Testament and the People of God*. Minneapolis: Fortress.
———. 1996. *Jesus and the Victory of God*. London: SPCK.
Yee, Gale A. 1989. *Jewish Feasts and the Gospel of John*. Wilmington, Del.: Glazier.
Zumstein, Jean. 2004. Die Endredaktion des Johannesevangeliums (am Beispiel von Kapitel 21). Pages 291–315 in *Kreative Erinnerung: Relecture und Auslegung im Johannesevangelium*. Edited by Jean Zumstein. 2nd ed. ATANT 84. Zurich: Theologischer Verlag.

Contributors

Armand Barus is Dean of Studies at Cipanas Theological College in Indonesia. He received his M.Div. from Trinity Theological College (Singapore) and his Ph.D. from Aberdeen University. His research focuses on applications of narrative theory to the Fourth Gospel.

Jaime Clark-Soles teaches New Testament at Perkins School of Theology, Southern Methodist University, in Dallas, Texas. She received her M.Div. from Yale Divinity School and her Ph.D. from Yale University. As an ordained American Baptist minister, Rev. Clark-Soles has served in both parish and hospice settings. She is the author of *Scripture Cannot Be Broken: The Social Function of the Use of Scripture in the Fourth Gospel* and recently completed a book that addresses views of death and afterlife in the New Testament.

Carsten Claussen is Wissenschaftlicher Assistent in New Testament Theology at the Protestant Theological Faculty, University of Munich, Germany, where he also received his doctorate. He is the author of *Versammlung, Gemeinde, Synagoge: Das hellenistisch-judische Umfeld der fruhchristlichen Gemeinden.*

Mary Coloe holds a joint position as Senior Lecturer at Australian Catholic University and Director of Biblical Studies at St. Paul's Theological College, Brisbane, Australia. She completed her Doctor of Theology through the Melbourne College of Divinity and is the author of *God Dwells with Us: Temple Symbolism in the Fourth Gospel.*

Alan Culpepper was formerly Professor of New Testament at Baylor University and currently serves as Dean of the McAfee School of Theology at Mercer University in Atlanta, Georgia. He received his M.Div. from Southern Baptist Theological Seminary (Louisville) and his Ph.D. from Duke University. He has written numerous papers and eight books, including *Anatomy of the Fourth Gospel, John the Son of Zebedee,* and *The Gospel and Letters of John.*

Brian Johnson teaches New Testament at Lincoln Christian College in Lincoln, Illinois, and has served in several parish settings. He is the author of several papers and articles on the Johannine literature and is currently completing his Ph.D. at the University of Aberdeen (Scotland) on the eyewitness statements in the Gospel of John.

Matthew Kraus was formerly Associate Professor of Classics and Chair of the Program in Jewish Studies at Williams College and is currently visiting professor of Classics at Wright State University in Ohio. He received rabbinic ordination from Hebrew Union College-Jewish Institute of Religion and a Ph.D. in Classics from the University of Michigan. He has published several papers on Judaism in the Greco–Roman period and is editor of *How Should Rabbinic Literature Be Read in the Modern World?*

Francisco Lozada Jr. teaches Biblical Studies at the University of the Incarnate Word in San Jose, Texas, and received his Ph.D. from Vanderbilt University. He is author of *A Literary Reading of John 5: Text as Construction* and is a member of the Program Committee for the Society of Biblical Literature.

Beth Sheppard teaches Biblical Languages and New Testament at Southwestern College, Kansas, where she also serves as Director of the Library. She earned her Ph.D. at the University of Sheffield. She has presented numerous papers on the cultural context of the Fourth Gospel.

Yak-hwee Tan teaches at Trinity Theological College, Singapore, and received her Ph.D. from Vanderbilt University. She has presented and published several papers on globalization and social location. As an ordained minister with the Presbyterian Church in Singapore, she is involved in ecumenical discussions regarding church and society.

Tom Thatcher teaches New Testament at Cincinnati Christian University in Ohio. He received his Ph.D. from Southern Baptist Theological Seminary (Louisville) and is an ordained minister of the Christian Churches/Churches of Christ. He is the author/editor of numerous books and articles, including *Jesus in Johannine Tradition* and *Why John Wrote a Gospel: Jesus–Memory–History*.

Index of Ancient Sources

Old Testament/Hebrew Bible

Genesis
- 6:5 — 130
- 6:5–6 — 33
- 8:21 — 33
- 18 — 76
- 18:3 — 76
- 18:4 — 75, 76
- 18:5 — 76
- 18:6 — 76
- 24:38 — 72
- 28:21 — 72
- 46:31 — 72

Exodus
- 12:3, 6 — 76
- 12:22 — 95
- 12:46 — 95
- 16:13 — 37
- 25:9 — 78
- 30:17–21 — 77

Leviticus
- 21:21–22 — 72

Numbers
- 11:31–32 — 37
- 28:2 — 72

Deuteronomy
- 16:16 — 126
- 18:15–22 — 111, 113
- 32:38 — 72

Joshua
- 2:13 — 72

1 Chronicles
- 28:9 — 130
- 28:11 — 78
- 28:12 — 78
- 28:18 — 78
- 28:19 — 78

2 Chronicles
- 4:6 — 77

Psalms
- 7:10 — 130
- 25:6 — 77
- 26:2 — 130
- 35:19 — 177 n. 12
- 44:21 — 130
- 68:10 — 129
- 69:4 — 177, 177 n. 12
- 69:9 — 136

Song of Songs — 156

Isaiah
- 11:1 — 70

Jeremiah
- 8:2 — 78
- 11:20 — 130
- 12:3 — 130
- 17:10 — 130

Ezekiel		Joel	
5:5	126	3:8	90, 96
38:12	126		
41:22	72	Nahum	
42:15	78	3:6	78
44:16	72		
47	63	Zechariah	
47:1–7	90, 96	6:12	70–71
		9:9	92
Daniel		14:8	90, 96
7	96		
8	96	Malachi	
11	96	1:7	72

Apocrypha/Deuterocanon

Ecclesiasticus		3 Maccabees	
44:16	78	2:5	78
2 Maccabees		4 Maccabees	
6:28	78	6:19	78
6:31	78	17:23	78

New Testament

Matthew		1:1–18	9, 57, 73, 91, 149, 189–92
13:41–42	49	1:4	130
27:37	70	1:6	33
		1:6–9	81
Mark		1:12	118, 125, 139
3:27	46	1:13	34, 37, 80, 191
8:27–30	94	1:14	37, 71, 77, 80, 110, 129, 132, 149, 191
10:51	92		
11:1–19	90	1:17	94
12:33	40	1:18	117–18, 118–19, 125
14:28	60	1:19–34	81
14:62	15	1:19–51	127
15:25	70	1:19–2:11	124, 125, 128, 137–38
16:7	60	1:26	62, 91
16:14–18	60	1:29	91
		1:29–34	190
Luke		1:31	60
23:38	70	1:32–34	93
		1:35	61
John		1:35–42	10
1	149	1:35–49	91

1:35–51	59, 64, 91, 125, 137	3	35, 162–63
1:35–2:12	64	3:1	124, 163
1:37	61	3:1–15	162–63
1:38	62, 92	3:1–21	144, 162–63
1:40	61	3:1–4:54	124, 140
1:40–42	61	3:2	92
1:41	62, 94	3:3	35, 163
1:43	61	3:4	39, 163
1:44–49	61	3:4–7	191
1:45	62, 115	3:5	35
1:45–51	64	3:6	37, 191
1:48	62	3:8	36
1:49	62, 91, 93	3:13	34
1:49–50	62	3:14	34, 44 n. 4, 79, 163
1:51	34, 129	3:16	117, 118
2:1	64	3:18	93
2:1–5	114	3:19	163
2:1–11	59, 61, 172 n. 5	3:22	124
2:3	61	3:25–30	81
2:6	61	3:27	33
2:7	63	3:36	46
2:10	33	4	33, 47
2:11	60, 62, 64, 124, 131, 132, 136, 139	4:4–42	172 n. 5
		4:13	37
2:11–12	131	4:19	34
2:12	124, 125, 128, 130, 131	4:22	83
2:12–25	123, 124–25, 128, 134, 136–39, 206	4:23	35
		4:24	35
2:13	95, 125, 126, 131	4:28	33
2:13–22	125–26, 134, 135	4:29	34
2:13–25	90	4:31	92
2:16	72, 77, 80 n. 9, 126, 127, 128, 129, 132	4:42	118
		4:45	134
2:17	128, 131, 133, 136	4:46–54	47
2:18	127, 139	4:48	133, 139
2:19	71, 77, 79, 127, 130, 133	4:53–54	139
2:20	127	5	34, 51 n. 8, 185
2:21	39, 71, 77, 79, 80, 90, 127, 129, 135, 136	5:1	124
		5:7	33
2:22	128, 130, 131, 132, 133	5:14	124
2:23	95, 130, 132, 133, 138–39	5:21	46
2:23–25	124, 125, 126, 127	5:24	42
2:24	137, 138	5:24–25	157
2:24–25	163	5:25	47, 93
2:25	33, 130, 137	5:27	34

John (continued)
5:28	47
5:28–29	57, 59
5:29	46
5:30	117–18, 118–19
5:36	116
6	32, 37, 47, 51 n. 8, 64
6:1	124
6:1–15	59, 61, 64
6:4	95, 126
6:7	63
6:9	61, 64
6:10	34
6:11	64, 65
6:15	92
6:24	62
6:25	92
6:27	34
6:30	133
6:33	37
6:35	62
6:37	139
6:38–42	115
6:39	32, 47, 57
6:40	32, 43, 47, 57
6:42	115
6:44	32, 47, 57, 65
6:49	37
6:50	42
6:51–58	57, 59
6:53	34
6:54	32, 37, 47, 57, 62
6:56	37, 138
6:57	37
6:58	37
6:59	93
6:60–71	59
6:62	34
6:63	35, 37, 46
6:64	67
6:66–71	61
6:67–71	61
6:71	61, 64
7	93, 94
7:1	124
7:2–10	131
7:4	60
7:11	62
7:34–36	62
7:37–38	90
7:38	39, 96
7:39	35, 44 n. 4, 131
7:42	92
7:49–52	144, 162, 163–64
7:50–51	164
7:53–8:11	172
8	42
8:15	37
8:21	62
8:24	42
8:28	34, 44 n. 4
8:35	49
8:40	34
8:44	87
8:51–52	42
8:52	43
8:52–53	43
9	34, 185
9:1	33
9:2	92
9:16	34
9:17	34
9:22	85
9:24	34
9:35	34
9:38	34
9:43	45
10:1–5	102
10:8	96
10:10	44–45
10:11	38, 96
10:11–18	79
10:14–16	138
10:15	38
10:17	38
10:17–18	35, 43
10:22–39	96
10:28	62
10:33	34
10:33–36	34

10:36	93	13:6–38	73
11	42, 186	13:7	78, 124
11:1–44	172 n. 5	13:8	79
11:4	43, 93	13:12–14	79
11:7	124	13:12–15	73, 74, 78, 79
11:11	43, 124	13:13–14	93
11:11–14	43	13:14	79
11:16	61	13:15	74
11:18	92	13:16	76
11:23	47	13:16–20	73, 74
11:24	43, 47	13:18	37
11:25–26	43, 47	13:21	35
11:26	62	13:21–30	73–74
11:27	93	13:21–38	73
11:33	35	13:23	61, 65, 194
11:39	43	13:24	66
11:47	139	13:26	76
11:50	34, 43, 44	13:26–30	76
11:55	126	13:26–31	61
12:1	125	13:30	73–74
12:1–8	175 n. 5	13:31	34, 44 n. 4, 74
12:4	61	13:31–35	73, 74, 79
12:7	157 n. 10	13:31–38	74
12:12–15	91	13:31–14:31	174 n. 6
12:20	126	13:33	62, 80
12:23	34, 44 n. 4, 74	13:34	74
12:24–26	44	13:34–35	79
12:25	38, 40	13:35	79, 176
12:27	38, 39	13:36–38	73, 74
12:31	46	13:37	38
12:32	44 n. 4, 65	13:38	38, 74
12:33	44	14	39, 48–49, 174
12:34	34, 44 n. 4	14:1	39, 74
12:40	39, 40	14:1–4	90
12:42	85	14:2	70, 72, 77, 80 n. 9
12:48	32, 57	14:2–3	48
13	72–73, 77, 78, 79, 81, 174	14:5	61
13:1	73, 76, 79, 95	14:6	117, 174
13:1–3	74	14:10	70, 110
13:2	39, 61	14:11	110
13:2–3	73	14:12	39
13:4	74	14:16	35, 69
13:4–5	73, 74, 77	14:17	70
13:6–11	73, 74, 78	14:18	44
13:6–20	73	14:23	46, 49, 70

John (continued)

14:25	70
14:26	131, 175
14:27	39, 74
15:1	174
15:1–11	169
15:1–17	174–76, 174 n. 6, 178
15:4	174
15:5	62, 65
15:6	45, 175
15:9	176
15:9–10	175
15:10–11	175
15:12	176
15:13	38, 79, 175
15:15	175
15:16	176
15:17	176
15:18	174, 176, 177 n. 11
15:18–27	174, 176–78
15:18–16:4	174 n. 6
15:18–16:11	4 n. 1
15:19	176, 177, 177 n. 11
15:20	177, 177 n. 11
15:22	177
15:24	177
15:25	177
15:26–27	178
16:1–2	44
16:2	45, 85
16:4–33	174 n. 6
16:6	44
16:11	46
16:13	36
16:21	33
16:32	44, 62
16:33	44
17	112–14, 178
17:2	38
17:2–3	118
17:3	47, 94
17:6	33, 113
17:9–10	113–14, 117, 119
17:15	46
17:25–26	73

18:1–24	186
18:2–5	61
18:3	62
18:5	70
18:7	70
18:7–8	62
18:15	66
18:17	34, 66
18:20	93
18:24–19:42	186
18:25–27	66
18:28	95, 106
18:28–19:42	188–89
18:32	44
18:39	95
19	58
19:5	34
19:7	93
19:14	95
19:18	188
19:19	70
19:19–20	107
19:25–27	71, 114, 172 n. 5
19:26	194
19:26–27	66
19:28	58, 124
19:29	95
19:30	35
19:31	95
19:31–37	95
19:31–40	39
19:34	90
19:34–35	57
19:38	58, 124
19:38–40	164
19:38–42	144, 162, 164
20	34, 58, 60, 65
20:1–8	66
20:1–18	172 n. 5
20:2	61, 194
20:9	47
20:11–18	58
20:12	39
20:15	62
20:17	71, 118

20:18	58	Acts	
20:19	58	1:15	65
20:19–22	48	8:27	126
20:19–23	58		
20:21	58, 61	Romans	
20:21–23	60	8	51
20:22	35, 37, 58	8:24	51
20:23	58		
20:24	64	1 Corinthians	
20:24–29	58	1:12	65, 66
20:25–27	62	3:3–4	66
20:26–29	58, 61	13:12	37
20:28	62	14:23–24	140
20:29	62	15	30, 47
20:30	66, 132	15:23	47
20:30–31	57, 58, 59, 65, 66, 83, 94, 133, 139, 194, 205	15:26	44
20:31	53, 93, 94, 110, 118, 124, 136, 140	2 Corinthians	
		1:22	47
21	29, 30, 45, 51 n. 8, 55, 56, 57–60, 61, 62, 63–64, 67–68	Galatians	
21:1	58, 60, 62, 124	1:18	65
21:1–3	58	2:11	65
21:1–14	60, 62, 64, 65	3:13	44
21:2	61, 64, 92		
21:2–3	62	Philippians	
21:3	63	2:6–11	44
21:4	58, 62		
21:6	65	1 Thessalonians	
21:7	62	4	30
21:9	65		
21:11	63, 65	Hebrews	
21:13	64, 65	4:11	78
21:14	58, 60	8:6	78
21:15–17	66	9:19	95
21:15–23	60, 65, 66	9:23	78
21:19	43, 44, 45, 65		
21:20	66	James	
21:21–22	66	5:10	78
21:22	51 n. 8		
21:23	45, 65, 67	1 Peter	
21:24	68	5:13	65
21:24–25	60		
21:25	57	2 Peter	
		2:6	78

1 John		2 John	67
2:2	45 n. 5		
2:18–20	67	3 John	67

Extrabiblical Literature

1QH	130	Justin Martyr, *1 Apology*	140
1QS	130	Justinian, *Digest*	107, 117, 118
4Q161	71	*m. Berakhot*	76
4QpIsa^a	71	*Mekilta Exodus*	130
Augustine, *Confessions*	146	*Midrash Qoheleth*	130
Didache	64	Philo, *On the Special Laws*	77, 77 n. 8
Gaius, *Institutiones*	113, 114, 116, 117, 118	Philo, *Questions and Answers on Exodus*	76–77
Genesis Rabbah	130	*Targum Neofiti*	75–76
Gospel of Thomas 114	34	*Testament of Abraham*	75, 75 n. 5
Horace, *Satires*	106, 107, 115–16	*Trimorphic Protennoia* 40:19–32	48
Josephus, *Jewish War*	126		

Index of Authors and Subjects

17   63–65
153   63–64

abide   see *menō*
Abraham   43, 74–76, 75 n. 4, 76 n. 7, 92
acceleration (narrative technique)   127–28
Adam, A. K. M.   17, 19, 21–22
Albright, W. F.   201
analepsis   128
Anderson, Paul   6, 110–11, 113, 117
Ando, Clifford   107
Andrew (apostle)   61, 94, 128, 131
anēr ("man, male") 32, 33–34
anistēmi ("to resurrect")   47
anthropology   31–32, 39, 40–41, 50, 52, 61, 141 n. 1, 142, 168, 205
anthrōpos ("person, human being")   32–34, 40, 163
anti-Jewish   see *anti-Semitism*
antilanguage   87, 97
anti-Semitism   97, 142, 145, 152, 160, 165–66, 193
Appleby, Joyce   108, 109
apocalyptic(ism)   see *eschatology*
apokteinō ("to kill")   41, 45
apōleia ("destruction")   41
apollymi ("to destroy")   41, 45
aposynagōgos ("to put out of the synagogue")   85
apothnēskō ("death")   41–42
aporias   6, 12–13, 14, 22, 56
Ashcroft, Bill   168, 170, 176
Ashton, John   111, 113
Augustine   22, 63, 146, 189

the author (as historical anchor)   16, 17, 23–24
autobiographical criticism   185, 186–89, 193, 195, 196, 203

Bacon, B. W.   3, 5
Bakhtin, M. M.   171
Balch, David   80 n. 9
Ball, David   203
Barber, Benjamin   101
Bar-Efrat, Shimon   134
Barrett, C. K.   4–5, 5 n. 2, 200, 201
Barthes, Roland   23–24
Barus, Armand   206
Bauckham, Richard   88, 123, 133, 134
BDAG   92
Beasley-Murray, G. R.   63, 201
Beck, David   203
Belle, Gilbert van   202
Beloved Disciple   13, 13–14 n. 3, 14, 39, 45, 49, 60, 61, 65–66, 67, 68, 71, 154, 155, 156, 157–58, 157 n. 10, 159, 160, 164, 165, 166, 192, 194–95, 201, 206
Berger, Peter   141 n. 1, 142
Bethany   158
Bethesda   33
Bhabha, Homi   169, 171, 178
binary opposition/thinking   148, 154–55, 156, 158, 159, 159 n. 11, 162, 163, 165, 171, 172–73, 175, 178, 191
Bingen, Hildegard von   189
bi-optic approach   6
Birkat Haminim ("Benediction against Heretics")   85, 86, 87
Biville, Frédérique   107

blind man (John 9)   33, 34
Blomberg, Craig   88, 95, 109
blood   see *haima*
Boer, M. C. de   202
Boismard, M.-E.   6
Bonney, William   203
book as a friend   193-94
Booth, Wayne   194, 202
Borg, Marcus   186
Borgen, Peder   4
Böttrich, Christfried   61
Boyarin, Daniel   87, 148-50, 152, 161-62
Boyer, Peter   152-53 n. 8
Boys, Mary   152 n. 8
Bradley, Keith   113
Brant, Jo-Ann   204
bread   37, 45, 61, 63, 64, 65, 72, 76, 95
bread of life/from heaven   35, 37, 42, 47
Bremmer, Jan   38
Brodie, Thomas   5
Brooks, James   177 n. 10, 177 n. 11
brothers of Jesus   see *family: of Jesus*
Brown, Raymond   4, 14, 57, 58, 59, 60, 79, 81, 92, 163, 172, 201, 202
Brownlee, W. H.   201
Brumberg-Kraus, Jonathan   141 n. 1, 142, 143, 144, 150, 153, 154
Bultmann, Rudolf   3-4, 4 n. 1, 6, 57, 58, 189, 200, 201

Caiaphas   34
call of the disciples (John 1:35-51)   59, 64
Cana   33, 59, 60, 61, 63, 64, 116, 124
Cana wedding   see *wedding at Cana*
Capernaum   124, 125, 127, 130
Cassem, N. H.   46 n. 6
Cassidy, Richard   104-5
Chancey, Mark   105
Charlesworth, James   9, 75 n. 6, 202
Chatman, Seymour   202
child(ren)   168, 187
   metaphor for believers   34, 80-81, 80 n. 9, 152

Roman legal status   113-14, 115-16
Chow, Rey   169
Christ/Messiah (messianic title)   7, 17, 34, 53, 91-92, 93, 94, 99, 110, 124, 133, 137, 145-46, 150, 157, 158, 166, 172, 194, 206
christological exclusivism   117-19
christological titles   see *titles (Christological)*
Christology   14, 15, 67, 71, 81, 89-97, 110-19, 130, 145, 147, 150, 158, 159, 203
Chrysippus   36
Clark-Soles, Jaime   205
Claussen, Carsten   64, 205
Cohn-Sherbok, Dan   144 n. 4
Coloe, Mary   35, 40 n. 2, 48-49, 51 n. 8, 70, 70 n. 1, 71, 72, 74 n. 3, 90, 203, 205
colonized/colonizer   168, 169, 170-72
compliant reader/reading   154-56, 159, 193, 194-95, 204
Cook, Michael   142-43, 144, 144 n. 4
Craven, Toni   141 n. 3
Crook, J. A.   114
cross   35, 39, 70-71, 77, 79-80, 90, 95, 107, 116, 136, 188
crowd(s), the   62, 63, 92, 125, 125, 133-34, 138, 139
crucifixion   8, 64, 66, 74, 79, 80, 95, 145, 147, 150-51, 188
crurifragium   95
Cullmann, Oscar   4, 13, 13 n. 3, 16, 202
Culpepper, R. Alan   4, 7, 24, 56, 59, 78, 117, 201, 202

D'Angelo, Mary Rose   112
Daube, David   144 n. 4
David(ic) (king)   71, 78, 92, 94
Davies, Margaret   203
Dead Sea Scrolls   8-9, 9-10, 30, 52, 81, 106, 150, 201
death   41-42, 43, 44, 48, 49, 50, 51, 130, 154, 156
deceleration (narrative technique)   127-28

INDEX OF AUTHORS AND SUBJECTS 241

Dedication   see *Feast of Dedication*
Destro, Adriana   115
developmental approach   13, 14
devil   46, 49, 73, 87
diachronic approach   16, 17–22, 30, 31, 49–50, 51–52, 59, 60, 205–6
Diaspora   55, 67, 106, 126, 149
Didache   64
difference   174–75, 176, 177, 178, 183, 184, 187, 188, 195, 197
disciples   32, 35, 36, 38, 39, 40, 43, 44, 51 n. 8, 58, 59, 60, 61, 62, 63, 64–65, 67, 70, 73, 77, 78, 79, 80, 80 n. 9, 81, 90, 92–93, 94, 98, 113, 118, 124, 125, 128, 129, 130, 131, 132, 133, 134, 135, 136, 137, 138, 139, 173, 174, 175–77, 178
discipleship   59, 60, 64, 67
discovery   see *tasks of scholarship*
Dixon, Suzanne   108, 113, 116
Dodd, C. H.   4, 11–12, 55, 201
dog(s)   187, 188–89
Duke, Paul   202
Dunn, James D. G.   65
dwell(ing)   see *menō*

Eisenbaum, Pamela   143, 144 n. 4
Encyclopedia Judaica Decennial Book   145 n. 5
engaged reader/reading   157–59, 193, 195, 204
epigenesis   112
eschatology   21–22, 29–30, 31, 32, 33–34, 37, 40, 41, 45, 47, 49–51, 51 n. 8, 52, 53, 57, 205
essentialism/essentialist   144, 149, 169, 169 n. 1, 171, 173, 196
eternal life   40, 41, 46, 47, 49, 62, 112, 118, 119, 146, 154, 155, 156–57, 166, 194, 206
ethical criticism   194, 195
Eucharist(ic)   57, 64
excommunication   44, 45, 56, 85, 152, 172
Eyben, Emiel   114

faith   9, 10, 39, 62, 70, 117, 124, 125, 130, 132, 133, 136–39, 140, 158, 159, 164–65, 166, 194, 203, 206
family   92, 153, 155, 168, 187
   first-century   80 n. 9, 102, 104, 106, 110, 111–19, 205
   metaphor for church   80 n. 9
   of Jesus   60, 125, 128, 130–31, 134
Farewell Discourse   38, 73, 174 n. 6, 177 n. 12, 203
Father-Son motif   94, 102, 106, 109, 110–14, 115, 116–19, 132, 205
Feast of Dedication   94, 96–97
Feast of Tabernacles   79, 90, 95–96
Feeding of five thousand   59, 61, 63, 64
feet   see *footwashing*
feminism/feminist   17, 31, 141 n. 3, 154, 159, 168, 172, 179, 185, 189–92, 193, 195, 196, 203–4
fish   62, 63, 64, 65
Fitzgerald, John   76
flesh   190–91; see also *sarx*
flesh-and-blood reader   see *real reader*
Flusser, David   144 n. 4
focalization   190
footwashing   72, 73, 74–80, 80–81, 205
Fortna, Robert   4, 6, 7, 202
Foucault, Michel   170, 171 n. 4
Fourth Gospel   see *Gospel of John*
Frankfurter, David   144 n. 4
Fredriksen, Paula   15, 150–53, 152–53 n. 8, 161
Frymer-Kensky, Tikva   144 n. 4

Gaius   113, 114, 116, 117, 118
Galilee/Galileans   15, 60–61, 126, 134, 151
Gandhi, Leela   169, 171, 171 n. 4, 175
Gardner-Smith, Percival   3, 201
Gärtner, Bertil   135
Gaventa, Beverly Roberts   58, 60
Geertz, Clifford   141 n. 1, 142
Gehenna   see *hell*
Genette, Gérard   202

Gentile(s)   14, 18, 86, 123, 126, 129, 130, 131, 132, 133, 136–37, 139–40, 172, 206
Gibson, Mel   143, 152–53
Giddens, Anthony   167, 168, 179
Glass, Zipporah   172, 174, 175, 175 n. 7
globalization   26, 101–2, 103, 105, 108, 109–10, 119, 167–69, 172, 178, 179, 206, 207–8
Gnostic(ism)   40, 42, 49, 50, 55, 67, 80, 81, 105
Goldhill, Simon   107
Goodenough, E. R.   201
Good Shepherd   79, 96, 102
Gospel of John
  composition history   2, 14, 204, 209
  historical value   7–8, 9, 10–11, 13, 14–16, 18, 19–20, 22, 23
  literary sources   3–7, 4 n. 1, 11–12, 58, 69, 80, 168, 183, 200, 202
  oral tradition behind   3, 4, 5–6, 7, 8, 11–12, 13, 14, 29–30, 50, 55, 69, 81, 102, 108, 159, 201–2, 205
  provenance   8, 9, 9–11, 12, 14, 15, 18, 200
  relationship to the Synoptics   2, 3, 4–6, 7, 9, 11, 13, 13 n. 3, 14, 15, 16, 18, 19–20, 60–61, 80, 92, 94, 145, 147, 200
great church   14, 65
Greenspoon, Leonard   144 n. 4
Griffiths, Gareth   168, 170, 176
Guha, Ranajit   175 n. 8
gynē   32, 33–34

Hades   see *hell*
haima ("blood")   32, 37, 38, 40
Hall, Stuart   169, 169 n. 1, 170–71, 174, 175
Hamid-Khani, Saeed   86, 98
Hamm, Dennis   144 n. 4
Hanukkah   see *Feast of Dedication*
Haran, Menahem   72
Hauser, Alan   71 n. 2

Hays, Richard   76 n. 7
heart   see *kardia*
heaven   48–49, 48 n. 7, 50, 51 n. 8, 77 n. 8, 152, 163
hell   45–46, 49, 50
Hellenistic   31, 32, 36, 40, 41, 50, 77, 84, 99, 102–4, 105, 107, 109, 111–12, 119, 148 n. 7, 200
Hellerman, Joseph   80 n. 9
Hengel, Martin   88, 151, 161
Herod   103
Heschel, Susannah   141 n. 1
hieros   126, 129, 132
Hill, Charles   209
historical Jesus   15, 17, 18, 22, 29, 30, 31, 52, 53, 55, 65, 81, 102, 105, 150
Holy Spirit   13, 16, 35, 36, 37, 40 n. 2, 42, 47, 48, 49, 50, 51 n. 8, 58, 60, 69–70, 131, 136–37, 138, 145, 178
Horace   106, 107, 115–16
Horst, Pieter van der   87
Hoskyns, Edwyn   60
household of God   72, 77, 79–81, 80 n. 9
Howard-Brook, Wes   175
Hultgren, Arland   74
Hunt, Lynn   108, 109
Huntington, Samuel   168
Hurtado, Larry   94
hybrid(ity)   169, 171, 173, 178, 179
hypodeigma ("model, example")   72, 74, 78–80
hyssop   95

identity
  communal   70, 71, 72, 80, 155, 170–72, 173, 174, 176, 178, 179
  personal   115–16, 152–53 n. 8, 153–54, 169, 169 n. 1, 174, 184, 186, 188, 190, 192, 193, 196–97, 206, 208
Ignatius   18
Ilan, Tal   104, 105
implied audience/reader   123, 128, 130, 134–35, 135–36, 185, 202

INDEX OF AUTHORS AND SUBJECTS

implied author 123, 127, 134–35, 192, 194
interlocks 5
irony 33, 34, 173, 202

Jacob 37, 38, 47, 99
Jacob, Margaret 108, 109
Jasper, Alison 184, 189–92, 195, 196, 203, 206
Jeffers, James 104, 105, 108
Jeremias, Joachim 201
Jerome (saint) 63
Jerusalem 8, 58, 65, 72, 90, 91, 101, 103–4, 105, 125–27, 129, 130, 131, 132, 133, 134, 135, 138, 151, 200
Jesus' brothers see *family: of Jesus*
Jesus Seminar 7
Jewett, Robert 31, 37
Jewish New Testament scholarship 141–44, 149–50, 152–53, 159, 160–62, 193–95, 196
"Jews," the (a character in the Fourth Gospel) 46 n. 6, 62, 70, 71, 83, 85–86, 87, 90, 92, 93, 94, 97, 103, 107, 115, 125, 126, 129, 130, 131, 132, 136–37, 139, 145, 146 n. 6, 148, 152, 155–56, 163, 164, 166, 206
John the Baptist 9, 10, 33, 60, 62, 81, 91, 92, 93, 94, 190, 201
John (apostle) 10–11, 12, 14, 15, 200, 201
Johannine community 6, 7, 11, 14, 45, 55, 56, 65, 66, 67, 69, 70, 71, 72, 75, 80, 81, 85, 86, 87–88, 97, 99, 131, 152, 155, 156, 157, 159, 160, 172–73, 174, 178, 179, 199, 201–2, 203, 205–6, 209
Johannine tradition see *Gospel of John: oral tradition behind*
Johnson, Brian 89, 205
Jones, Larry 203
Jonge, Marinus de 110
Joseph of Arimathea 164
Joseph of Nazareth 115, 117
Josephus 30, 126–27

Judaism 9, 13–14 n. 3, 55, 67, 71, 74, 75, 76, 77, 81 n. 10, 83, 84–85, 86–89, 90, 91, 92, 93, 97–99, 103, 104, 105–6, 126, 143, 144, 147–48, 148 n. 7, 149–50, 152, 156, 158–59, 162, 164–65, 166, 197, 200, 205, 206
Judas Iscariot (disciple) 61, 62, 64, 73–74, 76
Judeans see *Jews, the*
judgment (eschatological) 46, 47, 49
Justin Martyr 140
Justinian 107, 117, 118

kardia ("heart") 32, 35, 38–39, 40, 74, 130, 137
Käsemann, Ernst 4, 190
Keck, Leander 47–48, 48 n. 7
Keener, Craig 83, 87, 91, 105–6
kenosis hymn (Phil 2:6-11) 44
Kermode, Frank 202
Kerr, Alan 90, 95
Kilgour, Frederick 107
Kim, Jean 204
King of Israel (christological title) 91–92, 93, 94
Kit Carson 187
Kitzberger, Ingrid Rosa 189
Klenicki, Leon 144 n. 4
Koester, Craig 91, 203
Köstenberger, Andreas 88, 93
koilia ("belly, womb") 32, 39
koimaomai ("to sleep") 41, 43
koimēsis ("sleeping") 41
Kraemer, Ross 141 n. 3
Kraus, Matthew 206
Kristeva, Julia 191
Kümmel, Werner George 5
Kysar, Robert 4, 51, 204

LaBahn, Michael 6
lamb (of God) 44, 45 n. 5, 91, 95
lame man (John 5) see *Bethesda*
Larsen, Kasper 203
Last Supper 65–66, 76, 79
Latin 106–7, 109, 110, 119

Lazarus 39, 43, 47, 93
LeBeau, Bryan 144 n. 4
Lee, Dorothy 79, 203
Leuven School 5
Levine, Amy-Jill 144 n. 4
liberation(ist) 168, 179, 192, 193, 195, 196
Lieu, Judith 144 n. 4
Lightfoot, J. B. 106, 201
Lincoln, Andrew 86, 203
Lindbeck, Kristen 152, 152 n. 8
"line," the (timelines) see *diachronic approach*
living water see *water: living*
loaves see *bread*
Logos 36, 79, 148–50, 148 n. 7, 155
Long, A. A. 36
Loomba, Ania 176
Lozada, Francisco, Jr. 203, 206
Luckman, Thomas 141 n. 1
Luther, Martin 189
LXX see *Septuagint*

MacMullen, Ramsey 103, 107
Mailer, Norman 157–58
Malina, Bruce 85–86, 87
Manns, Frédéric 71 n. 2, 74–75, 81 n. 10
Marcus, Joel 144 n. 4
Martha 43, 47, 93, 158
Martyn, J. Louis 4, 7, 56, 84–89, 99, 202
Mary Magdalene 34, 39, 58, 62, 66, 71, 92, 118
Mary, mother of Jesus see *mother of Jesus*
Mary, sister of Martha 157 n. 10, 158
McGowan, Andrew 64
McNamara, Martin 76
Medved, Michael 152–53 n. 8
Meeks, Wayne 85–86, 88, 108, 202
memory 5, 11, 26, 51 n. 8, 55, 66, 96–97, 108, 128, 131, 137, 202
Memra 148–49
menō ("to abide, dwell, remain") 38, 46, 48, 70, 80, 174, 175, 176

Menoud, P.-H. 69, 201
Messiah see *Christ/Messiah*
Meyer, Ben 89
Meyers, Carol 141 n. 3
midrash 149–50, 156
misunderstanding (literary motif) 62, 78, 134–36
model see *hypodeigma*
Moloney, Francis 4, 174, 175, 203
monogenēs 117–18
Moore, Stephen 203
Morris, Leon 4, 5–6
Moses 37, 47, 77, 78, 92, 95, 99, 111, 163
mother of Jesus 66, 71, 112, 114–16, 117, 119, 128, 130
Motyer, Stephen 87, 88, 94

Nag Hammadi 48
Nanos, Mark 144 n. 4, 153
naos ("sanctuary, temple") 126
narrator 39, 43, 44, 90, 91, 92, 93, 115, 123, 124, 125, 126, 127–28, 129, 130, 131, 132, 133, 134, 135, 136, 137, 138, 139, 190
Nathanael (apostle) 61, 62, 64, 91, 92, 93, 128, 131
Navajo 187–88, 189, 196, 197
Nazarene (title for Jesus) 70–71
necessary heir 117–18
Neill, Stephen 84
Neirynck, Franz 5
nekros ("dead") 41
Neusner, Jacob 144 n. 4
new commandment 73, 74, 79
New Look, the 1–2, 4, 6, 7, 8, 9, 10, 11, 12, 13, 14, 15, 16, 17, 19, 20, 21, 22, 23, 25, 26, 55, 56, 85, 86, 89, 99, 146 n. 6, 150, 159, 160, 183, 199–200, 201, 204, 205
"New Look on the Fourth Gospel, The" (Robinson article) 1, 2, 12, 16, 17, 20, 24–25, 29, 30, 31, 50, 69, 108, 119, 141, 159, 168, 183, 199–200, 200–201, 207

Nicodemus   33, 35, 39, 144, 162–66, 206
Nielsen, Helge   141 n. 2
Niemand, Christopher   81
Nisbet, Robert   116
Noack, Bent   4, 201, 202
noeō ("mind")   40

O'Day, Gail   172, 172 n. 5, 202
orientalism   169
Osiek, Carolyn   80 n. 9
Other(ness)   33, 154–55, 155 n. 9, 158, 169, 169 n. 1, 170–71, 172, 174, 175, 178, 184, 190, 195, 197, 208
other-world   173
ouranos ("heaven[s]")   48–49

Paraclete   see *Holy Spirit*
paradeigma   see *hypodeigma*
parousia   30, 41, 51, 51 n. 8
Parry, Benita   174
Parsons, Mikeal   186
Passion of the Christ, The (film)   143–44, 152–53, 152–53 n. 8
passion narrative   34, 44, 91, 95, 142, 151, 188–89, 200, 203
Passover   73, 76, 91, 94–95, 96, 124, 125, 126–27, 130, 131, 132, 133, 134, 137, 138, 151, 156
paterfamilias   113–14, 115–16, 205
patria potestas   112–14, 116
Patterson, Stephen   9
Paulien, Jon   163, 164
Paul(ine) (apostle)   29, 30, 37, 39, 40–41, 43, 44, 47, 48, 49, 50, 51, 66, 76 n. 7
peculium   112, 116
Perry, Menakhem   57
Pesce, Mauro   115
Peter (apostle)   34, 38, 39, 45, 59, 60, 61, 65–66, 67, 73, 74, 78, 79, 94, 128, 131, 157
Petersen, Norman   202
phaneroō ("to reveal")   60
Pharisees   62, 146 n. 6, 162, 163, 166

Philip (apostle)   61, 128, 131
Philips, Peter   87–88, 98
Philo   75, 76–77, 148, 148 n. 7, 149
Pilate   34, 92, 93, 107, 164
Pippin, Tina   172
Plato(nic)   38, 41, 42, 50, 148 n. 7
Pliny   104
plot   123, 124, 134
pneuma ("spirit")   32, 35–37, 38, 40, 42, 49, 50
poetics of location   170–71, 170 n. 2
point of view (narrative)   123, 127–28, 129, 137, 195
politics of location   170, 170 n. 2
polloi   see *the crowd(s)*
postcolonial(ism)   17, 26, 31, 168–69, 170–73, 170 n. 3, 178–79, 185, 188, 204, 206, 208
postcolonial optic   170
postresurrection point of view   47, 51 n. 8, 128, 129, 130, 131, 132, 133, 136, 137, 138, 206
power relations   113, 170–71, 170 n. 2, 171 n. 4, 184, 208
Pratt, Mary Louise   171
Pregeant, Russell   172
primacy effect   57, 62
prolepsis   128
Prologue (John 1:1–18)   9, 57, 73, 80, 91, 130, 149–50, 152, 189–92, 196, 203
Prophet, the (messianic title)   34, 111
psychē ("soul")   32, 35, 38, 40, 42, 43, 44, 49, 50

Qumran   71, 135

rabbi (title for Jesus)   91, 92–93, 137
rabbinic exegesis/literature   70–71, 71 n. 2, 81, 106, 145, 150, 161, 164
Rad, Gerhard von   75 n. 4
Rand, Jan du   202
Rawson, Beryl   113
reader-response criticism   183, 185, 202, 203

real reader 170, 171, 173, 179, 183, 185–86, 202, 206–7
recency effect 57, 66
Reicke, Bo 201
Reinhartz, Adele 88, 111–12, 141, 143, 144, 153–60, 161, 161 n. 12, 163, 164, 165, 166, 184, 192–95, 196, 202–3, 203–4
remain see *menō*
Rensberger, David 172 n. 5
resistant reader/reading 154–56, 158, 159, 185, 186, 189, 193, 194–95, 204
Resseguie, James 203
resurrection
    eschatological 31, 42, 43, 46, 47–48, 50–51, 130
    of Jesus 36, 37, 39, 40, 44, 58, 47, 48, 58, 60, 62, 64, 80, 118, 128, 129, 130, 131, 132, 133, 136, 137, 138, 139, 140
    of Lazarus see *Lazarus*
    point of view see *postresurrection point of view*
resurrection appearances see *resurrection: of Jesus*
rhetorical mythology 190
Rhoads, David 202
Riesner, Rainer 93
Riley, George 104, 105
Rissi, Matthias 64
Robinson, John A. T. 1, 2, 3, 4, 5 n. 2, 6, 7, 8, 9–10, 11, 12, 14, 15–16, 17, 18, 19, 20–22, 23, 24–26, 29–30, 31, 49–50, 51–52, 55, 57, 67, 69, 80, 81–82, 84–85, 86, 89, 99, 101–6, 108, 110, 119, 141, 143, 144, 146 n. 6, 150, 159, 168, 179, 183, 199–201, 204, 205, 207, 208
Rohrbaugh, Richard 85–86
Roman family see *family: first-century*
Rome 65, 71, 102, 107, 117, 172
Roth, Philip 157–58
rûaḥ ("spirit") 36
Ruckstuhl, Ernst 4, 201

Sabbath 96, 157, 157 n. 10

Sabbe, Maurits 5
Said, Edward 169,
Saldarini, Anthony 95
Saller, Richard 108, 115
salvation 51, 83, 117, 119, 152, 159, 191, 194, 195
Samaritan woman 33–34, 47, 83
Samaritans 14
Sanders, E. P. 123
Sandmel, Samuel 144–48, 145 n. 5, 146 n. 6, 149–50, 151, 153, 154, 159, 161, 161 n. 12
Sanga, Jaina 171
sarx ("flesh") 32, 33, 37–38, 40, 190–91
Satan see *devil*
Saunders, Ernest 141 n. 3, 142
Schlier, H. 78
Schnackenburg, Rudolf 4, 138–39, 201
Schneiders, Sandra 32 n. 1, 39, 46, 69–70, 186, 203
Schüssler Fiorenza, Elisabeth 141 n. 3
Schwartz, Seth 103
Schweizer, Eduard 4, 201
Scott, J. Julius, Jr. 71 n. 2
Sea of Galilee/Tiberias 58
searching/seeking theme 62
secondary orality 6
second coming 30, 48
Segal, Alan 144 n. 4
Segovia, Fernando 170, 170 n. 3, 173, 174, 174 n. 6, 177 n. 12, 179, 183
sēmeia see *signs*
Septuagint (LXX) 38, 75–76, 75 n. 5, 78, 177 n. 12
Setzer, Claudia 144 n. 4
Sevrin, Jean-Marie 163, 164, 166
Shabbetai Zevi 157
shepherd(s) see *Good Shepherd*
Sheppard, Beth 205
signs (Jesus' miracles) 130–31, 132, 133, 136, 137, 138–39, 162, 163
Signs Gospel 6–7
signs source see *Gospel of John: sources*
Skinner, Christopher 91
Smith, D. Moody 4, 6, 14–15, 207

INDEX OF AUTHORS AND SUBJECTS 247

social location   170, 170 n. 2, 179, 183–85, 186, 189, 192, 193, 195, 196–97, 206–7, 207–8
Society of Biblical Literature   26, 105, 143, 145 n. 5, 202, 204
sōma ("body")   32, 39, 44
Son of God   47, 53, 91, 92, 93–94, 110, 118, 124, 133, 148, 154, 156, 194, 206
Son of Man   34, 45, 163
sons of Zebedee   13, 61
soul   see *psychē*
Sperling, David   141 n. 3, 144 n. 4
Speyr, Adrienne von   189
Spivak, Gayatri   169
Staley, Jeffrey   184, 185–89, 192, 195, 196, 202, 203
Stauffer, Ethelbert   103
Stibbe, Mark   51 n. 8, 203
Stoic(ism)   36, 42, 49, 148 n. 7
Strauss, David Friedrich   63
Streeter, B. H.   3
subordinationist Christology   106, 109, 110–12, 114–15, 117
suffering servant   44
symbol(ism)   70, 71, 77, 79, 80, 83, 85, 89–90, 91, 92, 96, 97–98, 123, 134–36, 151, 163, 165, 190, 191, 203, 205
sympathetic reader/reading   155, 155 n. 9, 156–57, 159, 193, 195, 204
synagogue   7, 12, 14, 44, 45, 56, 77, 85, 86, 88, 93, 152, 155, 156, 172
synchronic approach   49–50, 52–53, 56–57, 58, 59, 61, 63, 67, 205

Tabernacles   see *Feast of Tabernacles*
Talbert, Charles   177
Tan, Yak-hwee   206
Tanzer, Sarah   144 n. 4, 163, 164–65, 166
tasks of scholarship   142–44, 153, 160
temple (in Jerusalem)   14, 49, 51 n. 8, 71, 72 76–77, 78, 79, 81, 89–90, 93, 94–95, 96, 97–98, 99, 103, 123, 125, 126, 129, 131–32, 134, 135, 136, 139, 151, 203, 206

as christological symbol   39, 71, 79, 80, 90, 95–96, 97–98, 123, 129, 131–32, 133, 135, 139, 151, 203, 206
as symbol of the Johannine community   70–72, 77, 80–81, 123, 136–37, 138, 139, 203
temple incident (John 2:12–25)   90, 123–25, 127, 128–29, 131, 132, 134, 136, 137, 138, 151, 206
"text" (versus "work")   23–24
thanatos ("death")   41
Thatcher, Tom   202, 205, 207
Thomas (apostle)   58, 61, 62, 203
Thomas, John Christopher   75, 75 n. 5
Thompson, Marianne Meye   118
Thyen, Hartwig   57, 58–59
thyō ("slaughter, sacrifice")   41, 45
Tiffin, Helen   168, 170, 176
titles (christological)   34, 70, 89, 91–94, 97
titulus (on Jesus' cross)   70–71, 107
Tolbert, Mary Ann   170, 170 n. 2
Tolmie, D. F.   203
Tovey, Derek   203
tradition   see *Gospel of John: oral tradition behind*
transmission   see *tasks of scholarship*
trōgō ("to eat, chomp")   37
Trumbower, Jeffrey   41 n. 3
Twelfth Benediction   see *Birkat Haminim*
Twelve, the (disciples)   13, 13–14 n. 3, 61, 64–65, 131
"two worlds" model   173–78, 179, 206

VanderKam, James   96–97
Vermes, Geza   144 n. 4
Veyne, Paul   114
vine discourse (John 15:1–11)   168, 172–73, 174–79, 206
Visotzky, Burton   84

Waetjen, Herman   209
Wahlde, Urban von   4, 7, 202

water   36, 37–38, 61, 63, 75, 75 n. 5, 96, 162, 203
  living   39, 47, 90, 96
water to wine   see *wedding at Cana*
Waters, Malcolm   168
Watson, Duane   71 n. 2
Watson, Francis   87
Watt, Jan van der   80 n. 9, 203
wedding at Cana   33, 59, 60, 61, 63, 64, 116, 124
Weiss, Herold   77
Westcott, B. F.   201
Westermann, Claus   75 n. 4
Wevers, John William   75 n. 4
White, Michael   117
Wills, Lawrence   144 n. 4
Winbery, Carlton   177 n. 10, 177 n. 11
wine   see *wedding at Cana*
Wolff, Hans   32, 36
woman at the well, the   see *Samaritan woman*
Woodward, Kathryn   184
"work" (versus "text")   see *"text" (versus "work")*

world, the (character in the Gospel of John)   33, 37, 40 n. 2, 43, 46 n. 6, 60, 73, 79, 95, 118, 148, 155, 158, 159 n. 11, 173–75, 176, 177, 190
world-above   173, 176, 177, 178, 206
world-below   173, 174, 175, 176–78, 206
world behind the text   82, 183–84, 197
world in front of the text   82, 183–84, 197
Wrede, Wilhelm   19
Wright, N. T.   84, 89, 126

Yee, Gale   94–95, 96

zaō ("to live")   46–47
Zebedee   see *sons of Zebedee*
Zeno   36
zēteō ("to search, seek")   see *searching/seeking theme*
zōē ("life")   40, 42, 44, 46, 50
Zumstein, Jean   59

www.ingramcontent.com/pod-product-compliance
Lightning Source LLC
Chambersburg PA
CBHW021807220426
43662CB00006B/207